Material Lives

ALSO BY SERENA DYER AND PUBLISHED BY BLOOMSBURY

Material Literacy in Eighteenth-Century Britain, co-edited with Chloe Wigston Smith

Material Lives

Women Makers and Consumer Culture in the 18th Century

Serena Dyer

BLOOMSBURY VISUAL ARTS
LONDON · NEW YORK · OXFORD · NEW DELHI · SYDNEY

BLOOMSBURY VISUAL ARTS
Bloomsbury Publishing Plc
50 Bedford Square, London, WC1B 3DP, UK
1385 Broadway, New York, NY 10018, USA
29 Earlsfort Terrace, Dublin 2, Ireland

BLOOMSBURY, BLOOMSBURY VISUAL ARTS and the Diana logo are trademarks of Bloomsbury Publishing Plc

First published in Great Britain 2021
Reprinted 2021 (twice), 2023

Copyright © Serena Dyer, 2021

Serena Dyer has asserted her right under the Copyright, Designs and Patents Act, 1988, to be identified as Author of this work.

For legal purposes the Acknowledgements on pp. xiii–xiv constitute an extension of this copyright page.

Cover design by www.ironicitalics.com
Cover image: *Morning Dress of the Year 1785* from the *Collection of English Original Watercolour Drawings* by Ann Frankland Lewis, England, 1785. Costume Council Fund. AC1999.154.11. www.lacma.org

All rights reserved. No part of this publication may be reproduced or transmitted in any form or by any means, electronic or mechanical, including photocopying, recording, or any information storage or retrieval system, without prior permission in writing from the publishers.

Bloomsbury Publishing Plc does not have any control over, or responsibility for, any third-party websites referred to or in this book. All internet addresses given in this book were correct at the time of going to press. The author and publisher regret any inconvenience caused if addresses have changed or sites have ceased to exist, but can accept no responsibility for any such changes.

A catalogue record for this book is available from the British Library.

Library of Congress Cataloging-in-Publication Data
Names: Dyer, Serena, author.
Title: Material lives : women makers and consumer culture in the 18th century / Serena Dyer.
Description: London ; New York : Bloomsbury Visual Arts, 2020. | Includes bibliographical references and index.
Identifiers: LCCN 2020024851 (print) | LCCN 2020024852 (ebook) | ISBN 9781350126961 (paperback) | ISBN 9781350126978 (hardback) | ISBN 9781350126985 (pdf) | ISBN 9781350127005 (epub)
Subjects: LCSH: Material culture–England–History–18th century. | Women–England–Archives. | Women–England–Biography. | Women–England–Social conditions–18th century.
Classification: LCC GN585.E54 D94 2020 (print) | LCC GN585.E54 (ebook) | DDC 306.4/6082094209033—dc23
LC record available at https://lccn.loc.gov/2020024851
LC ebook record available at https://lccn.loc.gov/2020024852

ISBN: HB: 9781-3501-2697-8
PB: 9781-3501-2696-1
ePDF: 9781-3501-2698-5
eBook: 9781-3501-2700-5

Typeset by RefineCatch Limited, Bungay, Suffolk
Printed and bound in Great Britain

To find out more about our authors and books visit www.bloomsbury.com and sign up for our newsletters.

Contents

List of illustrations vii
Acknowledgements xiii
List of abbreviations xv

1 Introduction: Making material lives 1
   Material life writing 7
   The consumer culture of making 9
   Four material lives 14

2 Material accounting: A sartorial account book 21
   Barbara Johnson (1738–1825) 23
   Educating Barbara Johnson 30
   Accounting for herself 33
   Material literacy 39
   A chronicle of fashion 45

3 Dress of the year: Watercolours 49
   Ann Frankland Lewis (1757–1842) 50
   Sartorial timekeeping and the fashion plate 58
   Accomplishment and creative practice 78
   Society and fashionable display 89
   Selfhood, emotion and the mourning watercolours 99

4 Adorned in silk: Dressed prints 123
   Sabine Winn (1734–1798) 125
   Paper textiles, dress and the dressed print 131
   Sabine Winn's dressed prints 140
   Print and making at Nostell 156

5 Fashions in miniature: Dolls 161

    Laetitia Powell (1741–1801) 162
    The Powell dolls 164
    Mimetic dolls and miniature selves 177
    Dolls as sartorial social narrators 181

6 Conclusion: Material afterlives 189

Glossary of sartorial terms 195
Notes 197
Bibliography 229
Index 241

Illustrations

1.0 (chapter opening image) George Walker, *Industrious Jenny*, 1810s. Courtesy of The Lewis Walpole Library, Yale University.   xvi
1.1 Barbara Johnson's Album, 1746–1823. Copyright Victoria and Albert Museum, London.   2
1.2 Ann Frankland Lewis, *The Dress of Year 1775*. Los Angeles County Museum of Art, www.lacma.org.   4
1.3 Nicolas Larmessin IV, *Nicaise*, after Nicolas Lancret, dressed by Sabine Winn, 1761–1765. Copyright National Trust.   5
1.4 The Powell Collection of Dolls, 1754–1911. Copyright Victoria and Albert Museum, London.   6
1.5 Isaac Cruikshank, *Miseries of Human Life*, 1808. Courtesy of The Lewis Walpole Library, Yale University.   12
1.6 George Walker, *Industrious Jenny*, 1810s. Courtesy of The Lewis Walpole Library, Yale University.   13
1.7 William Henry Pyne, frontispiece to *Miseries of Human Life*, 1806. Courtesy of The Lewis Walpole Library, Yale University.   15
2.0 (chapter opening image) Barbara Johnson's Album, 1746–1823. Copyright Victoria and Albert Museum, London.   20
2.1 Barbara Johnson's Album, 1746–1823. Copyright Victoria and Albert Museum, London.   22
2.2 Engraving of the Great House, Olney, from *Sunday at Home*, 1857. Courtesy of HathiTrust.   24
2.3 Family tree of the Johnson family. Compiled from evidence in BOD: MS Don. c. 190, ff. 34–5 and 192, ff. 108–17 and LA: JOHNSON/1/3.   24
2.4 Thomas Beach, *The Honourable Mrs Craven*, 1776. Courtesy of the Walker Art Gallery, Liverpool.   27
2.5 Johan Zoffany, *Mrs Wodhull*, 1770. Copyright Tate, London.   29
2.6 'Lord Mountjoy, & Miss Barbara John-son, Dancing a Menuet together at a Ridotto in the Hay Market', Jane Johnson's Nursery Library, 1740s. Courtesy of the Lilly Library, Indiana University, Indiana.   31

2.7 Barbara Johnson's Album, 1746–1823. Copyright Victoria and Albert Museum, London. 35
2.8 Appearances of silk and cotton in Barbara Johnson's album, 1746–1823, arranged by decade. Source: VAM: T.219-1973. 40
2.9 Patterns of British Manufacture, from Ackermann's *Repository of Arts,* 1809. Private Collection. 42
2.10 Number of gowns purchased by and gifted to Barbara Johnson, arranged by decade, 1750–1819. Source: VAM: T.219-1973. 43
2.11 Barbara Johnson's Album, 1746–1823. Copyright Victoria and Albert Museum, London. 47
3.0 (chapter opening image) John Hoppner, *The Frankland Sisters*, 1795. Courtesy of the National Gallery of Art, Washington. 48
3.1 *Fashionable Dresses in the Rooms at Weymouth*, from the *Lady's Magazine*, 1774. Copyright Victoria and Albert Museum, London. 50
3.2 Ann Frankland Lewis, *The dress of year 1774*. Los Angeles County Museum of Art, www.lacma.org. 51
3.3 Woman's dress and petticoat, 1765–1775. Los Angeles County Museum of Art, www.lacma.org. 52
3.4 Family tree of the Frankland family. Compiled from evidence in NLW: Harpton Court Papers and Yorkshire Archaeological Society: DD94. 53
3.5 Unknown artist, *Sarah Rhett Frankland*, 1743. Courtesy of the Gibbes Museum of Art. 55
3.6 *The Ladies in the newest Dress*, published in the *Lady's Magazine*, 1775. Courtesy of The Lewis Walpole Library, Yale University. 60
3.7 Ann Frankland Lewis, *The dress of year 1776*. Los Angeles County Museum of Art, www.lacma.org. 61
3.8 *A Lady in the Dress of the Year 1766*. Courtesy of the Museum of London. 62
3.9 George Moutard Woodward, *Fashions of the Day, or Time Past and Time Present*, 1807. Courtesy of the Library of Congress. 64
3.10 Ann Frankland Lewis, *The dress of year 1777*. Los Angeles County Museum of Art, www.lacma.org. 66
3.11 Ann Frankland Lewis, *The dishabille of year 1778*. Los Angeles County Museum of Art, www.lacma.org. 67
3.12 Morning Dress in *Gallery of Fashion*, April 1796. Courtesy of the British Library. 68
3.13 Ann Frankland Lewis, *1779*. Los Angeles County Museum of Art, www.lacma.org. 69
3.14 Ann Frankland Lewis, *1780*. Los Angeles County Museum of Art, www.lacma.org. 70
3.15 Fashion plate from *Gallerie des Modes*, 1780. Courtesy of the Rijksmuseum. 71
3.16 Ann Frankland Lewis, *The dress of year 1781*. Los Angeles County Museum of Art, www.lacma.org. 72

3.17 Ann Frankland Lewis, *The half dress of year 1782*. Los Angeles County Museum of Art, www.lacma.org. 73

3.18 Morning Dress for March 1801, from *Lady's Monthly Museum*. Los Angeles County Museum of Art, www.lacma.org. 75

3.19 *Jan 1814 Promenade Dress*. Private collection. 76

3.20 Promenade Dress, January 1814, from the *Repository of Arts*. Los Angeles County Museum of Art, www.lacma.org. 77

3.21 The Court Dress as Worn on His Majesty's Birthday and Kensington Garden Walking Dress, June 1808, *La Belle Assemblée*. Courtesy of the de Beer Collection, Special Collections, University of Otago, Dunedin, New Zealand. 79

3.22 John Hoppner, *The Frankland Sisters*, 1795. Courtesy of the National Gallery of Art, Washington. 81

3.23 Evening dress, March 1812, from *La Belle Assemblée*. Courtesy of the Los Angeles Public Library. 83

3.24 Morning dress, June 1812, from *La Belle Assemblée*. Courtesy of the Los Angeles Public Library. 84

3.25 Ann Frankland Lewis, *The dress of year 1784*. Los Angeles County Museum of Art, www.lacma.org. 86

3.26 Ann Frankland Lewis, *Morning dress of the year 1785*. Los Angeles County Museum of Art, www.lacma.org. 87

3.27 Silk satin muff with a painted medallion depicting a dog. Copyright Victoria and Albert Museum, London. 88

3.28 Ann Frankland Lewis, *Morning dress January 1786*. Los Angeles County Museum of Art, www.lacma.org. 90

3.29 Ann Frankland Lewis, *The Court dress of the year 1787*. Los Angeles County Museum of Art, www.lacma.org. 91

3.30 Ann Frankland Lewis, *Morning dress 1788*. Los Angeles County Museum of Art, www.lacma.org. 92

3.31 Detail of Ann Frankland Lewis, *1779*. Los Angeles County Museum of Art, www.lacma.org. 94

3.32 Joshua Reynolds, *Seymour, Lady Worsley*, 1779. Courtesy of Harewood House. 95

3.33 *An officer in the light infantry, driven by his lady to Cox-Heath*, after John Collett, 1780. Courtesy of The Lewis Walpole Library, Yale University. 96

3.34 Ann Frankland Lewis, *The Windsor Uniform* 1789. Los Angeles County Museum of Art, www.lacma.org. 97

3.35 *Restoration Dresses*, 1789. Los Angeles County Museum of Art, www.lacma.org. Courtesy of The Lewis Walpole Library, Yale University. 98

3.36　Ann Frankland Lewis, *The Half dress of the year 1790*. Los Angeles County Museum of Art, www.lacma.org. 100

3.37　Ann Frankland Lewis, *Morning dress 1791*. Los Angeles County Museum of Art, www.lacma.org. 101

3.38　Ann Frankland Lewis, untitled watercolour, probably 1792. Los Angeles County Museum of Art, www.lacma.org. 103

3.39　Ann Frankland Lewis, *1793*. Los Angeles County Museum of Art, www.lacma.org. 104

3.40　Ann Frankland Lewis, *May 1794*. Los Angeles County Museum of Art, www.lacma.org. 105

3.41　Mourning Dresses, *Gallery of Fashion*, March 1797. Courtesy of the British Library. 107

3.42　Ann Frankland Lewis, *Morning dress 1795*. Los Angeles County Museum of Art, www.lacma.org. 108

3.43　Ann Frankland Lewis, *1796*. Los Angeles County Museum of Art, www.lacma.org. 109

3.44　Ann Frankland Lewis, *1797*. Los Angeles County Museum of Art, www.lacma.org. 110

3.45　Ann Frankland Lewis, *1798*. Los Angeles County Museum of Art, www.lacma.org. 111

3.46　Ann Frankland Lewis, *1799*. Los Angeles County Museum of Art, www.lacma.org. 112

3.47　Ann Frankland Lewis, *Morning dress December 1800*. Los Angeles County Museum of Art, www.lacma.org. 113

3.48　Ann Frankland Lewis, *1801*. Los Angeles County Museum of Art, www.lacma.org. 115

3.49　Ann Frankland Lewis, *1802*. Los Angeles County Museum of Art, www.lacma.org. 116

3.50　Ann Frankland Lewis, *1803*. Los Angeles County Museum of Art, www.lacma.org. 117

3.51　Ann Frankland Lewis, *Morning dress 1804*. Los Angeles County Museum of Art, www.lacma.org. 118

3.52　Ann Frankland Lewis, *March 1806*. Los Angeles County Museum of Art, www.lacma.org. 119

3.53　Ann Frankland Lewis, *Morning dress January 1807*. Los Angeles County Museum of Art, www.lacma.org. 120

4.0　(chapter opening image) Hugh Douglas Hamilton, *Sir Rowland Winn and his wife Sabine Winn in the Library at Nostell*, 1767. Copyright National Trust. 122

4.1　Nicolas Larmessin IV, *Les Troqueurs*, after Nicolas Lancret, dressed by Sabine Winn, 1761–1765. Copyright National Trust. 124

4.2　Family tree of the Winn family. Compiled from evidence in the Nostell Archive, WYAS: WYW1352. 127

4.3　Hugh Douglas Hamilton, *Sir Rowland Winn and his wife Sabine Winn in the Library at Nostell*, 1767. Copyright National Trust. 129

4.4　*Une Vendeuse des Images* from Martin Engelbrecht's *Métiers*, 1730. Courtesy of Kunstbibliothek, Staatliche Museen zu Berlin. 132

4.5 Antoine Trouvain, *Mademoiselle d'Armagnac en Robe de Chambre*, 1695. Courtesy of the Bibliothèque nationale de France. 134

4.6 Anna Magdelena Braun, *Trachtenbuch*, 1773. Courtesy of the Germanishes Nationalmuseum. 137

4.7 R. Page, *Caroline, Queen of England*, 1820. Private collection. 138

4.8 'Ladies in Fashionable Dresses' and 'An Interesting Scene from the Novel of Lussington Abbey', from the *Ladies Complete Pocket Book*, 1805. Courtesy of Kent Archive Service. 139

4.9 Reverse side of one of Sabine Winn's dressed prints, 1761–1765. Copyright National Trust. 143

4.10 Nicolas Larmessin, *Les Rémois*, after Nicolas Lancret, dressed by Sabine Winn, 1761–1765. Copyright National Trust. 143

4.11 Nicolas Larmessin, *Les Oyes de Frere Philippe*, after Nicolas Lancret, dressed by Sabine Winn, 1761–1765. Copyright National Trust. 144

4.12 Nicolas Larmessin, *Frere Luce*, after Nicolas Vleugels, dressed by Sabine Winn, 1761–1765. Copyright National Trust. 144

4.13 Pierre Filloeul, *La Matrone d'Ephes*, after Jean-Baptist Pater, dressed by Sabine Winn, 1761–1765. Copyright National Trust. 145

4.14 Nicolas Larmessin, *La Faucon*, after Nicolas Lancret, dressed by Sabine Winn, 1761–1765. Copyright National Trust. 145

4.15 Pierre Filloeul, *Le Glouton*, after Jean-Baptist Pater, dressed by Sabine Winn, 1761–1765. Copyright National Trust. 146

4.16 Nicolas Larmessin, *Le Fleuve Scamandre*, after François Boucher, dressed by Sabine Winn, 1761–1765. Copyright National Trust. 146

4.17 Pierre Filleul, *Le Coccu Battu et Content*, dressed by Sabine Winn, 1761–1765. Copyright National Trust. 147

4.18 Nicolas Larmessin, *Le Gascon Puni*, after Nicolas Lancret, dressed by Sabine Winn, 1761–1765. Copyright National Trust. 147

4.19 Nicolas Larmessin, *Les Deux Amis*, after Nicolas Lancret, dressed by Sabine Winn, 1761–1765. Copyright National Trust. 148

4.20 Nicolas Larmessin, *La Jument de Compere Pierre*, after Nicolas Vleughels, dressed by Sabine Winn, 1761–1765. Copyright National Trust. 148

4.21 Nicolas Larmessin, *Les Aveux Indiscrets*, after Jean-Baptiste Pater, dressed by Sabine Winn, 1761–1765. Copyright National Trust. 149

4.22 Nicolas Larmessin, *La Servante Justifiee*, after Nicolas Lancret, dressed by Sabine Winn, 1761–1765. Copyright National Trust. 149

4.23 Nicolas Larmessin IV, *Nicaise*, after Nicolas Lancret, dressed by Sabine Winn, 1761–1765. Copyright National Trust. 150

4.24	Nicolas Larmessin, *La Servante Justifiee*, after Nicolas Lancret, 1743. Courtesy of the Rijksmuseum.	154
4.25	Nicolas Lancret, *La Servante Justifiee*, 1743. Courtesy of the Metropolitan Museum of Art.	155
4.26	The yellow drawing room of the Nostell dolls' house. Copyright National Trust.	158
5.0	(chapter opening image) Laetitia Powell, *Mrs Powell's Wedding Suit*, 1761. Copyright Victoria and Albert Museum, London.	160
5.1	Family tree of the Powell family. Compiled from evidence in Edgar Powell's 1891 pedigree.	163
5.2	Laetitia Powell, *Fashionable Full Dress for Young Lady, 1754*. Copyright Victoria and Albert Museum, London.	165
5.3	Laetitia Powell, *Fashionable Full Dress for Spring 1759*. Copyright Victoria and Albert Museum, London.	167
5.4	*A Lady in the Dress of the Year 1758*, from Barbara Johnson's Album. Copyright Victoria and Albert Museum, London.	168
5.5	Laetitia Powell, *Mrs Powell's Wedding Suit*, 1761. Copyright Victoria and Albert Museum, London.	169
5.6	Laetitia Powell, *Doll dressed in a brunswick*, 1769. Copyright Victoria and Albert Museum, London.	172
5.7	Laetitia Powell, *Undress called a Levite*, 1784. Copyright Victoria and Albert Museum, London.	174
5.8	Laetitia Powell, *Fashionable visiting dress*, 1792. Copyright Victoria and Albert Museum, London.	175
5.9	Fashion plate from *Gallerie des Modes*, 1780. Courtesy of the Rijksmuseum.	178
5.10	*The History of Little Fanny*, 1810. Courtesy of the University of Nottingham Special Collections.	182
5.11	Harriet Johnson's paper doll, 1787. Photo © Historic Royal Palaces/Robin Forster/Bridgeman Images.	185
5.12	Letter from Harriet Johnson to her sister Maria, 1802. Courtesy of the Bodleian Library.	186

Acknowledgements

It is often said that historical research can be lonely. We spend months and years squirrelled away in libraries and offices eagerly searching for the remnants of the lives of the long-dead. Yet academia has furnished me with a cherished network of friends and colleagues, all of whom have contributed in large and small ways to the shape of this book. Conference wine receptions and lunches at the archives have fostered academic collaborations and friendships alike, and I am forever grateful for the ideas, commiserations and celebrations shared with fellow researchers. The ever fabulous and boundlessly kind travelling sisterhood of art and material culture historians has offered endless support throughout this journey. For help tracking down references, twitter comradery, deciphering artistic techniques and support in manifold ways, I thank Tabitha Baker, Jennie Batchelor, Sarah Bendall, Bethan Bide, Leanne Calvert, Elaine Chalus, Hilary Davidson, Christine Davies, Owen Davies, Holly Day, Laura Engel, Ariane Fennetaux, Christine Griffiths, Jade Halbert, Sally Holloway, Ben Jackson, Suzanne Karr Schmidt, Alicia Kerfoot, Elizabeth Lambourn, Sophie Littlewood, Hannah Lyons, Caroline McCaffery-Howarth, Matthew McCormack, Simon McCormack, Rebecca Morrison, Marina Moskowitz, Anne Murphy, Maddy Pelling, Sophie Pitman, Edward Potten, Vivienne Richmond, Lizzie Rogers, Kate Smith, Lizzy Spencer, Kate Strasdin, Jon Stobart, John Styles, Sally Tuckett, William Tullett, Laura Ugolini, Amanda Vickery, Lucie Whitmore and Kelley Wilder. I am especially grateful to Kerry Bristol, Karen Harvey and Chloe Wigston Smith, who have kindly read and commented upon various portions of this book. Their suggestions have enriched this text. I extend a particularly heartfelt thank you to Freya Gowrley, whose companionship and comradery got me through my final few months of writing, and the wonderfully knowledgeable Elisabeth Gernerd, whose generosity, friendship, and intimate understanding of prints have been invaluable.

As with most books, this one has been a long time in the making. I first came across Sabine Winn and her fabulously rich archive as a postgraduate student at the University of York's Centre for Eighteenth Century Studies. The seed of an idea which grew into this book was first planted as an undergraduate at the same institution. I would like to extend special thanks to Hannah Greig, whose support fostered my love of the eighteenth century, and her continued encouragement and enthusiasm has been inspirational. Giorgio Riello's patience, rigour and support throughout my PhD studies and beyond has had a transformative effect on my work. Colleagues at the National Portrait Gallery, the Museum of Domestic Design and Architecture, the University of Warwick, the University of Hertfordshire and De Montfort University have further deepened my understanding of history, objects and the obstacles and delights of academic and curatorial life.

The development of this project was not just made possible by the support of individuals, but by the societies, organizations and research funds who have seen the value of women's material lives. Funding for the research behind this project and the inclusion of so many beautiful colour images has been generously forthcoming in the form of research fellowships and grants from many sources, including the ESRC, the Pasold Research Fund, the Paul Mellon Centre for the Study of British Art, the British Federation of Women Graduates and the University of Warwick's Institute of Advanced Studies. For their support and enthusiasm throughout the publication journey, I would like to thank Frances Arnold, Yvonne Thouroude, Rebecca Hamilton, Amy Jordan, Merv Honeywood and the rest of the team at Bloomsbury.

Beyond the walls of the academy, my friends and family have supported this book in countless ways. Laura Coleman and Harriet Still have been on this journey with me since my York days, and have put up with me telling them more than they ever wanted to know about eighteenth-century women and 300-year-old objects. My love and eternal gratitude to James Davies, who has supported me in countless ways. His boundless belief in my abilities has sustained me when my own confidence floundered. And he makes a pretty decent cup of tea. For childhood visits to country houses, an endless willingness to supply me with books and having always been my biggest champions, I thank my parents. My father, sadly, is no longer here to see it, but this book is for him.

Abbreviations

BL	British Library, London
BM	British Museum, London
BOD	Bodleian Library, University of Oxford
CW	Colonial Williamsburg, Virginia
JRL	John Rylands Library, University of Manchester
LA	Lincolnshire Archives
LACMA	Los Angeles County Museum of Art
LWL	Lewis Walpole Library, Farmington
MET	Metropolitan Museum of Art, New York
NA	National Archives, Kew
NLW	National Library of Wales, Aberystwyth
NPG	National Portrait Gallery, London
NT	National Trust
VAM	Victoria and Albert Museum, London
WYAS	West Yorkshire Archive Service, Wakefield
YCA	York City Archives

1

Introduction: Making material lives

The lives of eighteenth-century women endure through a patchwork of archival remains. Some women's lives have been determined through pounds, shillings and pence, scratched out in homemade ink across the sprawling pages of account books.[1] Others have been reconstructed through women's social engagements, everyday practices and emotional lives in diaries and letters, detailing the minutiae of scandalous and quotidian lives alike.[2] A few select, celebrated women authored autobiographies and memoirs, retelling and crafting their exceptional tales for a clamorous readership.[3] Whether self-consciously constructed as memorializing ego-documents, or the incidental recording of daily life, women throughout history have left their mark. Yet, for all the information contained in the sheets and pages of missives, receipts, journals and periodicals, words and numbers have never been the only vocabularies used to express personal experiences, practices and narratives. The pen was only one tool amongst a diverse apparatus, which included the needle, the paint brush, scissors and pins. It is the lives of women as detailed through the products of this miscellany of creative material methods which form the focus for this book.

Eighteenth-century women constructed their material lives both deliberately, through concerted and continuous practices of self-reflection and structured documentation, and coincidentally, through spontaneous, procedural and incidental records of their interactions with the material world. The eighteenth century has been characterized as a period of material eruption, in which consumers were faced with an increasingly sophisticated and rich material world. In response to this abundance of goods, fresh behaviours for mediating individual relationships with the material world were fostered, diversifying from the household inventory or account book. These supplementary methods of reporting and recording functioned outside of traditional production and consumption paradigms and acted as forms of material diary. Genteel eighteenth-century women, I argue, fashioned narratives of their lives through series of objects – both purchased and homemade – which sat at the conjunction of the manual labour of making and cultures of consumption. This model of material life writing forces us to reconsider the boundaries often imposed between literary life writing, historical record and artistic endeavour, and offers an opportunity to reflect upon the mutability and multiplicity of roles played by material culture.

This book concentrates on four genteel eighteenth-century women: Barbara Johnson (1738–1825), Ann Frankland Lewis (later Hare, 1757–1842), Sabine Winn (née d'Hervart, 1734–98) and Laetitia Powell (née Clark, 1741–1801).[4] The women in this group share several key characteristics, which position them as the ideal protagonists in and proponents of the material life writing model. They all belonged to the 'genteel' strata of Georgian society and were financially equipped to engage in fashionable consumption and making practices.[5] They lived contemporaneously to each other, all having been born between 1734 and 1757, and they were all active in undertaking their material activities between the 1750s and 1820s. Finally, they all produced prolific material records of their lives, which were maintained consistently for extended periods. Collectively, they documented over 170 years through a range of material practices. These women have been selected because they represent four categories of material life writing. Johnson kept an album of fabric samples taken from her garments for nearly eighty years, which I position as a material system of accounting (Figure 1.1).

Figure 1.1 *Barbara Johnson's Album, 1746–1823, T.219-1973. Copyright Victoria and Albert Museum, London.*

Lewis painted annual watercolours of herself in significant garments, and Powell dressed dolls in miniature versions of her own clothes, which I classify as two types of repeated sartorial self-representation (Figures 1.2 and 1.4), and Winn consumed and embellished prints with silks as part of a portfolio practice of collecting, consuming and making (Figure 1.3). These women encapsulate four different approaches, yet all four embody material methods of chronicling a life through making.

Crucially, the material records produced by these women challenge us to re-evaluate and reinterpret scholarship on eighteenth-century production and consumption. The 'consumer society' and the 'industrial revolution' have been the dominant explanatory frameworks levied by historians to make sense of seismic social and economic change across the eighteenth century.[6] In their wake, they have given rise to a division between people who made things and people who bought things, which I refer to as the producer/consumer binary. This artificial distinction has shaped scholarship on shopping and consumption and has disguised the nuanced material knowledge and making skills possessed by many consumers. Johnson, Lewis, Winn and Powell are from the ranks of the genteel women consumers often positioned as driving forward the 'consumer revolution', and an examination of their bills, receipts and accounts alone would certainly support this established perspective. The conclusions reached through an exclusive focus on words and numbers are, however, fundamentally challenged by the material records kept by all four women. Instead, their material archives reveal an intimate knowledge of materiality, materials and material culture and, critically, an engagement with practices and processes of making. These collections resist straightforward categorization as records of production or consumption. They exist outside of this binary and compel us to question the rigidity of its construction.

The narratives which women stitched and sketched of their lives are as legible as those written in ink. Deciphering the objects at the heart of these stories has become vital to many historical studies, and material culture is no longer dismissed as ephemeral by scholars.[7] James Deetz argued four decades ago that while 'the written document has its proper and important place', it is imperative that sometimes we 'set aside our perusal of diaries, court records, and inventories, and listen to another voice'.[8] The object-centred and object-attentive studies which now flourish have cultivated a vibrant and ever-expanding field, which has both opened up lost and marginal areas for study, and allowed us to re-examine traditional historical perspectives. Barbara Burman and Ariane Fennetaux's *The Pocket*, for instance, uses 'accumulated shards of evidence' to enable the 'excavations of lost or marginal objects', while Giorgio Riello's *Cotton* mobilizes material culture methodologies in order to challenge conventional economic explanations for global change.[9] Elsewhere in the field, teapots, tables and tureens have been shown to have acted as agents of empire, while emotional tales of love and loss have been untangled from shoes and gloves.[10] The expansive studies of the 'material turn' have firmly revealed the emotional, cultural, political, economic and social agency which can be deciphered through things.

Figure 1.2 *Ann Frankland Lewis,* The dress of year 1775. *Los Angeles County Museum of Art, www.lacma.org.*

Figure 1.3 *Nicolas Larmessin IV, Le Cuvier, after Nicolas Lancret, dressed by Sabine Winn, 1761–1765, NT 960084.1. Copyright National Trust.*

Figure 1.4 *The Powell Collection of Dolls, W.183-1919. Copyright Victoria and Albert Museum, London.*

In spite of the maturation of the field, the inherent challenges of material culture studies still ring true and should not be left unacknowledged, even in work which champions their use. The vagaries of survival have presented a particular obstacle in the assembly of this book. Evidence of women's lifelong engagement with the practice of material life writing is an archival anomaly which this book readily exploits. Johnson, Lewis, Winn and Powell's archives are, although not unique survivals, unusual in their relatively comprehensive endurance. Comparable sources by other women survive as scrawls and scraps, fragmentary snippets of a fuller and consistent engagement with analogous material practices. When brought into conversation with their complete kin, it is possible to begin to make sense of these orphaned objects. The material records at the heart of this book are, indeed, joyous accidents of survival, but that does not mean they are any less representative or rich than their written equivalents. Three hundred years of retention, care and curatorial or archival decisions have shaped what is held within museum stores and archives alike; but the perceived ephemerality of dolls, watercolours and fabrics has caused them to suffer more indignities of separation and disposal than their written counterparts.

The legibility of this variety of material and visual sources is also a challenge to the recovery of material lives. The relative fluency of historians in the language of textual versus material sources has no doubt contributed to the privileging of the written word over the language of things. As with language, material culture consists of many dialects and vernaculars. The skill of reading the stitches of a doll's dress is very different from the brushstrokes of a watercolour, the design of a wallpaper or the carving of a chair. Each requires different modes of familiarity and knowledge, as well as a comprehension of specialist terminology. To learn the vernaculars of things is so often overlooked in holistic material culture methodologies, yet access to such knowledge is by no means the province of the connoisseur. Leonie Hannan and Kate Smith have demonstrated that such languages can be learnt through return and repetition, and that repeated exposure to an object can reveal new layers of knowledge.[11] Jules David Prown's instrumental methodology of description, deduction and speculation also continues to be influential in shaping how historians extract information from 'mute objects'.[12] Yet, as this book demonstrates, reading individual objects in isolation, and without literacy in their particular material dialect, has continued to obscure the tales which they were constructed to tell.

The narratives held within and communicated through objects and series of objects have been decoded from a variety of perspectives. Examinations of the lives of objects, which Igor Kopytoff famously characterized as the 'biography of things', position the objects as the subjects within their own life story.[13] In this model, objects were made, used, remade and eventually discarded, following an anthropomorphized material life-cycle. While objects may themselves be ascribed a biography, the study of the inverse – the ability of objects to act as agents within the biographies of their owners – is a more recent phenomenon. Paula Byrne's biography of Jane Austen, structured around shawls, notebooks and carriages, used objects as the springboard from which the themes of the author's life were explored.[14] Similarly, Neil MacGregor's *History of the World in 100 Objects*, and the imitations it spawned, mobilized objects as vessels of our shared human biography.[15] Works in this vein have made use of the power of things to encapsulate moments of meaning and significance, yet they draw upon objects as fragmented and even incidental vehicles for biographical knowledge. The idea that objects could consciously, cohesively and consistently act as a mirror for a life is absent from historical work.[16] Within the field of dress history, sartorial biographies, such as Kate Strasdin's work on Queen Alexandra, have married up the long-held understanding of the power of garments to act as a material reflection of the wearer and the biographical model.[17] Through such projects, object and human lifecycles and life stories have been brought into synchronization, and the symbiotic relationship between people and things gradually unpicked.

Material life writing

It is the contention of this book that biographical narrative was recorded, and can be read, through material objects, and that such readings can disrupt historical models drawn from written texts alone. This relationship between objects and biography is not conceived for the convenience of a neat conceit, but springs from the purposeful, conscious activity of eighteenth-century women. The field of literary life-writing is no longer constrained by Philippe Lejeune's familiar definition of the autobiographical genre as 'retrospective prose narrative produced by a real person concerning his own existence, focussing on his individual life, in particular on the development of his personality'.[18] To echo Felicity Nussbaum's words, such strict definitions highlight the failures of the generic expectations of autobiography to measure up to life writing practice.[19] As literary scholars such as Nussbaum and Amy Culley have demonstrated, autobiography is mutable, and broader approaches to life writing practice allow explorations of self-representation which spread beyond a 'narrow Romantic cannon which has privileged published autobiographies and linear narratives'.[20] Michael Mascuch has expressed concerns about discarding the rigidity of the genre, and has championed 'imposing limits on autobiographical emissions, placing narrative autobiography in a specific and meaningful historic environment', and it is certainly not my intent to draw false equivalencies between written biography and material objects which dilute the literary canon.[21] Rather, I aim to draw parallels and comparisons between the cultural practices of literary autobiography and material narratives, which mutually enrich our understanding of how women recorded their lives.

The creative practices which I define as material life writing developed concurrently with autobiography's emergence as a recognizable and distinct genre. For both, the eighteenth century was formative. Of course, material life writing practices were not unique to genteel eighteenth-century English women. Matthäus Schwarz's *Book of Clothes*, in which Schwarz recorded his garments through 136 commissioned watercolours, presents a similar commitment to sartorial biography in sixteenth-century Germany.[22] Since the eighteenth century, the material life narrative has flourished, from album and scrapbook culture in the nineteenth century to the perpetual stream of self-portraits evident in the selfie culture and digital storytelling of the social media age.[23] The eighteenth century presents a nascent and formative period of development for both literary and material life writing, to which genteel women were vital. Nussbaum has aligned the 'use of biography as a technology of the middle-class self' with the 'assertion of a female identity in public print'.[24] Concurrently, material life writing offered a platform for women to shape and resist the persistent and prevalent public tropes of women as frivolous consumers. Both acted as a means of negotiating rational selfhood, genteel feminine publicity and the maker/author's relationship with social and cultural norms.

That is not to say that we should treat the written and the material biography as cohesive. Instead, I suggest that they formed two arms of a collective body of cultural practice, which shared the intent of producing memorializing and self-reflective records. Many of the signifiers of autobiographical practice identified by literary scholars are also evident in material practices. Both are retrospective or concurrent acts of self-recording, they demonstrate an engagement with narrative and chronicling, they relate to factual lives and events, and act as crucibles for self-reflection and development. Much like autobiography, there is evidence that material life writing practices were conceived as part of imagined communities amongst women.[25] Just as manuscripts circulated, were read and discussed, material records were shared, continued and mimicked. Johnson's nieces continued their aunt's album-making, while multiple generations of Powell's descendants continued to dress doll-sized versions of themselves for over a century.[26] Friends and family members often gifted useful materials, patterns or instructions, or were commissioned to obtain things on the maker's behalf.[27] The opaque relationship between the real and the constructed nature of autobiographical discourse is also consistent across both forms. Without their full-sized companions for comparison, the veracity and accuracy of neither Lewis' watercolours nor Powell's dolls are verified. Whether they emerge from the pen, brush or needle, all vessels for the mediation of selfhood act as 'representations of our imagined relation to reality' and are entangled in the 'material reality of lived experience'.[28]

The consumer culture of making

It is well established within feminist scholarship that human stories can be told as effectively with the needle as with the pen. Since Rozsika Parker's landmark volume *The Subversive Stitch* was published over thirty years ago, the gendered material practices of women have presented rich opportunities for historians of craft and women's history.[29] These genteel women's making activities have been framed as accomplishments and pastimes.[30] Such studies aimed to rectify the emphasis within scholarship on women as consumers, and instead revealed the material strategies of women as producers.[31] Once unappreciated and understudied, the ways in which women have manipulated the material world are now understood as complex and worthy of scholarly interrogation. Yet, as crucial as it was to salvage women's needlework from its miserable and demeaning status as ephemeral pastime, a closer interrogation of the dynamics and symbiosis between women's consumer and producer selves remains vital. The material lives at the heart of this project disrupt this artificial divide between production and consumption, and it is my contention that within their stitches and brush strokes these four women capture the intense interdependence of women's consumer and producer practices.

Rather than rely on the traditional maker/consumer paradigm to understand the material lives of my subjects, I subscribe to a model of material literacy that allowed women to navigate and record their relationship with the world of goods.[32] The materially literate consumer acts as a usefully broad category, which incorporates both material knowledge and skill. Knowing how something was made and the ability to make it are certainly not the same thing, and material literacy allows for such variations. Borrowing from concepts of textual literacy, the term allows for the varying dialects and vernaculars of materiality, and for variation in the acquisition and application of that literacy. To be materially literate was not an absolute, and neither was it a straightforward spectrum of aptitude. It is possible to be fluent in the making of a dress, but unconversant in the structure of a chair. Whatever the medium, this comprehension of making was never the province of professional producers alone.

Making and buying are, in many ways, inseparable. At the most basic level, women's consumption patterns were shaped in a very real way by their making. If a woman were to make a garment for herself, she might consume cotton from a draper, but she would not patronize the associated labour market available through the mantua maker or seamstress. However, she would buy thread, wax, needles, pins, scissors and tapes amongst a plethora of other tools and accoutrements which, for the most part, were only required if their owner was engaged in some form of making.[33] Similarly, she would only buy paints, brushes and embroidery threads if she was going to pursue the related activities. The consumer marketplace contained not only finished goods, but the tools and materials to make things. Beyond this routine impact upon consumption models, the material strategies of Johnson, Lewis, Winn and Powell reveal more complex synergies between how they themselves conceived of their making and purchasing, specifically in relation to dress. At their heart, each of their material archives consists of material strategies which mediated their maker's consumption, whether as a form of management or memorialization. Instead of only recording purchases in pounds, shillings and pence, it is the materiality of garments which these women documented. That is certainly not to say that these records are indulgent reflections on sartorial consumer pleasures. Instead, I suggest that these practices acted as self-regulation and rationalization exercises within a world that was still negotiating what productive consumption entailed. To put it succinctly, consumption was chronicled through material production.

These strategies sought to intervene in the fraught relationship between women and consumption. The frivolous woman consumer was rhetorically depicted as morally and economically dangerous, aligned with female profligacy, dissolution and even prostitution.[34] Less extreme, but no less negative, has been the influence of conspicuous leisure, which positioned women as unproductive consumers, preoccupied by idleness and casual desire, rather than material or economic practicality or productivity.[35] Thorstein Veblen's enduring image of the self-indulgent women of 1890s New York has haunted scholarly work on the subject, and the trope of the shopping-obsessed middle-class woman is as alive today as it was in the eighteenth century.[36] The *Gentleman's Magazine* of 1731 positioned over-indulgence in shopping and luxury goods as evidence of 'weak Minds, vain, empty, and effeminate'.[37] Yet hours spent browsing, viewing and touching goods were far from empty. Browsing, as Helen Berry has pointed out, was a necessary tactic in order to navigate quality, value and taste within the marketplace, and ran alongside bargaining as a means of obtaining good deals.[38] Infusing the discussion with an attention to materiality, Kate Smith has demonstrated that the accrual of haptic knowledge and the development of the shopper's somatic memory was integral to this browsing practice.[39] As shoppers browsed, they touched, assessed and accumulated material knowledge which enabled them to make informed and rational consumption choices. The desirability of a silk was not only bound up in the fundamental information about where it was made or how new it was, it was also intensely material. The colour, the hand and the quality of the weave were all assessable through touch, sound and sight. Far from a frivolous and self-indulgent means of passing leisure time, browsing, and the familiarity with the materiality of goods which it engendered, was integral to rational and productive consumption.

Isaac Cruikshank's 1808 caricature series, *Miseries of Human Life*, includes an image which wonderfully sums up how haptic browsing practices were warped and twisted through hierarchical gendered binaries (Figure 1.5). Part of a series of caricatures which explored the calamities and woes of life in London at the turn of the nineteenth century, this image depicts two women as they carefully inspect a length of cloth, while their male companion waits in the carriage. The two women in the shop have brought the fabric into the natural daylight by the door and are prudently and judiciously assessing the fabric – quality, weight, suitability, colour – as they amass material knowledge and exercise their material literacy. Irritated by the raucous din of a saw being sharpened, the impatient man perceives nothing but his own inconvenience and frustration and is blind to the rationality and purpose of the task at hand. Primarily authored by the pens of men, the rhetoric of frivolous feminine consumption has obscured the powerful material literacy possessed by women, and the ways in which it shaped their interactions with the material world. The multi-sensory materiality of browsing, and the presence of making within the shop, directly influenced and informed the making practices of consumers. In the early 1790s, Elizabeth Woodhouse, the daughter of a successful York haberdasher, paid ten pounds to a local milliner to instruct her in her 'art'.[40] Stored amongst the receipts and accounts of Woodhouse's wedding trousseau, the attainment of making knowledge was explicitly framed as a transaction on an equal footing with the acquisition of crockery, recipe books and other accoutrements of genteel married life. Making skills existed as a commodity within the marketplace, and we must acknowledge that consumers were also in the market for making knowledge.

A watercolour by George Walker, captioned 'Industrious Jenny ever useful miss!! Employs her time in making a pelisse', depicts the domestic industry signalled by Woodhouse (Figure 1.6). The pelisse, a woman's coat-like outer garment, is an item of clothing which required an advanced range of cutting, construction and stitching skills. As such, it is usually ascribed to the hands of mantua makers and dressmakers, or sometimes male tailors. Yet 'industrious Jenny' is no professional maker. The Jenny depicted is probably Walker's sister, Jane.[41] The siblings' father had been a merchant, but the family also had ties to the landed gentry and, although not wealthy, were firmly part of genteel Yorkshire society. Jenny's engagement with making was not born of necessity but was part of a broader consumer culture of making. Even aristocratic women turned their hands to dressmaking. In a 1781 letter to her sister Louisa Stuart, Lady Carlow wrote, 'my chief amusement since I came from town has been making myself a white polonaise, in which I have succeeded to a miracle, and repent having given one to a famous mantua maker in Dublin who spoilt it entirely for me'.[42] Curatorial connoisseurship has tended to ascribe neat stitches to professional makers and shoddy work to amateur hands. A reinstatement of genteel women as knowledgeable garment makers, however, demands a reassessment of the dynamics between amateur and professional making.

Figure 1.5 *Isaac Cruikshank*, Miseries of Human Life, *1808. Courtesy of The Lewis Walpole Library, Yale University.*

Figure 1.6 George Walker, Industrious Jenny, *watercolour on paper, 1810s, B1975.4.974. Courtesy of the Yale Centre for British Art.*

Of course, it does not necessarily follow that all amateur women who engaged in making were inherently skilled or successful. The frustrations and failures of making are just as significant as the successes. William Henry Pyne's frontispiece to the original 1806 edition of James Beresford's *Miseries of Human Life* encapsulates the vexations of the book's female character, Mrs Testy, with a depiction of her frustrated attempts to thread a needle (Figure 1.7). The text continues on the theme of needlework grievances with Mrs Testy's complaint of 'receiving the first hint that your thimble has a hole worn through it, from the needle, as it runs, head and shoulders, under the nail'.[43] Sewing could be painful, dyes could run, pieces could be cut out wrong and hours spent stitching could result in miserable failure. We must recognize the trials and issues involved in building a knowledge of making and avoid constructing or relying upon a narrative of flawless feminine skill. Such failures are especially evident in Powell's dolls' garments, examined in Chapter 5, where progressive improvement in her skill in cutting and stitching is explicitly legible. Her dolls chart her trials, failures and improvement as a maker, as well as her sartorial biography.

The intersection between the consumer culture of making and gender is particularly significant. For some scholars, the attempts to reclaim women's history which dominated scholarship of the 1990s have been superseded by holistic studies of gender or complementary studies of masculinity.[44] Men, of course, both shopped and made things outside of professionalized or industrialized structures. Winn's husband, Sir Rowland Winn, engaged in correspondence shopping, which incorporated haptic browsing through samples of gilt buttons and gold braid.[45] Men also participated in making as a tool in identity formation and cultural practice.[46] The ways in which consumption and production have been fragmented are, however, highly gendered, and reflect period perceptions of gender rather than practice. The rigid feminization of the consumption of sartorial goods, and valorization of masculine industrial labour (much of which was also carried out by women) dominated eighteenth-century culture.[47] Between the civilizing but diminishing lens of women's accomplishment and craft, the privileging of men's professional making skill and the rampant vilification of frivolous and effeminate consumption, women must take centre stage within any attempt to dissolve the rigidity of the prevalent producer/consumer binary.

Four material lives

The four women who dominate this book created works of material life writing of astounding richness. The material archives of Johnson, Lewis, Winn and Powell are remarkable in their detail and extent, yet they are far from exceptional in their content or practices. In researching this book, I have located hundreds of scraps and snippets that mark similar material practices, some of which make cameo appearances in this volume. Having suffered innumerable indignities through classification as

Figure 1.7 *William Henry Pyne, frontispiece to* Miseries of Human Life, *watercolour on paper, 1806, 806.06.01.01. Courtesy of the Yale Centre for British Art.*

ephemeral curiosities, such morsels of material lives have been separated and scattered to archives around the globe. Even the archives of Johnson, Lewis, Winn and Powell have been broken up and dispersed over time. In completing the jigsaw of Johnson's life, pieces were found in no less than seven different archives on both sides of the Atlantic. Yet, in restoring the comparatively complete material lives of women like Johnson, we are able to begin to make sense of the fragmentary material remains of so many other lives.

This book is committed to a comprehensive reading of material and textual archives. Instead of attempting to counter a dependency on words and numbers with an equally unrepresentative over-reliance on material objects, this book interweaves the information gleaned from the traditional manuscript sources of these women with the products of their material practices. While it is the material objects which drive the narrative of this book, their contents are enriched and corroborated through their alignment with the letters, diaries, receipts, commonplace books, literary outputs, annotated books and ephemera, travel writing and accounts of the four women, their families and their peers. The discursive relationship between object and text which unfolds is, I suggest, representative of the holistic cultural practices with which eighteenth-century women engaged. In challenging the producer/consumer binary I have no intent of building up a material/textual equivalent. Material practices and literacy were understood alongside textual literacy and numeracy and must be brought into conversation with one another.

Each chapter of this book takes one of the four women as its starting point, and uses their robust, extensive and well-preserved archive as a means of making sense of four different approaches to material life-writing practice. Each material life dissolves the producer/consumer binary in distinctive but interlocking ways. Historiographical threads, such as print and periodical culture, feminine accomplishment and emotional labour run throughout the volume alongside the dominating narratives of consumption and making. To bring cohesion to the wealth of sometimes disparate or overlapping information contained within this unconventional sets of sources, all four of the chapters will follow the same fundamental framework. Each chapter opens with an introduction to its category of object and specific material archive. This is followed by a biography of the individual woman, offering a narrative framework against which her material life may be considered. This biographical section offers up an opportunity to consider what information eluded the pen but continues to resonate within stitches and fibres. Each chapter will then reinject materiality into each life story, and consider the vital role played by material accounts, watercolours, dressed prints or dolls in deconstructing the relationship between production and consumption, and constructing the material lives of their makers.

Chapter 2, 'Material Accounting', focusses on Johnson's behemoth album of fabric samples and fashion plates. Collated by Johnson over a span of nearly 80 years, the album contains 122 fabric samples, as well as notes and fashion plates taken from pocket books. Pasted into an old ledger, the album itself acts as a form of material account book, which presents material life writing as a self-regulatory and self-management exercise. Used as a record of Johnson's acquisition of garments and a place to accumulate fashion plates and engravings, the album merges the format of the account book with the scrapbook, seaming together the narratives of the financial, biographical, material and fashionable aspects of Johnson's life. The album, which sprang from her mother's didactic methods, was started at the tender age of 8, and through Johnson's life morphed from a pedagogical exercise to a vital accounting tool for this never-married woman. Johnson's album unveils a self-conscious use of material literacy to navigate the moral and commercial worlds of Georgian womanhood. Through this act of collaged consumption, Johnson recorded her story through her clothing, and fashioned a material account of her life.

While Johnson's album is a complete record of every garment acquired by its creator, Lewis' watercolours, which are the focus of Chapter 3, 'Dress of the Year', were purposefully elected as representatives of their maker's sartorial and social highlights. The thirty-two watercolours, completed by Lewis between 1774 and 1807, reveal how the increasingly popular fashion press influenced women's material practices. Stylistically derived from the fashion plate, these works acted as means of recording and mediating Lewis' consumption of fashion within the framework of print culture and the periodical press. Occasionally accompanied by descriptive notes, these images acted as repeated sartorial self-representations, which privileged the materiality and sartorial language of garments above the features of the face that wore them. Far from splintering fashion from selfhood, Lewis pours emotional, personal and intense feeling into each image. The loss of children, parents and spouses, as well as instances of social consequence are mediated and memorialized through each brush stroke.

Chapter 4, 'Adorned in Silk', brings the narrative material strategies employed by Johnson and Lewis into conversation with the vignette approach adopted by Winn. Instead of a single uniform methodology for the mediation of her material life, Winn engaged with a medley of material methods. The most significant of these centred on a series of sixteen French engravings, which were dressed by Winn using snippets of silk, between the 1760s and 1780s. Winn's craft and consumption practices were explicitly interwoven, and her archive also contains tantalizing glimpses of the fabrics she purchased from retailers in both Wakefield and London. These carefully constructed material scenes attest to Winn's knowledge of how to 'dress' figures. When considered in the context of Winn's own consumption, these adorned prints reveal a complex narrative of national identity, commercial practice and the emotional life-writing attached to textiles. Winn, along with her husband, have been cast as hungry consumers, who filled their Yorkshire home with Thomas Chippendale furniture and Robert Adam interiors.[48] Yet Winn's experiments in painting with fabric reveal more complex material strategies.

Finally, Chapter 5, 'Fashions in Miniature', turns to a fundamental fusing of consumer and producer practices: a series of twelve dolls dressed by Powell between 1754 and 1801. This chapter draws together the strands of making, fashion knowledge, consumption and material life-writing from throughout the book, and sets out a model for the hybrid maker-consumer. These dolls formed part of a wider culture of doll dressing, used as a means of training the material literacy of girls from childhood to adulthood. They chart Powell's growing skill as a maker in tandem with her choices as a consumer. Constructed as miniature versions of fashionable ladies, including garments specifically worn by Powell herself, these dolls enabled the development and maintenance of a vast material knowledge of garment construction. Traditionally examined as play things or mimetic social and domestic training tools, dolls are reframed by this chapter as vessels for material literacy. Captured in the tiny stitches, ruffles and ribbons of these dolls' garments, Powell's sartorial life writing underscores how vital making and materiality were to genteel eighteenth-century women.

The restrictions and boundaries which historians have placed upon the lives of eighteenth-century women have been determined by historical narratives often dominated by words and numbers. Far from a signifier of domestic drudgery and patriarchal dominance, women's material strategies were powerful acts of agency which were used to mediate the sophisticated world of goods. The lives of these four women, as reconstructed through their material archives, fundamentally reshape the moulds into which we place eighteenth-century genteel women. Johnson, Lewis, Winn and Powell compel us to reclaim the material literacy of making from a historical landscape dominated by economic frameworks of trade, industry and consumption. In the words of Deetz, the records of these women sing out to us: 'don't read what we have written; look at what we have done'.[49]

a Laylock figur'd Ducape
Negligee. twenty two yards
half ell wide.
five and ninepence a yard.
four dozen and half of
trimming. 6:6 a dozen.
Stamford Races. June 1767.

a purple & yellow Ducape
Night-Gown. fourteen yards
and a half. half ell wide
five & sixpence a yard.
a dozen & half of trimming
five & sixpence a dozen
1767

A lady in the Court Dress of
the Year 1768.

The Undress.   The Brunswick.

a Garnet Lustring Night-gown
three qrs wide. 1768:
nine yards. at 4: 6 a yard

a white Lustring Gown
five and sixpence a yard
eight yards. 3 qrs wide
1768

a purple and white
Cotton Gown 1768.
five & sixpence a yard

2

Material accounting: A sartorial account book

Barbara Johnson's material life begins not with silks or cottons, gowns or petticoats, but with money. In 1743, when Johnson was five years old, *The Lady's Preceptor* advised readers to teach any daughter 'enough arithmetic to prevent her being deceived by merchants'.[1] Economic literacy was considered essential for eighteenth-century women, whether they were wives, mothers, daughters or single. Financial education equipped women with the required skills to navigate the perilous commercial market. Consumers were pitched against retailers and merchants, who were in turn advised to always pursue 'the main Chance of getting Money'.[2] Economic self-awareness was tied into an expectation amongst the genteel that women should document their consumer lives: what they owned, what was owed to them, and what they owed. Money and objects were inextricable. To keep accounts was a defence against what moral writers perceived to be the encroachment and corruption of the capitalist world.[3] Thrift and self-control sat alongside the desire to consume and possess objects from the increasingly sophisticated world of goods. Such accounts were microcosmic expressions of the complexities of consumer knowledge and practices. Buying a new dress was far from a simple commercial exchange of money for goods. Instead, the transactions recorded in accounts represent expressions of a vast and detailed material knowledge and skill. Traditional financial accounts have regularly fuelled economic and social histories of eighteenth-century women.[4] Yet records of consumer transactions were documented in diverse formats. Materials, as well as numbers and words, could regulate and record consumption.

The culture of material accounting underpinned the activities of eight-year-old Barbara Johnson, as she sat down with her mother to begin a project which would last a lifetime. Taking a snippet of the fabric left over from her first full-length sack gown, Johnson pinned the small rectangle of fabric, measuring four by eight inches, to a slip of paper. Upon the paper, she wrote in a neat hand 'a flower'd calico long sack 1746'.[5] This process would be repeated by Johnson over 120 times before she turned 85, replicated for each and every garment that she had made. Every note and fragment of fabric, which were compiled within a large album, were not uniformly executed. Some notes contained the price, or the amount of fabric purchased. Others referenced a special occasion, perhaps a ball or social gathering, or whether a gown was worn for familial or royal mourning. Several made mention of where the fabric was acquired, who made the garment or even if the fabric was given as a gift. In spite of this inconsistency, a common thread runs between every garment recorded: the materiality of Johnson's accounting method. Pounds, shillings and pence, the tactile samples of silk and cotton and the articulation of sartorial vocabulary sat together within this material account book.

Johnson made a monolithic material investment in her album. Its collation represented more than a passive pastime and an outlet for an interest in 'fashions and fabrics'.[6] Alongside the fragments of fabric and their accompanying notes, Johnson also collected the small engraved fashion plates found in pocket books, the epitome of eighteenth-century frugality and fashionability. Arranged together, these materials fed into a culture of self-regulation. The album represents an intentional, considered and active project for Johnson: a means of accounting for herself.[7] It reflects the serious application and continued investment evident in the collecting practices of Johnson's contemporaries.[8] Yet it also

Figure 2.1 *Barbara Johnson's Album, 1746–1823, T.219-1973, f. 1. Each page in the Album is arranged differently, with samples, notes and fashion prints collated in a loosely chronological order. Copyright Victoria and Albert Museum, London.*

intertwines the enlightenment exercise of collation and display with the commercial world of fashionable consumption. The album interweaves Johnson's moral and material selves and aligns her religious upbringing with her commercial engagement with the marketplace. It is a complex document, which compounded disparate strands of Johnson's life. Her biography as a never-married woman, a churchman's daughter and a materially literate woman is legible through each snippet of fabric, fragment of text and collated fashion plate preserved by Johnson within her album.[9]

Barbara Johnson (1738–1825)

Barbara Johnson is perhaps the most well-known of the four women at the heart of this book. The album is regularly called upon by textile scholars and historical reenactors alike. When the Victoria and Albert Museum published a facsimile of the entire album in 1987, the volume was prefaced by biographical essays on Johnson and her family. Drawn from the archival collection at the Bodleian, as well as papers still in private family hands, this narrative of Johnson's life is now familiar to scholars of dress and textiles. Indeed, Johnson is the only woman studied in this book whose material life has, arguably, already been uncovered. And yet there is still more to find. Her story has been told in part; but Johnson demonstrates that a material life-narrative is as worthy of reassessment as a written one. Further paper archives and two decades of material culture scholarship have transformed and sharpened the lenses through which the album may be read. Johnson's is a familiar material tale well worth retelling.

Barbara Johnson was born on 17 May 1738 in the sleepy village of Olney in Buckinghamshire. She was the eldest and only daughter of the Reverend Woolsey Johnson (1696–1756), a prosperous and ambitious man.[10] Woolsey Johnson had attended Clare College, Cambridge in his youth, and in 1720, at the age of only 24, he was appointed deacon at Peterborough. Woolsey Johnson was a religious pluralist and a career-churchman. Throughout his career he held posts as rector at Wilby in Northamptonshire (1729–56), Olney in Buckinghamshire (1735–53), another family seat at Witham-on-the-Hill in Lincolnshire and several posts in London. His portfolio of positions meant he generated a significant income. He could afford an impressive London property at Warwick Court, Holborn, and was able to build a new manor house at Witham-on-the-Hill.[11] When Barbara Johnson was born in 1738, the family lived in the Great House at Olney. Built in the seventeenth century, this imposing Jacobean property had been in the Johnson family for generations and was a far cry from a modest rectory (Figure 2.2).[12] The Johnsons were not provincial and bucolic, but upwardly mobile and ambitious.[13]

Woolsey Johnson had inherited the Olney parish from his father, William Johnson (1665–1736). It was there that, in 1735, he married his wife, Jane (neé Russell 1706–1759). Jane Johnson was the

Figure 2.2 *Engraving of the Great House, Olney, from* Sunday at Home, *1857. Johnson's childhood home was a Jacobean mansion, not a modest rectory. Courtesy of HathiTrust.*

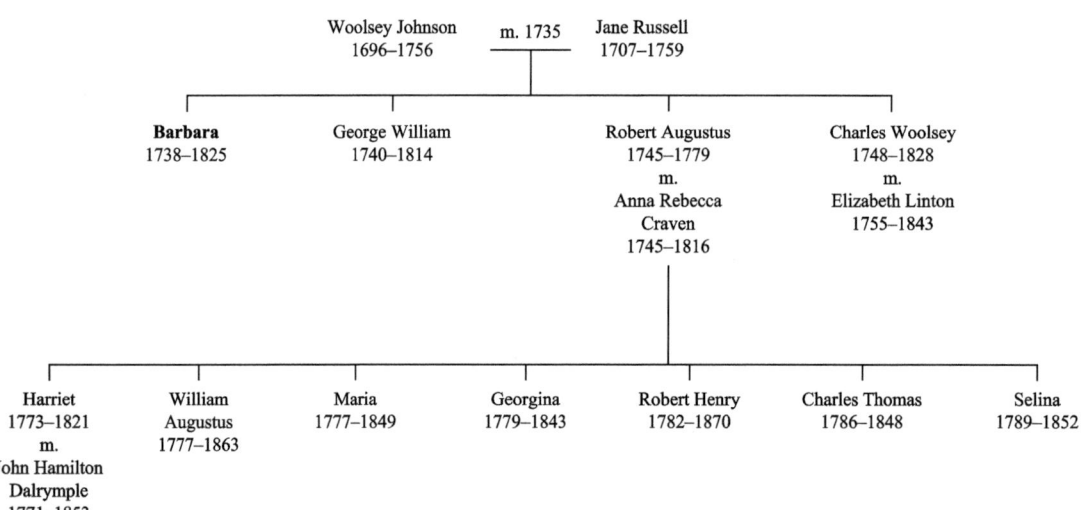

Figure 2.3 *Family tree of the Johnson family. Compiled from evidence in BOD: MS Don. c. 190, ff. 34–5 and 192, ff. 108–17 and LA: JOHNSON/1/3.*

daughter of a Warwickshire gentleman, and was a pious and literary woman who actively supported her husband's work. 'Ever since I was a girl,' she wrote to a friend in the 1740s, 'reading the scriptures has always been my favourite study.'[14] She was deeply passionate about charitable works and took her responsibility to help the poor extremely seriously.[15] Yet her piety and wifely duty often sat in contradiction to her literary and creative talents. Novels, periodicals and poetry fuelled Jane Johnson's love of the written word, and she has been credited with writing the first fairy tale in English for children.[16] Humanist, scientific and religious ideas come together through her writing, which was self-reflective and moralistic. It was into this intellectual, self-improving and religious environment that Barbara Johnson was born.

Barbara Johnson was the couple's first child, and her parents were deeply attached to her. Writing to a friend a year after her daughter's birth in 1738, Jane Johnson wrote:

> Your inquirys after my little Girl are very obliging, I wish you would come and see how you like her. She is I thank God at present very well, and as much like her self as you ever saw a little girl in your life, but as to who she is like besides there are various opinions, I think her the very picture of Mr Johnson's mother whom you never saw. She is extremely fair her cheeks look as tho' they are cover'd with Rose leaves and her lips are like the Coral she wears. Her Papa and Mama think her the very finest Child they ever saw with their eyes.[17]

Barbara Johnson's devoted parents had several more children over the following decade (Figure 2.3). Their daughter was followed by four younger brothers, George, Frederick, Robert and Charles, the latter being ten years Barbara Johnson's junior.[18]

Barbara Johnson's idyllic and stable childhood in rural Buckinghamshire proceeded a peripatetic and unpredictable adulthood. Both of her parents passed away before she was 21, leaving her to take care of her younger brothers. Her father died first, in 1756, followed swiftly and unexpectedly by her mother in 1759. In spite of their early demise, their influence on Barbara Johnson's own literary, religious, financial and material outlook remained strong throughout her life. Crucially, they left her enough money to equip her as a woman of independent means, relieving the financial strain associated with her position as a never-married woman.[19] Officially, the children were left to the care of the executor of Jane Johnson's will, the Reverend Edmund Smythe, a cousin of Jane Johnson, and a family friend. In her will, Jane Johnson left her daughter and each of her younger sons £1,500.[20] This sum was to be paid to Barbara Johnson whenever she wished, with interest of 3 per cent in the intervening period. Though supplemented later in her life, this bequest provided Barbara Johnson with a steady, respectable and reliable income of £45 per annum.

For the remaining sixty years of her life, Barbara Johnson remained unmarried. Whether by choice or circumstance, around a third of women in the early modern period remained single.[21] As an unmarried genteel woman, Barbara Johnson provides historians with evidence of a consumption pattern which fell outside of the traditional household structure that has dominated narratives of consumption.[22] Johnson was neither wife nor mother, and did not have the household management responsibilities which, for genteel women, inevitably accompanied those roles.[23] Instead, she was responsible for managing her own 'Money Matters', and cannot be placed within traditional, economic consumption models.[24] The longevity of her engagement with the album may have been, to some extent, the result of her never-married status. Barbara Johnson focussed on the self rather than the home, fashions rather that furnishings, clothing rather than children. The album was a positive and proactive means of managing this very personal consumption, and as a historical document it provides a refreshing counter to the consumption of other never-married women. Her contemporary Gertrude Savile, for instance, lived a financially and materially restricted life.[25] The album is a celebration of Johnson's never-married status, and a testament to her freedom to account for herself in an idiosyncratic and personalized way.

Barbara Johnson did, however, have a difficult task on her hands: how to maintain an appearance of fashionable gentility on her £45 a year; especially when surrounded by wealthy relatives. In 1773, her brother Robert, who now lived in Witham Hall, had married Anna Rebecca Craven (1745–1816), the wealthy younger sister of Sir William Craven (1738–1791).[26] Robert's new wife was decidedly fashionable, aristocratic and wealthy, and William Craven generously provided Robert with a lucrative Shropshire living, which was maintained by a curate. The Cravens had commissioned Henry Holland and Capability Brown to design their family seat of Benham Park in the 1770s, and the union brought Barbara Johnson into close contact with the fashionable landed elite. Barbara Johnson and her brothers were also members of Lady Anna Miller's (1741–1781) Bath Easton literary circle, and one of Barbara Johnson's poems was published anonymously in Miller's *Poetical Amusements at a Villa near Bath* (1775–81).[27] Barbara Johnson socialized on the fringes of the aristocracy. She attended balls and assemblies frequented by the *beau monde* and exchanged gossip about the fashionable elite. Keeping up sartorial appearances was vital.

Unusually for a never-married woman, Johnson did not position herself as a dependant in the household of one of her brothers.[28] Instead, Johnson's lifestyle was rather peripatetic. She visited friends and family on an almost annual rotation, and divided her time between Buckinghamshire, Lincolnshire, Northamptonshire, London and Bath.[29] One of the biggest influences on her life, both personally and financially, and one of her closest friends, was Catherine Ingram (1744–1808), who had married Michael Wodhull (1740–1816) in 1761.[30] The Wodhulls provided Johnson with surrogate kinship and, though close to her brothers, Johnson seems to have spent more time as a resident within the Wodhull household.[31] Michael Wodhull was a wealthy and learned man, who translated the classics, was a contributor to the *Gentleman's Magazine*, and had books of his own poetry published.[32] He was famed for his library and, shortly after his marriage, he rebuilt his family seat at Thenford in

Figure 2.4 Thomas Beach, *The Honourable Mrs Craven, oil on canvas, 1776, WAG 8632. Mary Craven (1714–1791) was Robert Johnson's mother-in-law, and appears regularly in Barbara Johnson's letters. Courtesy of the Walker Art Gallery, Liverpool.*

Northamptonshire. The refashioning was, purportedly, to provide his books with a better home. Even the design for the house came from a book by Abraham Swan, who had been architect of nearby Edgecote.[33] In this new library hung a portrait of Catherine Wodhull by Johan Zoffany (Figure 2.5). Painted in the classical grand style, the portrait was a testament to the couple's fashionable and artistic aspirations, and their classical literacy. Barbara Johnson stayed with her friend and her husband frequently at both their house in Thenford, and their address at fashionable Berkeley Square in London. She even had her accounts with mercers sent to this address and became a permanent part of the household later in life.[34] When Barbara Johnson died in 1825, it was at Thenford House. She is buried, alongside Catherine Wodhull, at Thenford church.[35]

Between her association with the Cravens, the Wodhulls and the glittering literary gatherings she attended in Bath, Barbara Johnson mixed in fashionable and wealthy social circles. Although she managed on the income from her mother's bequest throughout most of her adult life, this income was supplemented in her later years. When her brother George died in 1814, he left his elder sister an annuity of £50 per annum, which doubled her income. Then, when her friends the Wodhulls died, they left their estate to Catherine's remaining sister Mary Ingram (1748–1824), to whom Barbara Johnson became a companion. Upon Mary Ingram's death, Barbara Johnson received a further annuity of £200. This left Barbara Johnson with a total income of £295 per annum at her death, a sizable sum for a genteel woman on her own.[36] On 14 April 1814, after her brother's death and the discovery of her newfound income, Barbara Johnson wrote to her nephew William Augustus Johnson (1777–1863) that:

> I have always learn'd to be content with a slender income and have gone very well thro' the World to an advanc'd age. I have I believe met with as much real friendship, affection and esteem (the true blessings of life) as if I had posses'd a much larger fortune, I have always kept myself independent and as I have all the comforts of life, I am not likely to grow rapacious in my old age.[37]

Barbara Johnson was financially astute throughout her life, and invested the money she received from her brother George into stocks.[38] Writing to him in 1773, she responded to an offer of a financial gift, saying 'I am very much Oblig'd to you for your kind offer to gift me more money, but I don't want any now, and I hope I shall with some management be able to live upon my income at least at present.'[39] Even when given the opportunity to receive additional funds, Johnson prized her ability to self-sufficiently manage her money. As a financially independent and conscientious single woman, especially one who was not a permanent resident in a relative's house, economic prudence was essential. The socio-economic position of the never-married woman was precarious, and financial irresponsibility disastrous.[40] For Barbara Johnson, rational, self-reflective management of her consumption was indispensable, and had been a lesson taught to her from an early age.

Figure 2.5 *Johan Zoffany, Mrs Wodhull, oil on canvas, 1770, T02217. Catherine Wodhull was Barbara Johnson's closest friend. Copyright Tate, London.*

Educating Barbara Johnson

Let us return to Olney in 1746, decades before Johnson was compelled to concern herself with stocks, shares and money from her brothers. Eight-year-old Johnson, the apple of her parents' eyes, had two little brothers, and was being educated at home by her mother, Jane. Pious, intelligent and literary, Jane Johnson's character appears rather at odds with the traditional picture of her daughter as a fashion-loving consumer. Yet the educational materials constructed by Jane Johnson for her children reveal the inextricable links between the visual, material, religious and moral education of the Johnson children.[41] Self-regulation and productivity were prized by the Church, and religiously devout women often used diaries and other forms of reflective writing as a means of expressing critical religious self-reflection.[42] This link between moral regulation and the material world sheds light on the core purpose of Johnson's album. From dutiful daughter to financially diligent never-married woman, the album was an exercise in self-regulation. Through the album, Johnson channelled material desires and sartorial interests into an exercise in reflective self-improvement.

Jane Johnson was not averse to the pleasures of silks, lace and embroidery. She was adept at sewing, drawing and cut paper work, and in 1749 she wrote to her aunt of the 'intoxicating pleasure' she felt when she spent her time making 'Prizes, Flowers, Stomachers, needle books, cutting watch papers, & many other pretty things'.[43] Yet, when she visited poor families in want of a change of linen, she keenly felt the disparity of their material circumstances, and chastised herself for her own enjoyment of pretty things.[44] Much of this charitable work was carried out as part of Jane Johnson's role as a churchman's 'incorporated wife'.[45] Her role as an aid to her husband and his religious calling was a driving force in her life, and Jane Johnson wrote that she considered it a wife's 'Principal Duty, to do as her Husband commands her, according to St. Paul'.[46] Yet she found ways to align her duties as a churchman's wife with her love of making things. This is most tangibly evident in the educational materials she produced for her four children, of which 438 separate pieces remain, as well as a children's book in manuscript form, entitled *A Very Pretty Story to Tell Children*, and other literary compilations.[47] Haptic, visual and literary, the subjects of these handmade materials ranged from the fundamentals of reading to moralizing tales.

It is striking that, throughout these pedagogical aids, Jane Johnson placed immense importance upon visual stimulus as a supplementary means of reinforcing text. This was in line with the contemporary pedagogical theories of François Fénelon (1651–1715).[48] This approach was by no means unique to Johnson; visual and material means were often used to reinforce lessons, and were commonplace by the start of the nineteenth century.[49] These visual and textual tales were often moral stories, in which the visual reinforced important ethical codes.[50] Jane Johnson's use of the visual to strengthen the textual emerges at an early point in her children's education. A set of alphabet cards created by Jane Johnson contained phrases to help her children recall their alphabet, accompanied by images of the person or thing which began with that letter.⁵¹ An empress, for example, was used for the letter E, and a monkey for the letter M. The cards also contained worldly warnings; 'T Was a tra-der, and ga-ther'd pelf', for instance, instilled an early wariness of the tricks and greed of merchants amongst the young Johnson children.⁵²

Many of the cards produced by Jane Johnson depicted ladies and young girls in fine and elaborate dresses. She took meticulous care in colouring these miniature depictions of fashionable dress, and presented specific identifiable garments rather than generic clothing. As her children got older, Jane Johnson placed them as the subjects of some of the images. In one series of cards, Barbara Johnson was herself named as the central figure. The image depicts her in fashionable dress as she dances a minuet with Lord Mountjoy, possibly referring to Herbert Windsor (1707–1758), the last Baron Mountjoy (Figure 2.6). Through such images, Barbara Johnson was simultaneously trained how to read, and taught about the social world she would inhabit as an adult. Aristocratic men and women inhabited these cards, living in a little paper world full of dances, social activities and clothes. Other cards in this series, which also included flowers, animals and country scenes, are explicit in their intention to teach the Johnson children what they would need to know as adults, especially in regard to dress. A series of four cards all depict fashionable young ladies, three of which mention the style and fabric of the gowns worn. Card number four of the series, for instance, depicts 'Miss Carpenter, in a yellow Lutestring Sack, and a red knot, dancing a Rigadoon by herself at Mr Lally's School'.⁵³ The other images depict 'Miss Cherry Lily dress'd in a blue Sattin Coat; walking with a Fan in her hand, to Church', and the fictional 'Lady Margaret Morduant, Daughter to the Earl of Peter-borow' in a 'red lutestring coat'.⁵⁴ In a similar fashion to the paper doll story books which were to become popular at

 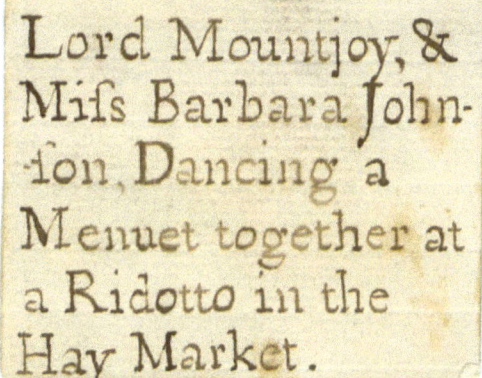

Figure 2.6 *'Lord Mountjoy, & Miss Barbara John-son, Dancing a Menuet together at a Ridotto in the Hay Market', Jane Johnson's Nursery Library, LMC 1649, Set 19, no. 3. Courtesy of the Lilly Library, Indiana University, Indiana.*

the beginning of the nineteenth century, Jane Johnson's story cards brought together fashionable dress, social status and a specific activity.[55] It was in the context of these sartorial reading lessons that Barbara Johnson made the first entry into her album. Just like her mother's didactic materials, Johnson's notes referenced the style of the garments, the terminology used to identify the fabric and the purpose for which it was worn. The resemblance between the two practices is unquestionable.

By the time Johnson was 13, her notes also recorded the price per yard and the length of fabric she had purchased. The album was transformed into a material account book. This practice resonates with the virtues espoused in contemporary pocket books for children. These little volumes championed practical financial self-regulation and aligned moral goodness with economic responsibility. In the 1690s, John Locke had argued that children should be encouraged 'to learn perfectly merchants' accounts, and not to think it is a skill that belongs not to them, because it has received its name from, and has been chiefly practised by, men of traffic'.[56] Locke framed accounting as a useful means of self-regulation rather than financial frugality. To Locke, such records enabled a reflective analysis of spending habits, rather an absolute dissuasion to consume. Pocket books provided an apparatus for this financial self-regulation, and titles were published which specifically targeted women and girls, as well as men and boys. John Newbery (1713–1767), the prolific publisher of pocket books for both adults and children, explicitly stated that by keeping accounts children would learn to maintain their social and economic security: '[h]e that keeps his Accounts may keep his family, but he that keeps no Account may be kept by the Parish'.[57] In a similar vein, the preface of Newbery's 1753 *Ladies Compleat Pocket Book* advised his adult women readers that 'Common Prudence teaches us, that there is nothing more necessary to make Life easy and comfortable than to keep an exact, plain and explicit Account of our daily expenses, that we may be able to regulate them in Time'.[58]

Pocket books emerged in the 1750s and were instrumental in the development of the eighteenth-century periodical press for women.[59] They were small pocket-sized books, measuring only twelve by eight centimetres. Their format was heavily indebted to the almanac, and they often contained diary and accounting space, as well as information on etiquette, poems, stories, fashion plates, practical information on hackney coachmen's rates and tables of social precedency. They were priced at one shilling and were available from at least 1753. The influence of Newbery on Johnson's education is evident both in the album and in Jane Johnson's didactic materials. As Victor Watson has pointed out in his work on Jane Johnson's writing, it is an extraordinary coincidence that she wrote her short story, 'A Very Pretty Story to Tell Children in 1744', the very same year that Newbery published *A Little Pretty Pocket Book*.[60] Newbery's ongoing impact on the Johnson family continued to be felt in 1754 when, aged 16, Johnson included her first pocket book fashion plate in the album. The image was from one of Newbery's own pocket books.[61]

As within the pages of a pocket book, the economic and the fashionable persistently sat side by side throughout Johnson's album. At the same time as Johnson began to learn how to manage her small income, she also learnt the social and sartorial rules of dress. During these childhood years, Johnson purchased an average of two to three garments per year.[62] The terminology used by Johnson refers to 'gowns' and 'robe-coats', as well as the standard sartorial terminology of nightgowns and negligées. In this early period of her life, however, the sack and the coat dominated Johnson's wardrobe. Previous analysis of the album has queried what Johnson may have meant by the term 'coat', as this term was used both as an abbreviated term for petticoat, and a name for a specialized children's garment.[63] Two of the pedagogical cards produced by Jane Johnson depict young girls wearing what is described as a 'coat'.[64] In both cases, this appears to be a gown with a closed skirt and bodice. The style depicted in Jane Johnson's drawings, and referred to as a 'coat', bears a strong resemblance to extant children's dresses.[65] There were several key features of this coat style which differed from adult dress. The skirt tended to be cut all in one, rather than with an open front over a petticoat. They also often fastened with lacings down the centre back, with no opening at the centre front, which gave the gowns a more flexible fit, extending their wearability as the child grew.[66] Both these characteristics are in line with Jane Johnson's drawings. The last garment which Johnson describes in the album as a 'coat' was purchased in 1755, when she was 16 or 17, and on the cusp of adulthood. After this point, Johnson never used the term again.

Through these formative years, the album charted Johnson's sartorial maturation. At 8 years old, the sack gowns were probably Johnson's first adult-style dresses; at 16, the coats were her final children's garments. As part of Jane Johnson's wider pedagogical plan, the album provided a means through which Barbara Johnson could manage and self-regulate both her love of fashion, and her consumption of it. Moralistic and religious as the atmosphere in the Great House at Olney may have been, it provided an ideal environment for the creation of an album which would last a lifetime. Johnson's early entries to her album were her primer for the methods of economic and material self-regulation she would turn to throughout her life.

Accounting for herself

In 1759 Johnson found herself orphaned and deprived of her mother's guiding hand. The fourth page of the album contains exclusively black, brown and dark grey fabrics. Johnson denoted these as the fabrics she wore for 'mourning for my mother' and 'mourning for my father'.[67] Striking in its sombre reverence, this page of the album marks a watershed in Johnson's life. Yet, instead of abandoning her childhood practice of sartorial recording, she strived onwards. For the next sixty years, the album's construction remained comparatively consistent. Now a woman of independent means, the album presented Johnson with an imaginative strategy for managing her income. It contains 122 samples in total, with an average consumption of two to three garments per year from the age of 8 to 85. The ledger in which Johnson kept this record had previously been used as an account book by a George Thompson, and how Johnson came to possess this book remains somewhat of a mystery. As Thompson's ledger dates from 1738 to 1748, and the first sample is dated 1746, the earliest samples were certainly accumulated into the book retrospectively. The chronology in these early years is also not entirely consistent, as the samples were probably stored elsewhere, attached to their little paper labels, and later deposited and arranged within the album itself.

In spite of the immense number of samples, it is clear that the album is not quite complete. There are several gaps in Johnson's acquisition of garments. Some of these gaps are single years, while other larger gaps, such as 1773–75 and 1783–84 coincide with periods when Johnson was socially active in Bath and was highly likely to have been active as a consumer. We also know that Johnson received or inherited items of clothing which do not appear in the album, such as 'a flowered silk and a suit of point lace', which was inherited from a Mrs Williams in 1780.[68] These absences were likely a necessary consequence of Johnson's collection methods. The fabric samples, even when taken from items described as gifts, must have been acquired from the offcuts from the construction of the garment. It would have been impossible to take such large samples from a completed gown. As such, the album is as much a record of garment making and manufacture as it is of consumption. It captured moments of dress construction.

Although clearly commenced as a means of self-regulation and material accounting, a closer look as a single page from the album reveals that these practical purposes ran alongside other rich veins of meaning and motivation. The seventh page of the Johnson's album contains fabrics dated to 1758 and 1759, as well as one fashion plate dated 1759, and another undated engraving (Figure 2.7). Although the mourning garments were confined to a single, earlier page, these fabrics also date from the same years. Johnson's decision to confine the mourning garments to their own page, and consequently break the chronology of her garment acquisition, shows an intent to memorialize and honour a specific affective biographical moment within the album. Feelings, as well as finance, shaped the album. Yet, extracted from the mourning garments which they were purchased alongside, the samples on this page offer no hint of the emotional turmoil of grief. The information logged with these fabric samples is typical of that recorded throughout the album. On this page, the brown silk at the top left is accompanied by a note which reads: 'a brown figur'd lutestring night gown July 1758 3s 6 a yard, half yard wide'.[69] The blue silk is described as 'a Strip'd buff & blue Taffety negligée June 1758, four guineas the piece sixteen yards, yard wide'. Finally, the red fabric is described as being for 'a Scarlet Stuff Gown December 1759 1:7 a yard, seven yards'. This pattern of describing the fabric, its intended use, the price, length and width was Johnson's standard practice, and very much reads like the contents of a traditional account book. Finance, fashion and familial memorialization ran side by side.

Johnson's album chimes with many of the characteristics of eighteenth-century accounting. Often used to access the economic narrative of the life-cycle, account books provide quantifiable measures

Figure 2.7 *Barbara Johnson's Album, 1746–1823, T.219-1973, f. 7. Johnson's album was kept in rough chronological order, although there are a handful of discrepancies. Here, fashion plates from 1759 and c.1800 are side by side. Copyright Victoria and Albert Museum, London.*

of consumer practice.[70] Although it was only her consumption of dress which she recorded, rather than her full personal accounts, this was not unusual in eighteenth-century accounting. As Amanda Vickery has noted, 'even keen accountants may have chosen to capture only one area of their lives in a record book'.[71] For genteel women, fashionable consumption was certainly an area which they were encouraged to account for. Like many publications of its kind, the 1782 edition of *Harris's Original British Ladies Complete Pocket Memorandum Book* preceded its usual accounting section with an address to the ladies on dress, cautioning them to remain astute in their consumption.[72] Johnson's focus on fashionable dress clearly marks out her sartorial consumption as an area in which she felt the need for additional tools to mediate her self-regulation as a consumer.

As a material form of the account book, the album was a defence against the rhetoric around overindulgent fashionable consumption, and the problems which surrounded a credit-based consumer economy. When not warning consumers about the ploys of tradespeople, moral literature from the period often presented an image of the consumer in control, particularly in financial terms. This control chiefly operated through economy of credit, and was enacted through how, when and to whom credit was paid off.[73] This culture of credit came about as part of the financial revolution of the seventeenth and early eighteenth centuries and provided the precedent for the majority of the consumer's financial transactions throughout the eighteenth century. Credit was granted based almost entirely on the appearance of the consumer. Did they look respectable? Were they well-presented and dressed in appropriate clothing? Dress acted as proof of credit-worthiness. As Margot Finn has stated, '[c]reditors sought constantly and unsuccessfully to read debtors' personal worth and character from their clothing, their marital relations, their spending patterns and their perceived social status'.[74] If consumers could be trusted to keep accounts, then retailers and merchants would, in theory, have their bills paid on time. Money would continue to flow through the country, and the national economy would be maintained.

The most credit-worthy clients were permitted to pay off their debts after a period of months, even years; and could conduct their business at a distance. Augusta Irby (1747–1818), wife of Thomas de Grey, the second Baron Walsingham, ran up debts of nearly £1,000 with her London milliner between 1784 and 1796, which she paid off by small and irregular instalments of £50.[75] This was not an unusual arrangement. Charles Wyndham, the Earl of Egremont (1751–1837) ordered items from the same milliner for his mistress Elizabeth Ilive, which were to be sent to Petworth House in Sussex, and added to the Wyndham's credit account.[76] The viability of an individual as a consumer was based on a subjective assessment of objective means, and was often compounded by conducting business at a distance. Ideally, regular repayments created a systematic cash flow for the retailer, but this economic stability relied upon consumers who retained control of their accounts.

The consumer who was misjudged by the retailer, and could not, or would not, pay their debts, caused a break in the financial flow of business, and led to financial ruin for retailers and consumers alike. Account books seized when business owners were unable to pay their own debts provide an insight into how and why issues with the credit system were compounded by the poor money-management rife amongst consumers. The accounts of retailer-turned-debtor William Barwick, a Haberdasher working in York in the 1820s, were arranged under the names of each customer, and reveal that the vast majority of customers left their bills unpaid months, or even years, after they received the goods.[77] The Johnsons had recent family experience of the pitfalls of the credit system, as Woolsey Johnson's grandfather, Thomas Johnson, had been imprisoned for debt in the Marshalsea.[78] This near miss of a family disaster must have left the Johnsons keenly aware of the fragility of the credit system, the risks of financial irresponsibility, and the disconnect between wealth and credit. Indeed, Barbara Johnson wrote to her brother of a mutual acquaintance who 'was greatly distressed in his circumstances, though the world thought him very rich'.[79]

Much of the literature which criticized consumer abuse of the credit system stemmed from moral religious writing, of the kind Johnson's religious parents would have read.[80] Josiah Hort (1674–1751), Bishop of Kilmore and Ardagh, published a sermon in 1738 entitled *Of Righteousness in Paying Debts*, in which he stated that: '*The Spoil of the Poor is in your Houses*; for how can we call it by a better Name when we see Luxury in Dress ... supplied by poor Tradesmen, who are unmercifully kept out of their Money, till they are ruined and undone by supporting the Vanity of those who despise them.'[81] Hort's complaint places social and economic responsibility on the shoulders of the consumer. The tradesman was actively 'kept out of their Money', the payment withheld as a deliberate and controlling act.[82] Hort was not alone; other publications from the mid-century made similar calls for women to keep accounts of their financial and moral lives. In his *Complete System of Family Book-Keeping* (1758), Adam Walker (1731–1821) wrote that:

> I am very conscious how dry and ungenteel Subjects of this Nature, as well as Oeconomy in general, appear to the polite and very enlightened Ladies of the present Age; but, so far as my Abilities would admit, I have removed the Drudgery, and leave it to better Judges how far I have succeeded. Oeconomy is still a Virtue amongst the Wise and Prudent, and not, I hope, so to be corrupted by the Contagion of Fashion, as to rob even an honest Design of its due Praise.[83]

Walker would have been unimpressed with Johnson's album. It realized his fears of the 'contagion of fashion' corrupting the virtuous design of accounting.

Accounting for oneself, whether in words on numbers, was a significant activity for the Johnsons. Jane Johnson had been an avid keeper of commonplace books. Before her marriage she had compiled a book of neatly arranged recipes and useful household remedies.[84] Later in life she compiled extracts and pieces of her own writing for her own moral improvement, and stitched these together into small volumes.[85] Jane Johnson encouraged her children to mimic this practice of compilation, and the family letters refer to a communally produced memorandum book. Robert Augustus, Barbara Johnson's brother, maintained a journal from 1771–1777, which contained a record of his tours around England, as well as extracts from books he had read.[86] Similarly, Barbara Johnson wrote to her brother George when he returned from a trip around Europe, to express her hope that he had recorded his journey in a journal or album, and requested to view it.[87] George's process of recording his travels also included painting watercolours of places he had visited.[88] This habit of constructing literary, visual and material records of their experiences was a family trait, and a practice the siblings shared with one another. They were kept accountable to each other, and they circulated the records they produced within the family.

The practice of preserving and compiling collections of fabric samples was not unique. Accounts for the refurbishment of houses often contained samples of the fabrics for soft furnishings, retained as a means of recording the scheme that had been agreed.[89] In the nineteenth century, women like Anne Sykes (1816–1880), Annie Hayslip (1835–1898) and Thomas Hardy's sisters Mary (1841–1915) and Katharine (1856–1940) maintained records of the garments owned and worn by their friends and relatives.[90] Like Johnson, they pinned explanatory notes to small fragments of textile, memorializing their social and familial worlds. Similar records were kept of the ensembles worn by Queen Charlotte and the princesses in the 1790s, and Catherine Milburgha Hartshorne (1836–1907) kept albums containing samples from garments with aristocratic and royal connections.[91] Across the channel, Marie Antoinette's *Gazette des Artours de Marie-Antoinette* is also similar to Johnson's album.[92] Like Johnson's album, it contained samples of fabric taken from each garment in the Queen of France's possession, along with a short written description to identify the garment. However, these wardrobe accounts acted as a material index. This directory of fabrics allowed easy visual identification and acted as an *aide-mémoire* for an immense collection of garments.

Johnson's album also displays similarities to the nineteenth-century scrapbook.[93] Beverly Lemire, in her seminal book on the consumption of cotton fabrics in Britain, specifically referred to Barbara Johnson's album as a 'scrap-book and clothing diary'.[94] There are precedents for ladies collecting and making albums from prints, trade cards and fashion plates in the eighteenth century, such as the collection of Sarah Sophia Banks (1744–1818).[95] These organized collections, however, were based around specific genres of print, rather than incorporated as a supplement to a more personal record. The scrapbook as a genre did not fully emerge until the nineteenth century. Johnson's niece, Selina, created a scrapbook in the 1860s that included paintings and drawings of houses, table decorations, the church, fashionable hairstyles and portraits of people she knew.[96] This record, although begun in 1863, contained earlier scraps from her childhood, and was continued by family members into the following century.[97] Similarly, Barbara Johnson's nephew, George Wolsey Johnson created a scrapbook memorializing the family history, and included drawings of the various Johnson family homes.[98] These scrapbooks, and the many others like them, allowed their creators to 'make a place for themselves and their communities by finding, sifting, analysing, and recirculating' the writing and images that mattered to them.[99] They helped to make emotional sense of traumatic experiences, such as war and grief, as well as enabling them to create an object which acted as a material articulation of personal identity and family history.

Accounting for the self, these records show, extended beyond financial self-regulation. Self-memorialization – the desire to be remembered – is also consistently present. Johnson's album, like those of Sykes, Hayslip and the Hardy sisters, presents an alternative format of the memory quilt, in which fragments of fabric from old and treasured textiles were stitched together into something new.[100] Garments and curtains, table clothes and upholstery were brought together in these objects, which retained and conjoined the collaged memories attached to the various fragments into one comprehensive object of remembrance. In quilts, 'curiosities' of the past were arranged together into a grid format which defied linear narratives of historical construction.[101] The patchwork quilt was a material space in which a personal or family history could be pieced together, each milestone marked out through fabrics. Fragments of the past could be collated, organized and made sense of through an act of making, just as they were in Johnson's album. A similar correlation between fragments of fabric and memory can be found in the Foundling Hospital's tokens.[102] Founded in London in 1739, the hospital provided a home for the babies of mothers who, for social or financial reasons, could not take care of them. The babies, who were given new names and detached from their former identities, were only identifiable through the tokens left with them by their mothers. If a mother were able to reclaim her child in the future, she need only bring a matching token. Usually a swatch of fabric, these material markers were often a fragment of the mother's clothing. Left behind with their children, these textiles provided a poignant link between the mother and child; a fractured remnant of their previous lives. These scraps and snippets encapsulated memories and, pinned into a large ledger, recorded and organized identities through fabrics.

Johnson's album defies categorical classification. It is a financial record, a self-reflective chronicle, a biographical narrative and a memorializing ego-document. Yet it does not fit neatly into any of these categories. It deals almost exclusively with Johnson's interest in and consumption of fashion, but its focus on the point of consumption separates it from other established genres of scrapbook. As an idiosyncratic compilation of standardized methods of record-keeping, the album is intensely biographical and personal, and yet the chronology is uneven. Despite its similarities to comparable genres, Johnson's album undoubtedly sits most comfortably as a peculiar and distinctive form of account book. Critically, Johnson recorded garments at the nascent moment of their purchase and creation as items of dress. Unlike the practices of Lewis and Powell, discussed later in this book, Johnson did not select specific, emotionally affective garments to memorialize in her album. Every garment made for Johnson, from her childhood in 1740s Buckinghamshire to her old age in 1820s Thenford, was carefully and unfailingly logged and recorded.

Material literacy

The notes which accompanied Johnson's fabric samples reveal a diverse and complex vocabulary of textile knowledge: her material literacy. Johnson was an able maker, and regularly sent her brothers gifts of netted purses and garters which she made herself, and she even fashioned a stool for her young niece.[103] This material knowledge was not only expressed through making itself; Johnson was also fluent in the language of textiles. The didactic tools created by Jane Johnson had specifically used terminology such as 'lutestring' rather than simply the basic fibre, 'silk', and Johnson continued to update, refine and use this terminology throughout the album. Johnson was not a passive consumer, willing to purchase whatever she was told was fashionable. Her agency as a consumer, and her knowledge of the materials and materiality of the textiles she purchased, are explicit in her meticulous record. While many of the consumption trends recorded in the album can be explained by broader narratives of trade and industry, it is the terminology and material knowledge displayed in the accompanying notes which highlight Johnson's intense material understanding.

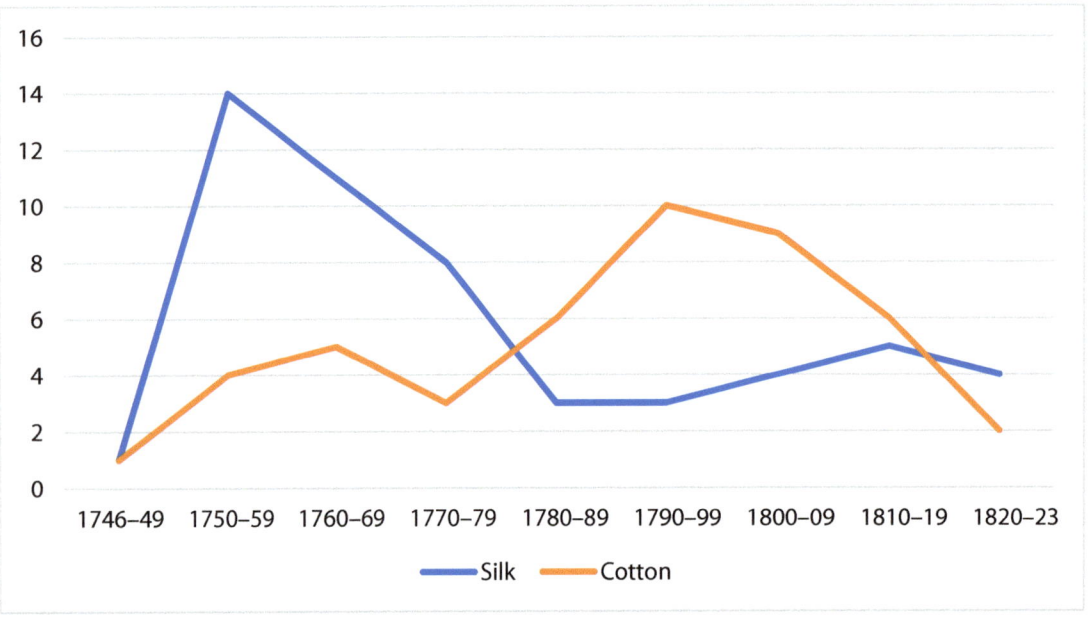

Figure 2.8 *Appearances of silk and cotton in Barbara Johnson's album, 1746–1823, arranged by decade. Source: VAM: T.219-1973.*

Johnson's relative consumption of cotton and silk textiles across the seventy-seven years covered by the album reveals the impact of changing patterns of global trade on Johnson's shifting and evolving consumption, and underlines the need to continually update material vocabulary (Figure 2.8).[104] During her teens and young adulthood in the 1750s and 1760s, Johnson demonstrated a clear and decided preference for silk textiles, and an awareness of the terminology used to denote the abundance of available varieties. Silk brocade, tabby, satin and lustring dominate the samples Johnson collated. Throughout the final decades of the eighteenth century, however, silk satins and brocades were replaced by purchases of cottons in the form of calico, muslin and chintz. Silk and cotton had consistently been the most popular imported fabrics into Britain.[105] In the late eighteenth century, the domestic cotton industry began to boom, and this cheaper, novel fabric enjoyed a burst of popularity amongst consumers.[106] Further nurtured by the mercantilist banning of imported Indian cottons earlier in the century, this protectionist attitude to domestic economics had fostered a shift in consumer spending. These fabrics were comparatively inexpensive, meaning better prices for consumers and better profits for retailers and merchants. This substantial and sophisticated array of new textiles required fluency in a new and continually evolving material vocabulary.

Johnson's material literacy is evident throughout her accompanying notes. She carefully recorded specific attributes of the cottons she consumed, and confidently used correct and up-to-date vocabulary. Her recognition of the fibre content of each fabric was not universally correct, for instance in her teens she misidentified a linen as a cotton.[107] Her textile lexicon, however, was robust and well informed. In the 1780s, David Murray, Viscount Stormont (1724–1796, later the Earl of Mansfield) protested in Parliament against the growing tide of weavers leaving British shores, and set up his own mill.[108] Johnson engaged with Stormont's patriotic action, purchasing a 'Stormont cotton' in 1788, and explicitly recorded this connection in the album.[109] Johnson was conversant in the politics of the contemporary textile market, and was conscious in her decision to support the British textile industry in an act of patriotic consumption. We know from her letters that she took a keen interest in politics, and did not approve of Lord North's taxation policies.[110] She also engaged in a lengthy correspondence with Sir Hugh Inglis (1744–1820), a relative via marriage and a Director of the East India Company from 1784.[111] Johnson's material literacy connected politics and trade with fashion and fabrics.

The correlation between patriotism, the vocabulary of textiles, consumption and fabrics was reinforced through the innovative marketing techniques employed in publications such as the *Repository of Arts*. Begun by Rudolph Ackermann (1764–1837) in 1809, this periodical included a page entitled 'patterns of British manufacture' in each issue.[112] Surrounded by a patriotic allegorical woodcut, these 'patterns' were samples of fabrics and ribbons, accompanied by textual descriptions of the items, and directions to retailers from whom they could be purchased. This was a comparatively innovative inclusion, at least amongst British periodical publications.[113] Aside from its persistent insistence on the pre-eminence of British textiles, these samples also championed the development of material vocabulary. The first issues, like those that followed it, elaborated on the material properties of the fabrics included (Figure 2.9). The first fabric was described as a 'plush, manufactured from mohair'. It was framed as ideal for the cold weather:

> The utility of this fabric for vests is sanctioned by sporting gentlemen, who have the lower part of the vest for six or seven inches lined with the same. After a hard chase, the loins do not experience that chill and cold which is often felt in the ride home, owing to the gentle irritation and warmth of the plush, which absorbs the perspiration.[114]

The periodical presented readers with both terminology and purpose, linking the material properties of the textile with bodily problems and practical utility. Terminology and materiality were also championed in a 'brocade of tissue' and a 'flowered satin', fabrics three and four in the same issue. Visually similar, the descriptive text uses specific textile vocabulary to differentiate and distinguish. Not one to miss an opportunity to promote the manufacturers of Britain, Ackermann concluded this section by attributing these two silks to the weavers of Spitalfields:

> The three last patterns are the manufacture of Spitalfields. The introduction of silks among our ladies of fashion, has revived the almost declining employment of the silk-weavers, and if it has the effect of excluding the fine fabrics of Indian manufacture, to the increase of our artizans at home, we shall feel very happy in the exchange.[115]

Figure 2.9 *Patterns of British Manufacture, from Ackermann's* Repository of Arts, *1809. Fragments of real fabrics were pasted into every copy of this periodical. Private Collection.*

For Ackermann, patriotic consumption was a fundamental facet of material literacy. National industry, material properties and a robust textile vocabulary were promoted in unison.

The resumed popularity of silk in the 1810s, signalled by Ackermann, is reflected in Johnson's album. However, her loyalty to British manufacture was not so steadfast. In contrast to Johnson's patriotic purchases of British manufactured cottons in her middle age, during her old age she recorded her acquisition of various French imports. As a never-married woman, Johnson benefited from a kinship network of gift-giving. She accepted a gift of French silk from her friend Catherine Wodhull in 1795, and another of French sarsanet from her brother in 1811, at a time when the two countries were actively at war. Her brother had given her gifts of gowns throughout her life as a signal of fraternal patronage and familial care.[116] These significantly intensified as she progressed in age, as did gifts from Wodhull. Between 1799 and 1804 all of the garments which Johnson recorded were made from gifted fabrics. Following the death of Catherine Wodhull in 1808, her husband continued in the stead of his wife, gifting Johnson the material for two further gowns. A gift of fabric, however generous, still required financial outlay by Johnson. A gift of 'Pompadour broad cloth' from Johnson's brother in 1760 required her to spend a further eight pounds on the services of a maker.[117] The corresponding bill from Henry Paulin, a London haberdasher and habit maker, broke down the additional costs required to convert this length of fabric into a riding habit for Johnson.[118] There were two dozen silver buttons, seven yards of silver binding, buckram and lining fabrics, then the making of the habit itself and a

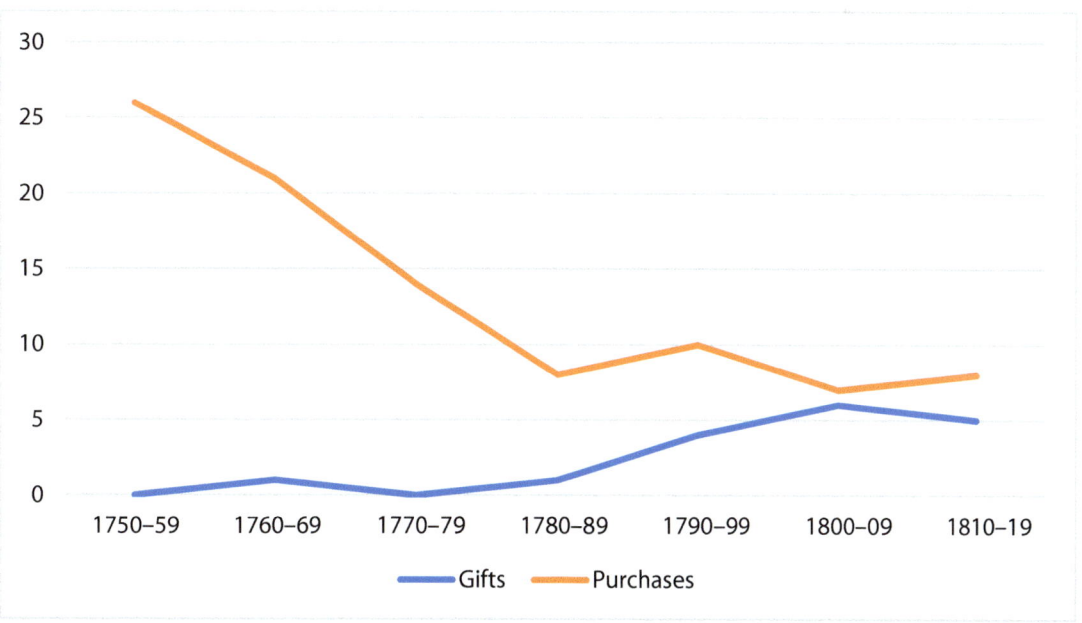

Figure 2.10 *Number of gowns purchased by and gifted to Barbara Johnson, arranged by decade, 1750–1819. Source: VAM: T.219-1973.*

contrasting waistcoat. In total, Johnson's outlay exceeded her brother's. Gifts of cloth did not alleviate the financial burden Johnson may have felt; instead, they necessitated additional engagement with the commercial market.

When Johnson purchased fabrics for herself in her later years, she overwhelmingly favoured plain fabrics, often in dark colours. While the earlier dashes of deep and dark shades were identified as mourning wear, no specific purpose was recorded for these later purchases. Vickery has commented that this preference for darker colours, small, busy prints and figured silks indicated a clear decision to dress for older age.[119] Johnson's fabric choices in these later years contrast sharply with the fashionable light, white muslin gowns depicted in the fashion plates scattered amongst the fragments of fabrics. On the few occasions Johnson purchased a muslin, it was either a printed muslin, or a dark coloured Chambery muslin, which was a delicate silk and cotton mix. Despite not engaging with the fashion for white muslin in her old age, Johnson did consume several new fabrics, such as the sarsanet gifted by her brother in 1809. This soft, flowing silk contrasts with the stiff silks of Johnson's youth, which would not have been appropriate for the high-waisted fashionable styles of the regency. Johnson kept up with fashion, but, as with all her material endeavours, it was in her own idiosyncratic way. Johnson's up-to-date material literacy and consumption habits are also revealed through the terminology used in these later years. From 1798, she regularly used the new terminology of 'round gown', and purchased two pelisses in 1803 and 1811.[120] Both styles were unique to this period and followed the new raised waistline.[121] As Johnson aged, there was a clear decline in the number of garments acquired year-on-year. The average dropped from two to three per year in her youth, to only one per year in her old age. Up to date as her purchases may have been, Johnson's consumption of garments was a cumulative process. While some earlier garments were possibly disposed of, others were kept, remade, reused and recycled in a cycle which is absent from the album.[122] Each entry in the album reflects an initial moment of investment in a fabric that might have gone on to experience various incarnations as it was updated, remade and refashioned.

Although Johnson was keen to keep sartorially up to date, she also actively commented on the more radical changes in fashion and was not always complimentary. In the 1770s she passed on news from the Wodhulls to her brother, and wrote that 'they send me surprising accounts of the latest fashions, and of the ladies heads which are quite enormous'.[123] 'Ladies heads', in this context, referred to the towering hairstyles fashionable in that decade. Similarly, as she planned her outfit for the Stamford race weekend, she quipped, 'I don't know whether the ladies at Stamford dress in the whimsical manner I have lately heard of some being equip'd.'[124] Johnson also turned her humoured but critical tongue towards women who dared to wear youthful fashions, and even her relative Elizabeth Twisleton, Lady Say (1740–1816), also a distant relative of the novelist Jane Austen, was not immune. 'Lady Say,' Johnson wrote in the 1780s, 'dresses as youthful as ever, a yellow gown with pin gawz ornaments, so that she very much resembles a cousin Betty.'[125] In eighteenth-century slang, a cousin Betty was someone of limited understanding. Johnson may have been a chronicler of fashion, and an avid consumer, but she was not blind to its foibles.

A chronicle of fashion

Johnson was keenly interested in the evolution of fashionable styles, and she used the album to chronicle the evolution of fashion throughout her lifetime. This hybrid purpose is explicitly evident in the fashion plates collated and arranged throughout the album. First inserted in 1754, fashion plates from pocket books were relatively novel when Johnson first began to collect them. These small engraved images were included in the pocket books for women published by booksellers like Newbery, and they rapidly grew in popularity from the mid-eighteenth century. The images depicted dress from the previous year, so were always notoriously out of step with fashion. However, crucially, their captions provided pocket book readers with the descriptive terminology used to articulate evolving styles. Almost all of the 134 prints in the album originated from pocket books.[126] Their accumulation and roughly chronological layout was, however, far from a straightforward cavalcade of costume. Pocket books, established to have played a significant part in Johnson's education, carried self-regulatory connotations. These undertones of rational self-regulation extended to their fashion plates.

Pocket books appeared under an enormous number of different titles and were published both in London and by local booksellers. Although their titles were diverse, their content was remarkably similar. It is, however, possible to trace several of the prints within the album to the pocket books from which they originated. Johnson, this process reveals, was not loyal to one title or publisher through her life. Instead, she purchased a variety of different publications, with occasional exceptions and favourites. Most of the titles were printed in London and can be identified clearly through the text which accompanied the image, such as the *English Ladies Pocket Companion or Useful Memorandum Book* of 1792, the title page of which was included in the album. In the 1750s and 1760s Johnson was relatively loyal to the *Ladies Complete Pocket Book*, with at least twenty-one of the prints probably originating from this publication. This pocket book, published by Newbery, was one of the earliest which appeared. Other titles which Johnson sporadically purchased include *Wayland's Annual Present or Pocket Book, Lane's Pocket Book, The Ladies Museum or Complete Pocket Memorandum Book* and the *Polite and Fashionable Ladies Companion*. There are plates from at least nineteen different pocket books published in London, and Johnson certainly showed a preference for these metropolitan publications.

As with the construction of albums, it was not unusual to collect and collate pocket book fashion plates. Johnson's contemporary, Sarah Sophia Banks collected over 400 such images between 1760 and 1818, and there is significant cross over in the images gathered by both women.[127] In 1819, Mary White

(1759–1825) also created an album of fashion plates, and Catherine Hutton (1756–1846), daughter of successful merchant William Hutton, also recorded her engagement in a similar practice: 'I have been a collector of costumes … and I now have 650 English figures … They are composed eight large folio volumes … I have written on each opposite page of the English figures explanations and remarks of my own, which constitute a history of the habits of this country.'[128]

Banks, White and Hutton thought of themselves as collectors, who had curatorial authority over the narrative of fashion which they built in their albums. Their audience was posterity. Johnson's fashion plates, and the juxtaposition of these images with records of her own consumption, offer up evidence of a more active engagement with these images. Johnson did not copy verbatim the garments they depicted. They did, however, maintain her material literacy and present her with new sartorial vocabulary. Fashion knowledge once learnt is not static, and pocket book fashion plates provided a regular refresher for the consumer's material literacy.

Johnson's own evolving terminology directly echoed the vocabulary of the fashion plates' captions. In 1772, Johnson recorded her purchase of a brunswick made of Manchester cotton in a checked pattern.[129] A brunswick was a very unique garment: a three-quarter length jacket with a hood, button front and detachable lower sleeves. This distinctive style was exclusively fashionable between 1764 and the early 1770s.[130] Upon leafing back through the pages of the album, this same, specific terminology appeared on one of Johnson's fashion plates (Figure 2.11).[131] Although undated, this trend was relatively short lived. The correlation between fashion plate and purchase offers the first quiet hint of the resonances between print and dress which recur throughout this book. Textiles and paper, image and object, materials and words were symbiotic in eighteenth-century culture. Significantly, these prints were not purchased independently as fashion engravings, but were incidentally acquired by Johnson as part of the complete publication of the pocket book. As fashion plates evolved and diversified into the colourful concoctions of the late eighteenth century, Johnson remained loyal to her little monochrome images. Connotations of frugal fashion, self-regulation and indulgence in moderation enhanced their appeal as reflections of the album's moral, financial and sartorial ethos. Both pocket book and album were instruments for self-regulation.

One of the first engravings collected by Johnson depicted a lady and a gentleman in fashionable attire of the 1750s. Engraved by the French artist Louis Peter Boitard, its quality and detail cause it to stand out from its surrounding prints. Although it is unusual for a pocket book fashion plate, the print is the same size as its companions. Its caption, however, is rather more verbose. It reads:

Well regulate your Cash; to Trade attend;
Mark from Receipts and payments what you spend
Pay every Debt, exact each just Demand;
So shall fair Fortune wait upon your hand.[132]

Figure 2.11 *Barbara Johnson's Album, 1746–1823, T.219-1973, f. 11. Pocket book fashion plates often included captions which used specific sartorial terminology. Copyright Victoria and Albert Museum.*

Positioned almost at the front of the album, this print approximates an epigraph. As an espousal of economic values, this verse reflected the ethos instilled in Johnson's album from her youth. In the face of her economic instability as a never-married woman, Johnson retained this extensive financial, material and sartorial record of dress for seventy-seven years. She regulated her cash and her consumption and fashioned her biography through clothing. Begun as a pedagogical exercise at the apron strings of an intellectual mother who valued self-regulation, the volume evolved with Johnson as she grew and matured. The material literacy expressed within the volume developed too, as fashion plates nurtured and maintained this sartorial knowledge. Johnson deployed specific and specialized textile terminology, littered between records of pounds, shillings and pence. The album fostered Johnson's combined material and economic literacy and, in essence, is Johnson's material biography.

3

Dress of the year: Watercolours

The 1770s saw Britain's loss of the American colonies, James Hargreaves' successful patent for the spinning jenny, a credit crisis and James Cook's final voyage. They also saw the earliest fashion report printed in the *Lady's Magazine* and the inclusion of the first fashion plates in the British periodical press.[1] In 1774, the same year that the *Lady's Magazine* published 'Fashionable Dresses in the Rooms at Weymouth' (Figure 3.1), a young woman in Yorkshire also began a project to depict attire that would engross her for the next thirty-three years. Sitting in the parlour of Thirkleby Hall, a Jacobean manor house near Thirsk in North Yorkshire, 17-year-old Ann Frankland Lewis dipped her paintbrush into a striking blue pigment and began an annual ritual of sartorial self-representation.[2] Captioned 'The dress of the year 1774', and signed with her maiden name, Lewis' first watercolour depicts a sack-back gown with a buttoned compere front (Figure 3.2).[3] Ruched white gauze embellishes the stomacher, robings and the bottom edge of the petticoat, and a deep matching flounce adorns the petticoat, while triple-layered engageantes sit at the ends of the sleeves.[4] The hair, dressed in the towering styles at the height of fashion in 1774, is neatly pomaded, powdered, dressed and decorated with blue rosettes and twisted silk ropes. The gown that Lewis depicted closely resembles extant fashionable garments of the 1770s, from the compere front to the precise arrangement of the decorations (Figure 3.3). Sitting between the materiality of a real, owned, and worn garment, the artistic creativity of watercolour painting and the structures and customs of the emerging genre of the fashion plate, the watercolours showcase the fluid boundaries between visual and material culture, and women's consumption and making practices. Like all her watercolours, Lewis' 'dress of the year' for 1774 is a microcosmic social, cultural and fashionable time capsule.

Between 1774 and 1807, Ann Frankland Lewis completed thirty-two of her 'dress of the year' watercolours, composed as full-length views of a fashionably attired woman. Begun as an unmarried girl of 17 and set aside as a widow and bereaved mother of 50, these sartorial self-representations chronicle an enduring and dedicated relationship with fashion.[5] They depict lavish court dress, momentary crazes and longer-term trends, relaxed and informal dishabille, cosy fur cloaks and sombre mourning dress. Yet, behind the frills and feathers, muffs and bonnets, it is the creativity, artistic experimentation, engagement with commercialized fashion and print cultures and creative labour

Figure 3.1 Fashionable Dresses in the Rooms at Weymouth, *1774, published in the* Lady's Magazine. *This group of five women are dressed in an eclectic range of garments. Courtesy of the Victoria and Albert Museum, London.*

embodied by these images which is most striking. Far from a frivolous feminine pursuit to fill the hours of genteel leisure time or a giddy and distracting impediment to self-understanding, these images encapsulate an emotive, skilled and culturally engaged biographical narrative told through dress.

Ann Frankland Lewis (1757–1842)

Without the tantalizing information held within the watercolours, we would know little of Ann Frankland Lewis' life. She would be remembered only in her roles as daughter, sister, wife and mother, and she would be defined forevermore through her relationship to the powerful and politically minded men who surrounded her. The paper archives held by both the Frankland and Lewis families are crowded with long and tedious pedigrees.[6] The Frankland family's decent from Oliver Cromwell was carefully charted, and manorial rights in Wales, Yorkshire, London, Hertfordshire and Berkshire enshrined in documentary law; but Ann Frankland Lewis, her mother, sisters, nieces and daughters

Dress of the Year: Watercolours 51

Figure 3.2 *Ann Frankland Lewis,* The dress of year 1774. *The first of Lewis' watercolours depicts a woman in a blue sack-back gown with a compere front. Los Angeles County Museum of Art, www.lacma.org.*

Figure 3.3 (facing page) *Woman's dress and petticoat, 1765–1775. Made from silk brocade and decorated with lace, this ensemble closely resembles Ann Frankland Lewis' first watercolour. Los Angeles County Museum of Art, www.lacma.org.*

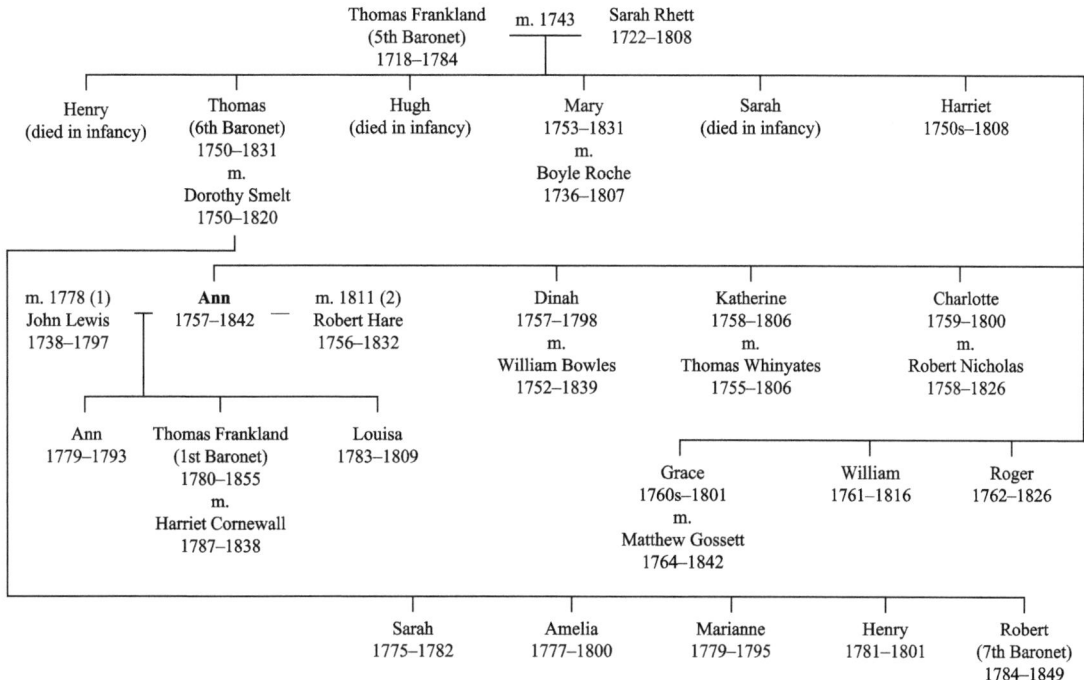

Figure 3.4 *Family tree of the Frankland family. Compiled from evidence in NLW: Harpton Court Papers and Yorkshire Archaeological Society: DD94.*

were but footnotes in the stories of their family's lineage and political dealings.[7] Whittled away over time, the letters, diaries, accounts and belongings of the Frankland and Lewis women are represented by a handful of survivors, mostly from years of widow or spinsterhood. The historical record, so decidedly masculine, has left Ann Frankland Lewis as a ghost in her own story – faint and partially erased by centuries of familial and archival filtering of her penned and printed remains.

From the records of her male relations, and the smattering of her own archival remains, Ann Frankland Lewis' life can be coarsely and unevenly pieced together. Her early years are only traceable in the historical record through the career of her father, Admiral Sir Thomas Frankland, fifth baronet (1718–1784). Born the younger son of the brother of the third baronet, he did not expect to inherit the estate and title, nor did he until 1768 at the age of 50. Instead, he had carved out a very prosperous career in the navy and as a member of parliament for Thirsk in Yorkshire. The son of the Governor of Fort William in Bengal, Henry Frankland (1690–1738), the Admiral was born in the East Indies, and joined the navy in May 1731.[8] He served under Captain Philip Vanburgh in the West Indies, North America and on home waters before his promotion to Captain in 1740.[9] His wealth and professional success was the result of capturing privateers or Spanish *guarda-costas*, and the *Boston Post* fêted him in 1743 as a 'galant and vigilant' naval officer.[10] It was a high-risk but lucrative enterprise; four privateers captured in 1758 raised a total value of £24,276, enough in the 1750s to buy over 3,000 horses.[11] Alongside his ventures in capturing pirate and privateer vessels, Admiral Frankland also amassed wealth through the exploitation of enslaved people.[12] As Simon Smith notes, 'the Franklands have been largely absent from accounts of colonial history, but they were remarkably active'.[13] Partnered with Gedney Clarke, Admiral Frankland was involved in the trade of enslaved people in South Carolina. It was against this backdrop of slavery and privateering that he met and married Sarah Rhett (1722–1808), the daughter of wealthy Charleston merchant William Rhett (1695–1728) and granddaughter of plantation owner and enslaver Colonel William Rhett (1666–1722). Painted to honour the marriage in 1743, Sarah Rhett Frankland's portrait (Figure 3.5) speaks to the family's newly amassed wealth in colonial America. The shimmering silk and aristocratic posture would equally grace the walls of her grandfather's Charleston plantation house, Rhettsbury, or her new husband's Jacobean ancestral home, Thirkleby Hall in North Yorkshire.

The couple permanently returned to England in 1757, first living at Kirby House in Inkpen, Berkshire before taking up residence at Thirkleby Hall upon the Admiral's succession to the baronetcy in 1768. Together, they had thirteen children, ten of whom survived to adulthood, of which Ann Frankland Lewis was the third surviving daughter (Figure 3.4). Lewis' eldest brother, Thomas (1750–1831), would succeed to the baronetcy upon their father's death in 1784. Educated at Eton and Oxford, Thomas was a friend of Sir Joseph Banks and an eminent botanist.[14] *Franklandia fucifolia* and *franklandia triaristata*, two varieties of a species of shrub, were named after him. Her elder sister, Mary (1753–1831), married Sir Boyle Roche (1736–1807), the Irish politician who was chiefly remembered for the witty remarks, metaphors and malapropisms with which he peppered his parliamentary speeches. Of her younger sisters, Dinah (1757–1798) married William Bowles (1752–1839), part of the Wiltshire gentry, Katherine (1758–1806) married naval captain Thomas Whinyates (1755–1806), Charlotte (1759–1800) married member of parliament for Cricklade, Robert Nicholas (1758–1826) and Grace (1760s–1801) married Matthew Gossett, Viscount of Jersey (1764–1842).[15] The family was well-educated, well-connected and generally well-liked in polite social circles.

Ann Frankland Lewis' teenage years as the daughter of a land-owning, parliamentary, naval officer in 1770s Yorkshire were replete with sociability and genteel entertainments. Annual lists of the 'Nobility and Gentry' who appeared at the York Assembly Room balls during the city's famous race week were published each year, and show the Frankland daughters attending together every year between 1771 and 1776.[16] The attendees with whom they mingled and danced between the grand Corinthian columns included local aristocrats the Earl of Carlisle, Lord John Cavendish, the Duke of Devonshire and the Earl and Countess Fitzwilliam, as well as York's doctors, merchants and professional families. Seymour Fleming, later the infamous Lady Worsley, appeared in 1775, and Sir Rowland

Figure 3.5 *Unknown artist,* Sarah Rhett Frankland, *1743. Courtesy of the Gibbes Museum of Art.*

Winn, husband of Sabine Winn, the subject of Chapter 4, attended each year. These formative social occasions, full of both the well-to-do elites of the *beau monde* and the newly wealthy professionals of bustling York, would have offered a buffet of sartorial sensory delights. Bursting with rustling silks, flowing lace and glittering jewels, such spaces have been characterized as a 'market place for beauty'.[17] The alluring fashionability of these spaces no doubt contributed to the choice of the Weymouth assembly rooms as the backdrop to the *Lady's Magazine*'s 1774 fashion plate (Figure 3.1). It was in the midst of Ann Frankland Lewis' foundational visits to these balls and parties that the 'dress of the year' watercolours were begun. Perhaps Lewis' depicted blue silk concoction of 1774, with its fashionable, high hairstyle and sumptuous trimmings, was once worn at one of these events (Figure 3.2).

In the late 1770s, probably at a ball in London, Ann Frankland Lewis met her first husband, John Lewis (1738–1797). Like her father, he was a member of parliament, and was returned for the family's historic parliamentary seat of Radnor in 1768 and 1774. Unlike her father, his political career was ineffective and futile, and he was unseated on petition in 1769 and 1775. Writing to the Duke of Portland in 1769, Beaumont Hotham enquired whether the Duke wished him to attend the Radnor petition 'for little Peter Pathetik', and John Lewis' speeches were even condemned as tedious and verbose by his own uncle.[18] His first wife, Mary Colby, had died in 1774, leaving him to care for their three daughters, Elizabeth, Sarah and Marianne. He quickly sought a new wife, and he and Ann Frankland Lewis were married on 24 March 1778. He was 40, she was 21. The couple lived between the Lewis family's house, Harpton Court in Radnorshire, Wales and their London home on Great Ormond Street. They soon had three children of their own, born in quick succession: little Ann, born a year after their marriage on 20 May 1779, swiftly followed by Thomas Frankland, born on 14 May 1780, and finally Louisa, born on 8 July 1783.

In 1780, John Lewis finally abandoned his parliamentary career. There was a double return for Radnor that year and his more eloquent Tory opponent, Edward Lewis, succeeded in winning the seat. The dramatic events of the Gordon Riots may also have influenced the couple to raise their young children in the safety of the Welsh countryside. With little Ann only 1, and Thomas a tiny 2-week-old infant, 23-year-old Ann Frankland Lewis found herself at home on Great Ormond Street, quite alone aside from her very young children and the servants and right at the heart of the infamous riots. Nearby in Bloomsbury Square, Lord Mansfield's furniture and papers had been seized from his house, piled high, and set alight in the street, the family barely escaping by the back door.[19] Bloomsbury was in turmoil, and Ann Frankland Lewis' sister, Harriet Frankland, wrote the morning after that 'the square is covered with pieces of parchment', fluttering down as the fires settled.[20] She witnessed panicked and petrified politicians scrambling to escape and, without time to pack, piling drawers full of clothes onto their over-laden carts. On 6 June, terrified at the news that the mob would soon descend upon the house of her neighbour, Edward Thurlow the Lord Chancellor, Ann Frankland Lewis gathered up her two tiny children and, at two o'clock in the morning, sought sanctuary a few streets away. She was right to run; the Lord Chancellor's rooms were soon invaded and ransacked by the mob.

Back in Wales the family lived quietly and happily, occasionally returning to London for court events and the London season, until the inevitable tragedies of family deaths began to strike. In 1784, her father Sir Thomas Frankland's death was the first major loss felt by Ann Frankland Lewis. The loss of her eldest daughter Ann in 1793, aged just 15, must have proven an even more heart-wrenching blow. Her husband died just four years later in 1797. In one of Ann Frankland Lewis' few surviving letters, she recounts her husband's death to her sister Mary, Lady Roche, writing that:

> Mr Lewis long foresaw his end approaching as he said a few days before we left town "When I now leave London I shall never return to see it again", and some weeks ago when he took to only wearing his slippers he said "you may give away my shoes I shall never wear them again" and many other little things of the same kind.[21]

Upon John Lewis' death, their son, aged only 17, inherited the Harpton estates, while widowed Ann Frankland Lewis remained his guardian. For these four years between her husband's death and her son's majority, she kept detailed accounts of the estate's finances, which totalled an income of around £4,000 per year.[22] Upon her son's majority in 1801, her role shifted, and she instead received a widow's quarterly jointure of £125. Tragedy struck again with the deaths of nieces and sisters, but the death of her elderly mother in 1808 hit her especially hard.[23] As a widow in 1809, Lewis travelled with her daughter Louisa to Dublin to visit her sister Mary, whose own husband had died in 1807.[24] On their return, Louisa also passed away, at the premature age of 26. She had suffered with shortness of breath, extreme fatigue and weight loss over an extended period, and it seems extremely likely that she was a victim of consumption.[25] Her mother felt the loss of the 'dear creature' keenly and recalled in a letter to her sister that 'it was not til that time that I felt what it was to be alone in the world'.[26] The only child to outlive her would be her son, Thomas. Throughout these tumultuous years Ann Frankland Lewis had consistently maintained her annual ritual of sartorial watercolours; but after this flurry of deep emotional blows, she painted her last 'dress of the year'.

To piece together the archival scraps and fragments of the final decades of Ann Frankland Lewis' life, we must turn to the archival records of her son and her second husband. Sir Thomas Frankland Lewis, born just weeks before the Gordon Riots of 1780, achieved the political success to which his father has aspired. He gained and retained the seat for Radnor and worked actively as a Whig politician from 1812 until his death in 1855. He was an active reformer, and intensely interested in land reform and agriculture. In 1820 he was elected as a Fellow of the Royal Society and acted as Chairman of the Poor Law Commission from 1834–1839. He and his wife, Harriet Cornewell (1787–1838) moved into Harpton Court, and Ann Frankland Lewis began a brief peripatetic lifestyle typical of a woman on her own. She visited her husband's daughters by his first wife, who were now married and settled, as well as her sisters, and often stayed on Welbeck Street in London and at Cambray House in Cheltenham, an established place of 'repose for ageing spinsters and widows'.[27] Whilst in the fashionable but sedate spa town of

Cheltenham, she met the widower clergyman Robert Hare (1756–1832), the younger son of Robert Hare Naylor (1730–1797) of Herstmonceux. They married on 7 July 1811, and the newlyweds, both in their fifties, moved to the rectory at Herstmonceux in Sussex.[28] The final breadcrumbs of Ann Frankland Lewis' life take the form of a handful of letters to her sisters, and to her grandchildren, who would become prominent politicians and scholars in Victorian Britain.[29] Widowed for a second time in 1832, she lived for another decade in a smart regency townhouse of her own in Cheltenham, accompanied by her companion, Louisa Berrington.[30] She died in Cheltenham in 1842, and left her entire estate, which consisted of the Cheltenham house, another house on Welbeck Street in London, furniture, jewels, shares and over £2,000, to her surviving son and his wife.[31] This brief biographical outline, consisting predominantly of the parliamentary failures and successes of her father, husband and son, and the procedural details of birth, marriage and death, is all that would remain of Ann Frankland Lewis' eighty-five years of life, were it not for her material life-writing through her thirty-two watercolours.

From the youthful woman at the York assemblies of the 1770s to the grieving wife and mother in 1800s Cheltenham, Lewis' watercolours visually chronical the life laid out in the Frankland and Lewis letters and family pedigrees. Yet, their brush strokes offer details which evade the pen. As cultural crucibles, each image mediated multiple strands of Lewis' life. Her social, marital and maternal status, her participation in political and court life, her consumption of emergent forms of fashion capital and communication and her manifold skills in making and material production are all recorded and reflected upon in the images she produced. Far from neatly compartmentalized production or consumption activities, these behaviours dissolve and merge into one another as she navigated and fashioned her own material life. To commence our exploration of Lewis' material tale, let us journey back through to her youth in 1770s Yorkshire and reanimate her story through the injection of the colour, depth and materiality bound up in her watercolours.

Sartorial timekeeping and the fashion plate

Upon first encountering Lewis' watercolours, now held in the collections of the Los Angeles County Museum of Art, their striking resemblance to fashion plates is immediately apparent.[32] The influence of this budding genre is intrinsic to the representative modes and visual literacies which Lewis deployed with her paints. The watercolours' composition and visual construction developed concurrently with their printed cousins, and Lewis' life in the genteel yet remote Thirkleby Hall positioned her as the ideal target consumer of the early periodical fashion plates. Directed towards fashionable women who desired regular access to London's cultural capital, periodicals like the *Lady's Magazine* recognized a market for the inclusion of fashion news, both textual and visual, from 1770 onwards. While the pocket book fashion plates collected by Johnson, discussed in Chapter 2, had offered annual and retrospective views of cosmopolitan fashions, the periodical fashion plate was presented as a solution which promised constant and fast access to cosmopolitan novelty.[33] To bemoan the slow transference of changes in fashion had been a popular cultural trope of the 1770s, and in 1773 the *Lady's Magazine* famously lamented that:

> If a lady of elevated rank ... should ... dress herself in a particular manner, all the rest of the sex would adopt her ton of dress ... the contagion commences from those who are familiar with the person who introduces the new mode; after which it communicates itself to their acquaintances or those who behold them ... from the city it spreads to the country, and foreign parts ... the fashion which reaches Amsterdam in 1773 was both born and expired in Paris is 1771.[34]

The fashion plate and periodical fashion reports were presented as a superior and efficient means of maintaining the temporal rhythm of changing fashions, keeping the women of Paris and Amsterdam sartorially in step. While London to Yorkshire may not be quite so significant a distance as Paris to Amsterdam, the intended appeal of the fashion plate was clear. Fashions could be summarized, packaged and sent around the country, across the channel and even across the Atlantic in a matter of mere weeks and months. Yet, the transition from the annual format of the pocket book fashion plate of the 1750s onwards to the monthly fashion plates of the periodical press was fragmented and uneven. It would not be until the 1790s that monthly updates began to appear consistently in some of the more expensive periodicals. Lewis' interactions with the genre reflect the fluidity between pocket book and periodical fashion plates. Of Lewis' thirty-two watercolours, eleven were explicitly captioned as 'dress of the year' or a near variant (Figure 3.7), the standard legend associated with pocket book fashion plates (Figure 3.8) which was swiftly abandoned within periodicals. Lewis' watercolours uniquely sit at the juncture of these two stages in the evolution of the fashion plate. They reflected the visual composition of the periodical style, but retained the terminology and temporal framing of the fashion plates in pocket books.

Scholarly treatments of the fashion plate have often assumed a passive consumption of fashionable trends on the part of the viewer, and a straightforward adoption of the styles depicted.[35] The material limitations of the two-dimensional printed image, however, curbed the practical transferability of the styles represented. The intricacies of cut and stitching, even the material properties of the textiles depicted, were lost in translation from garment to engraving.[36] The material literacy required to decipher and infer how a two-dimensional image might transform into a three-dimensional garment had not yet developed as a crucial skill set amongst fashion makers, as it would do in the twentieth century. Yet, Lewis' watercolours demonstrate a different type of engagement with the genre, which extends beyond the regurgitation and replication of recycled trends. The watercolours, instead, were a response via making, which captured the mode and memorializing qualities of the fashion plate, not necessarily the precise details of seams and stitches.

To read the fashion plate as a simple vehicle for fashion dissemination is to ignore the capacity of such images to commemorate and capture the cultural essence of a precise moment in time. Contemporary

Figure 3.6 The Ladies in the newest Dress, *published in the* Lady's Magazine, *1775. Although at first glance this image appears to present front and back views of the same ensemble, two different dresses are depicted. Courtesy of The Lewis Walpole Library, Yale University.*

Figure 3.7 *Ann Frankland Lewis, The dress of year 1776. Lewis depicts a rust-orange gown and a blue petticoat. The hair is extravagantly adorned with ostrich feathers. Los Angeles County Museum of Art, www.lacma.org.*

Figure 3.8 A Lady in the Dress of the Year 1766. *This fashion plate from a pocket book depicts a back-view of a woman in a nightgown, accessorized with an apron, fichu and bergere. Courtesy of the Museum of London.*

audiences explicitly read images of fashion as time capsules and epitaphs of their cultural context. As Timothy Campbell has convincingly argued, comparative sartorial satires, such as George Moutard Woodward's *Fashions of the Day* (Figure 3.9) conflated history and fashion, and actively situated the fashion plate as a vehicle for capturing each tick and tock, each month and year, in the passing of time.[37] Interlocked with dress, time became tangible, material and measurable. Woodward even 'respectfully dedicated' his satirical image to 'the Fashionable Editors of La Belle Assemblée – Le Beau Monde &c &c', citing and acknowledging the periodical press' role as chroniclers and keepers of fashion history as well as fashion present. The serialization of dress placed chronometric limits on material culture, articulating and codifying the limited fashionable lifespans of garments and accessories. A pocket book 'dress of the year' was a materialized moment, defined as analogous with its specific year. A precise combination of gown, petticoat, hat, cap, apron and cape, with hair styled in a particular fashion and rosettes placed in specific spots, the plate sartorially embodied that year on the printed page. Irrespective of whether or not it accurately reflected what was generally being worn, or if it differed to any great extent from the fashions of 1765 or 1767, it was classified for posterity as the sartorial incarnation of 1766.[38]

As periodicals adopted and adapted the fashion plate, morphing it from the pocket-sized twelve by eight centimetres to the periodical's seventeen by thirteen centimetre proportions, it was swallowed up into the serialized practices of the periodical press, alongside news, essays and novels. Bound together and placed on library shelves, the fashion plates within periodicals were transformed from arbiters of a modish present into historical record keepers. As Anne Hollander has argued, epochs are often crudely defined through their aesthetic styles.[39] Such sartorial time capsules interlock with periodization. In Britain, a Georgian panier or a Tudor doublet, a Victorian corset or Medieval hose act as symbols of eras. Viewed through the lens of hindsight, the gradual fluctuations and transformations are blurred, and fluency in the intricacies of cut and trim risks dilution. In fashion plates, the memorialization of sartorial biography – whether personal or general – is entrenched not necessarily in the detailed materiality of garments, but through representational summarization.

Lewis adopted the annual pocket book publication cycle as her own rhythm of sartorial recording. The act of captioning her watercolours as 'dress of the year' directly acknowledged the temporal pattern of fashion which had dominated print throughout her youth in the 1760s. Diarised through fashion, Lewis entangled the material reality of her lived experience with the representational functions and form of the fashion plate. Much like fashion plates, the watercolours acted as a historicizing record of Lewis' sartorial life, and an indication of her precise alignment with each new trend and style. This leads to intriguing and, to some extent, unanswerable questions around whether the garments were accurate representations of real clothing, either owned and worn by Lewis, amalgamated impressions of garments worn and seen that year or entirely imaginary. This opaque relationship between what was 'real' and what was representational discourse is inherent to any and all autobiographical forms, and should not be read as a comparative failing on the part of a material versus textual life narrative.[40]

Figure 3.9 George Moutard Woodward, Fashions of the Day, or Time Past and Time Present, 1807. *Courtesy of the Library of Congress.*

Lewis' watercolours mediated her imagined relationship with a sartorial reality and, while the authenticity of some of the outfits can be verified through other sources, the status of the watercolours as truthful mirrors of fashionable concoctions of silk, wool and cotton is as questionable as it is within fashion plates themselves. All visual representations are, after all, artificial constructions, be they professional portraits or amateur watercolours. It is the watercolours' role as a form of creative and reflective practice, formulated in response to a genre usually discussed in terms of consumption and dissemination, which reveals the complexity of contemporary interactions with fashion plates.

Lewis' adoption of the tropes and conceits of the fashion plate genre was not static. As the fashion plate evolved, so too did the elements that she embraced. In the watercolour of 1778, the first signed using her married name of Lewis, she adapted the formula she used in previous years at the foot of the image, instead captioning the image as 'dishabille of the year' (Figure 3.11).[41] Similarly, in 1782 she presented 'the half dress of the year' (Figure 3.17) and by 1791 she had dropped the 'dress of the year' model entirely, instead using 'morning dress' (Figure 3.37), the year by itself or occasionally the month and year. This gradual shift from the 'dress of the year' paradigm to the partially descriptive or more precisely timed captions parallels the same changes as they occurred in fashion plates. In some cases, she even pre-empted the shift becoming widespread. *Gallery of Fashion* (1794–1803), for instance, the most expensive and exclusive fashion periodical of the late eighteenth century, did not adopt the model of specifying 'morning', 'afternoon', 'full' or 'court' dress until June 1794, after which point it was a protocol they used regularly (Figure 3.12).

This correlation between print and paint is not only textual, but visual. Alongside the British pocket books and periodicals, it seems likely that Lewis was also heavily influenced by the French fashion periodical, *Gallerie des Modes* (1778–1787). First published as loose prints, before being sold as bound editions from 1779, the images were the work of renowned French illustrators such as Claude-Lois Desrais and Pierre-Thomas Le'Clerc.[42] Unlike the British equivalents of the 1770s and 1780s, they were large, bright and colourful. Their composition very closely mirrored Lewis' style, although, intriguingly, Lewis was using this layout four years before the *Gallerie des Modes* was first published.[43] Their aesthetic influence is palpable, as a comparison between Lewis' 1780 watercolour (Figure 3.14), and a 1780 print from *Gallerie des Modes* (Figure 3.15) demonstrates. Before even considering the style of the garments themselves, there are marked similarities in the compositions. The side-back view, the face in profile, the positioning within the frame and even the tiny foot peeking out below the hemline are consistent. The garments depicted are both *robes á la Polonaise*, consisting of looped up skirts over matching petticoats. Although the colour palette and fabric choices appear different – the print is a silk taffeta, while the watercolour appears to be an embroidered cotton – the positioning of borders and bows is consistent. This evenness between the published French print and the personal English watercolour indicates more than straightforward consumption and influence.[44] In signalling these connections, Lewis used her watercolours to display her fashion knowledge, and to situate herself as being in step with the newly defined rhythms of sartorial change delineated through fashion plates.

Figure 3.10 *Ann Frankland Lewis, The dress of year 1777. This bright pink, closed-front gown is trimmed with white silk gauze. Her hair is dressed with a black pouf decorated with black ostrich feathers, possibly for mourning. Los Angeles County Museum of Art, www.lacma.org.*

Figure 3.11 *Ann Frankland Lewis,* The dishabille of year 1778. *Lewis marks the year of her marriage with a simple white cotton dress trimmed with mauve ribbons. The figure holds a needle between her fingers and is mid-stitch on a small piece of sewing. Los Angeles County Museum of Art, www.lacma.org.*

Figure 3.12 *Morning Dress* in Gallery of Fashion, April 1796. *The fashion plates in* Gallery of Fashion *were more detailed and precise than their pocket book predecessors. Published by Nicholas Heideloff. Courtesy of the British Library.*

Figure 3.13 *Ann Frankland Lewis, 1779. This military-style riding habit was part of a trend from 1778–1783 for masculine informal women's dress. Los Angeles County Museum of Art, www.lacma.org.*

Figure 3.14 *Ann Frankland Lewis, 1780. This cotton* robe á la Polonaise *is decorated with embroidered boarders and green ribbon. Los Angeles County Museum of Art, www.lacma.org.*

Dress of the Year: Watercolours 71

Figure 3.15 Jeune Dame en robe á la Polonaise de taffetas garne a plat de bandes d'une autre couleur / *Young woman in a* robe á la Polonaise *of taffeta decorated with flat bands of a different colour. Fashion plate from* Gallerie des Modes, *1780. Courtesy of the Rijksmuseum.*

Figure 3.16 *Ann Frankland Lewis, The dress of year 1781. This formal court dress is trimmed with chain-effect blue and white loops. Los Angeles County Museum of Art, www.lacma.org.*

Dress of the Year: Watercolours 73

Figure 3.17 *Ann Frankland Lewis, The half dress of year 1782. The deep red silk of the gown is echoed in the bow on the cap. The dress is accessorized with a large white apron. Los Angeles County Museum of Art, www.lacma.org.*

The semblance of sartorial similarity with fashion plates reaches across all thirty-two watercolours, and spills over into the settings and accoutrements which are scattered across the images. The playful appearance of dogs in 1791 and 1795 (Figures 3.37 and 3.42), for instance, maps onto the appearance of pets in fashion plates. Painted shortly before the imposition of the Dog Tax in 1796, Lewis positioned herself within broader cultural discussions of dog ownership as luxury display, to which fashion plates were complicit.[45] Another 1780 print in *Gallerie des Modes* depicted its subject playing with a large black cat, while a 1784 image included a tiny poodle.[46] Similarly, the *Lady's Monthly Museum* included a dog in an 1801 plate (Figure 3.18). Furniture, too, which regularly appeared in the *Belle Assemblée* and *Repository of Arts* fashion plates of the 1800s and made appearances in Lewis' watercolours (Figure 3.50, for example). In print, such inclusions have been interpreted as holistic reflections of fashionable lifestyles and practices which extended beyond the clothes alone.[47] In a similar vein, the watercolours act as self-reflective microcosms, through which Lewis professed her own awareness, knowledge and ownership beyond the garments themselves. This constantly evolving dialogue between the consumed print and produced watercolour unveils a complex and creative alertness to fashion news.

Lewis' creative responses to the fashion plate were not unique, and instead open a window upon a varied but widespread culture of creative interactions with fashion plates. Women from across genteel society did not simply see fashion plates as passive commodities or sources of information, but as tools for their own making activities. Numerous imaginative and ingenious artistic interactions with these prints are littered across archives, ranging from highly inventive and idiosyncratic appropriations to more widespread practices. Perhaps the most unusual creative application of fashion plates was undertaken by bluestocking Mary Berry (1763–1852) and her sister, Agnes (1764–1852). Berry wrote a play entitled *Fashionable Friends*, which was performed at Horace Walpole's magnificent Gothic Revival villa Strawberry Hill in 1801.[48] As part of the preparations for this staging, Berry created an album of watercolour stage sets, which included twenty-nine figures cut from the fashion plates of *Gallery of Fashion*, which could be moved about this miniature stage like paper puppets.[49] Usually discussed as an inordinately expensive, exclusive and precious publication, this willingness to cut out and transform the *Gallery of Fashion*'s costly fashion plates into paper performers demonstrates a very fluid, active and productive response to such images.

This creative interaction is also evident in precise watercolour copies of fashion plates. A copy of the 'promenade dress' from the January 1814 issue of the *Repository of Arts* (Figures 3.19 and 3.20), for instance, positions the fashion plate as an artistic model. It is certain that this image was not the original design, but a retroactive copy.[50] Although the hand of the watercolourist is unpolished, every detail is mirrored; the feathered bonnet, the fur muff, the gown peeking out beneath the pelisse, even the colours are carefully imitated. The only perceivable difference in the composition is the lack of waistband on the pelisse in the watercolour copy. Copying was an integral part of learning to draw,

Figure 3.18 *Morning Dress for March 1801, from* Lady's Monthly Museum. *Los Angeles County Museum of Art, www.lacma.org.*

Figure 3.19 Jan 1814 Promenade Dress, *watercolour*. This watercolour was copied from the plate in *Ackermann's* Repository of Arts. *Private collection.*

Figure 3.20 *Promenade Dress, January 1814, from the* Repository of Arts. *Los Angeles County Museum of Art, www.lacma.org.*

and engravings made up a substantial portion of the fodder for hungry amateur watercolourists and commercial producers alike.[51] Much like allegorical scenes or copies of notable paintings, copying fashion plates simultaneously developed artistic skill and cultural knowledge. Allegorical or pastoral scenes did, of course, carry an intellectual weight which the commercialized fashion plate was seen to lack. In practice, however, fashion plates were a regular part of the amateur student-artist's intake. Through artistic engagement, fashion plates were transformed into tools for creative production.

The most widespread example of creative interaction with the fashion plate was simply to colour it in. Many periodicals, especially in the early years of the nineteenth century, sold two versions of each issue; one with hand-coloured plates and one left uncoloured. Frequently, the copies of these periodicals found in libraries and archives include both coloured and uncoloured plates side by side, indicating that the colouring occurred after purchase (Figure 3.21). The skill with which these coloured plates have been treated varies enormously. Some are neatly and carefully coloured, showing good knowledge of watercolour technique. Others have bright red doll-like cheeks and crude applications of the pigment.[52] This wide range of skill levels reflects an informal and uneven practice of colouring fashion plates. Much like copying, colouring in outlines was an established part of amateur artistic education. Prints acted as 'emblematic and illustrative aids to learning', and both copying and colouring prints were framed as rudimentary skills within contemporary educational texts.[53] George Brookshaw's *A New Treatise on Flower Painting or, Every Lady her own Drawing Master* (1816), for instance, presented the student artist with both drawn and painted flowers, with the intention that the uncoloured outlines would be filled in.[54] The outline fashion plates offered a similar canvas upon which women could practise and perfect their skills as amateur watercolourists, and sat within a broader culture of cultivating accomplishment.

Accomplishment and creative practice

Derided as amateur, degrading and frivolous, but a marriage-market essential, women's 'decorative efforts' have not been viewed kindly by history.[55] Accomplishments have been framed as a 'pantomime of elegant feminine poses', which required women to performatively parade their skills in art, music, singing, needlework, languages and reading.[56] The highly gendered framework of men as producers and women as consumers has been perpetuated through the exclusionary treatment of women's making and artistic endeavours as a means to ensnare men. Contemporary literature is peppered with treatments of women's creative practices as entertainments for a future husband. Maria (1768–1849) and Richard Edgeworth (1744–1817) wrote in *Practical Education* (1798) that 'if, for instance, a woman were to marry a man who was fond of music, or who admired painting, she should be able to cultivate those talents for his amusement and her own'.[57] Historically read through the patriarchal lens

Figure 3.21 *The Court Dress as Worn on His Majesty's Birthday and Kensington Garden Walking Dress, June 1808, La Belle Assemblée. Courtesy of the de Beer Collection, Special Collections, University of Otago, Dunedin, New Zealand.*

of husband-hunting, scholars have only recently begun to appreciate that women could engage in self-improvement or creative endeavour because of enjoyment, aptitude or vocation.[58]

Scholarly work on the accomplished woman watercolourist has often concentrated on the painting of flowers and landscapes and has maintained a focus on the rhetoric of the virtuous and feminine.[59] Since Rozsika Parker's ground-breaking work on embroidery, however, scholars have recognized making in many forms as integral to the shaping of women's selfhood and identity formation.[60] For Ann Bermingham, 'accomplishments should not simply be understood as ways for women with increasingly too much time on their hands to fill idle hours, but as ways for women to perform their subjectivity through certain allotted modes of artistic expression'.[61] Whether articulated with the needle, pencil or brush, the creative practices packaged as accomplishments enabled women to imagine and articulate the self in terms of self-representation, self-exploration and aesthetic. When disentangled from the misogynistic veil of accomplishment rhetoric, such practices reveal complex and determined approaches to self-exploration and self-reflection. As a genteel woman's personal creative endeavour, Lewis' watercolours were a tool with which she could negotiate her individual subjectivity and engage in shared and socially and culturally engaged artistic practices.

The Frankland family were artistically active, and the gendered ways in which the artworks of Lewis' brother, nephew and nieces have been treated act as a reflection of contemporary attitudes to art. Lewis' brother Thomas had been a pupil of watercolourist John Malchair (1713–1812) during his time at Oxford, and his name appears as a collaborator-pupil on a number of Malchair's works.[62] Her nephews and nieces were even more artistically minded. Robert (1784–1849), who would become the seventh baronet and adopt the surname Frankland-Russell, was especially prolific. He turned his hand to an abundance of hunting scenes and character sketches and completed two self-portraits, as well as portraits of his three daughters.[63] He is best remembered, however, for his collaborations with prominent satirist James Gillray (1756–1815), having provided the original sketches for a number of Gillray's published prints. Most notable amongst these is his 1810 depiction of Billy, George III's gamekeeper.[64] Although no evidence has survived of their artistic outputs, there is reason to believe Lewis' nieces, Amelia (1777–1800) and Marianne (1779–1795), were also artistically able. Their joint portrait, painted by John Hoppner in 1795 (Figure 3.22), presents the teenage sisters in a romantic landscape symbolizing their familial love.[65] On her lap, Amelia clasps an artist's portfolio, from which a profusion of papers threatens to escape. In her hand, the golden nib of a pen glistens, while her sister grasps a rolled piece of paper. The depiction of amateur artistic endeavour within professional portraiture was widespread and certainly formed part of the display of accomplishment.[66] Filtered through the brush of a professional artist, whatever skills the sisters may have possessed can only be imagined. While their brother and father might be able to collaborate with successful professionals, we do not see the produced work of the Frankland daughters, but a rhetorical representation of their femininity. Tempting as it might be to read images like the Frankland sisters' portrait as purely

Figure 3.22 *John Hoppner,* The Frankland Sisters, *1795. Both sisters died of consumption before 1800. Courtesy of the National Gallery of Art, Washington.*

performative, such narrow interpretations perpetuate a misogynistic obliviousness towards women's artistic agency. It was, after all, Hoppner's brush which confined the sisters' presumed artistic skill to symbolic visual motifs.

Aside from the plethora of things made by women which fill museum stores, auction rooms, antique shops and attics, evidence that women's artistic engagement was more than a performance of marriageability can be read through the dynamic and vibrant commercial culture which it generated. With the rise of women's amateur artistic endeavour and the rhetoric of accomplishment, one of the key concerns felt by commentators was the commercialization of art. The contemporary distinction between professional and amateur work was not based on monetary value or payment for labour. Professional artistic practice involved the 'production of original works of genius intended for public exhibition', while amateur works were 'derivative' and 'intended for domestic decoration'.[67] The popularity of commercial centres for women's amateur art aided in the construction of this binary distinction. When Lewis began her watercolours in 1774, watercolour paint was still the provision of apothecaries, who would grind and mix their own colours for their clients. William Reeves' invention of solid, soluble watercolour cakes in 1780 has been credited with inspiring the spike in the medium's popularity.[68] Portable, tidy and affordable, neat little watercolour boxes containing the cakes were quickly commercially available. At the same time, destination shops for art supplies flourished in London, following in the stead of the print sellers like Matthew and Mary Darly, who were already giving lessons and selling instruction books by the 1770s.[69] Cavernous spaces, full of prints, painting and artistic supplies, Samuel and Joseph Fuller's Temple of Fancy (which opened in 1809) and Rudolph Ackermann's Repository of Arts on the Strand (which opened in 1794, having moved from an earlier premises on Pall Mall) encapsulated the 'mingling of art, education, and commerce'.[70] Ackermann's artistic empire included a drawing school, a gallery of 'ancient and modern' paintings and drawings and a circulating library of prints and drawings, and from 1809 he published the periodical embodiment and namesake of his shop, the *Repository of Arts*.[71]

Inside establishments like Ackermann's, the fashion plate was placed side by side with the paints, brushes, papers and instructive manuals needed to engage in painting as an accomplishment. Within these spaces, both physical and textual, production and consumption were explicitly placed next to each other. Visitors to the shop consumed in order to produce, and produced things which were influenced by what they consumed. Bermingham has credited fashion plates with acting as models for appropriate habits and practices within the culture of accomplishment.[72] Akin to the inclusion of dogs and furniture as luxury accessories, depictions of fashionable feminine activities also acted as a means of positioning fashionable dress within a wider social and cultural landscape. Two plates from 1812 issues of *La Belle Assemblée* explicitly merged fashionable dress with fashionable activities (Figures 3.23 and 3.24). The first, which depicts a woman in a 'white cambric frock', positions its subject at a stylish table.[73] Its drawer partially ajar, papers covered with watercolour landscapes threaten to escape

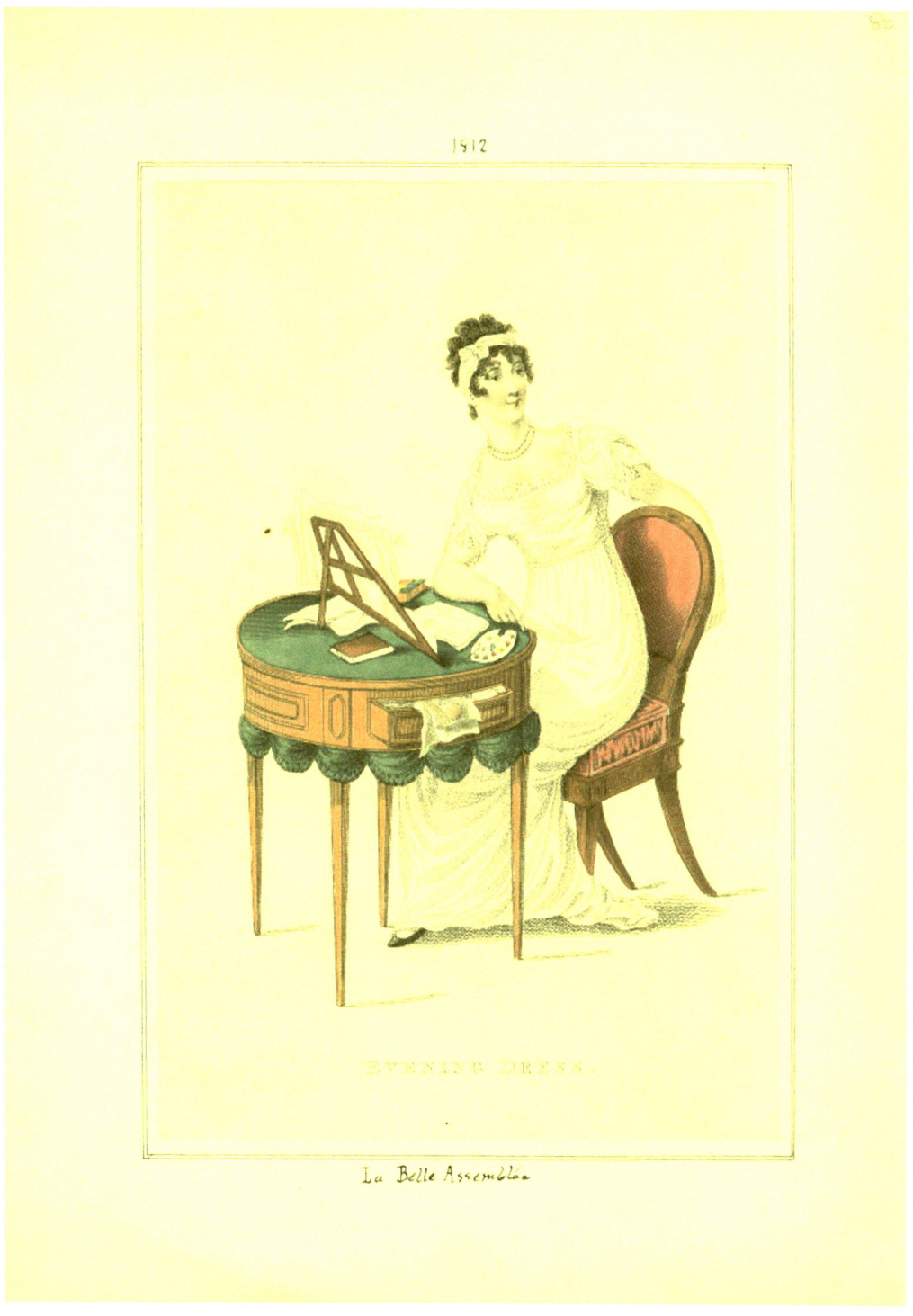

Figure 3.23 *Evening dress, March 1812, from* La Belle Assemblée. *Although captioned as 'evening dress', other versions of this image present it as 'morning dress'. Courtesy of the Los Angeles Public Library.*

Figure 3.24 *Morning dress, June 1812, from* La Belle Assemblée. *Courtesy of the Los Angeles Public Library.*

and flutter to the floor. Its subject sits at her easel, with a box full of the innovative watercolour cakes at her side. On the one hand, her watercolour accoutrements are fashionable accessories and a display of accomplishment. The inclusion of this activity is also, however, an extension of the plate's reflexivity and commercial power. It shrewdly advertised the very watercolour boxes which were probably available in the same shop as the periodical itself and acknowledged the interests and practices of the magazine's readership. This custom is extended in the June plate, which presents its subject mid-stitch. Dressed in 'French cambric or plain India muslin richly embroidered round the bottom with a deep border', the woman concentrates on the task at hand.[74] The piece of white muslin she holds between her fingers, poised to embroider, blends seamlessly with her dress, reinforcing the connection between the consumed fashionable image and the making activity being undertaken. Such plates actively recognized that women knew how to make things, and explicitly aligned the consumption of print, paint and threads with the material productivity of the periodical's readership.

Lewis' watercolours regularly capture this juncture between fashionable dress and women's creative practices. Her 'dishabille of the year 1778' (Figure 3.11) captured Lewis mid-stitch, at work on a similar muslin piece to that depicted in the *La Belle Assemblée* plate. In a comparable vein, her 'morning dress of the year 1785' (Figure 3.26) portrayed knitting, with the two long needles busily at work. Knitted pincushions, stockings and purses were often made in the drawing rooms and parlours of the gentry, and Hannah Robertson remarked in her *Young Ladies School of Arts* that 'as soon as a girl has learned to read properly, she is commonly put to the knitting of stockings'.[75] In 1785, as a young mother of a 6-, 5-, and 2-year-old, Lewis may have memorialized the knitting of garments for her children in this image.[76] Other watercolours depict garments Lewis may well have made herself, such as the apron depicted in 1790 (Figure 3.36). Intriguingly, Lewis never depicted the act of painting, but these ventures into the fibre arts evidence a more holistic engagement with making, which bridged and brought together the paint brush and the needle. Lewis presented these activities of painting and stitching as integral to her fashionable self. While her skill with watercolours is to be inferred from the image itself, her broader material literacy is clearly articulated, enjoyed and exhibited.

Perhaps the best example of the marriage between the visual, commercial and sartorial in Lewis' creative practice is her depiction of satin prints or painted silk medallions.[77] These small, round or oval decorative images can be seen in both Lewis' 1784 and 1785 watercolours (Figures 3.25 and 3.26), although it is unclear whether they are of the painted or printed variety. As the name suggests, the images were either popular prints transferred onto silk satin, or unique designs painted directly onto the fabric.[78] The satin was then cut into a medallion shape and incorporated into consumers' craft projects. Satin prints and medallions were advertised by print sellers in newspapers and on trade cards throughout the 1780s and 1790s, and muffs and work baskets were explicitly suggested as appropriate projects.[79] The survival of muffs which include satin prints or painted medallions is rare, but those that do exist very closely resemble Lewis' depiction.[80] One such muff from the 1790s was

Figure 3.25 *Ann Frankland Lewis, The dress of year 1784. Dressed in pink silk with black trim to mourn the death of her father, Admiral Sir Thomas Frankland, Lewis' figure grasps an example of a silk muff decorated with a satin print. Los Angeles County Museum of Art, www.lacma.org.*

Figure 3.26 *Ann Frankland Lewis,* Morning dress of the year 1785. *Lewis' watercolour depicts a woman knitting. She is dressed in a blue redingote and large black hat. Los Angeles County Museum of Art, www. lacma.org.*

constructed of ivory silk satin and embellished with trailing embroidered flowers and a painted medallion depicting a small dog (Figure 3.27). While the painted images are often rather idiosyncratic, the satin prints often bore allegorical designs copied from popular paintings, or recognizable symbolic figures.[81] Another muff from the 1790s is adorned with a satin print depicting Hope.[82] Resting on an anchor, which almost dwarfs the full-length female figure, Hope was regularly deployed as a wearable nautical symbol of patriotism, honouring the naval battles of 1794–1805.[83] While it is not possible to clearly identify the image on Lewis' muff, which is bordered with pearls and framed with coloured silk embroidery, it bears the hallmarks of a similar figurative allegorical design. Adorning clothing with these images did, on the one hand, align the wearer with the notions of patriotism, feminine beauty and virtue encapsulated in these allegorical images. But alert contemporary viewers would have been able to decipher something more. Although it was possible to purchase muffs with these images pre-applied, the vast majority were advertised as craft supplies.[84] As such, the muffs were transformed into displays of material literacy and making, which exhibited the wearer's taste, their awareness of the dialects of contemporary visual culture, their eye for composition and, perhaps most importantly, their skill with the needle.

Figure 3.27 *Silk satin muff with a painted medallion depicting a dog. Copyright Victoria and Albert Museum, London.*

Lewis' depiction of another medallion on her work box in 1785 (Figure 3.26) extends her articulation of this resonance between consumed image and produced craft. The adornment of work boxes and baskets was another of the uses endorsed by print sellers in their advertisements, and Lewis' use was firmly positioned within this fashionable and commercial culture. As with the medallion on Lewis' muff, it is too loosely rendered to confidently identify whether it represented a print or a hand-painted image, although it is also likely to have been in a similar vein to the allegorical figures.[85] Positioned on the work box, the receptacle for Lewis' tools and trappings for textile work, the myriad symbolic and practical meanings of the satin print materialize. Alongside their direct application on muffs and other dress accessories, satin prints were also used for embroidery outlines, and could be used to create textile maps, as well as figurative scenes.[86] Much like the skeletons provided by uncoloured fashion plates or within watercolour manuals, these satin prints offered a pre-prepared ground for embroidery. The direct link between this decorative image and the types of textile work facilitated by the box's contents in turn reinforces Lewis' engagement with both making and the commercial world. It is also no coincidence that Lewis depicted a wide-brimmed hat on both the woman in the satin print, and as part of the 'morning dress of the year 1785' worn in the watercolour. On the one hand, this visual echo makes an active comparison between the allegorical figure and Lewis' own character, and fits within the gendered representational rhetoric around accomplishment and the performance of feminine virtue. On the other, this layered representation feeds back to the reflexivity of the fashion plate, with Lewis as a maker of an image depicting making. Lewis' merged consumer and producer activity reminds us that women's making practice was highly involved. Making was, indeed, a performative act through which women enacted femininity and mobilized received visual literacy to embody allegorical virtues and craft public selfhood. It was also, however, an act of intense and varied material ability and literacy. Drawing, painting, stitching and embroidering were meshed with rigorous cultural knowledge of commercialized fashions and print practices.

Society and fashionable display

Lewis' cultural knowledge of fashion extended beyond the pages of fashionable periodicals or, indeed, the polite society of genteel Yorkshire and Wales. As much as print liked to declare its centrality to the dissemination of dress, face-to-face interactions and social osmosis were integral to the spread of fashion. As the daughter and later wife of members of parliament, Lewis regularly found herself bundled up in a coach and travelling towards London most autumns for the season. Living on Great Ormond Street in the 1780s, Lewis was positioned at the heart of fashionable Bloomsbury.[87] Her neighbours were the nobility, the fashionable select of the *beau monde* and, as was underlined by her experience of the Gordon Riots, the political elite. Both the Frankland and Lewis families were at the

Figure 3.28 *Ann Frankland Lewis, Morning dress January 1786. This cape trimmed with yellow fur closely resembles one in a 1778 print from* Gallerie des Modes. *See Rijksmuseum: RP-P-2009-2105. Los Angeles County Museum of Art, www.lacma.org.*

Figure 3.29 *Ann Frankland Lewis,* The Court dress of the year 1787. *The court mantua was often idiosyncratically and symbolically decorated. Los Angeles County Museum of Art, www.lacma.org.*

Figure 3.30 *Ann Frankland Lewis, Morning dress 1788. A pink striped shoe peaks out under this white cotton dress. Los Angeles County Museum of Art, www.lacma.org.*

peripheries of the cohort of privileged men and women who made up the *beau monde*.[88] The leaders of this world of fashion were high-ranking peers and, as much as the Franklands and the Lewises might trace and obsess over their connections to powerful seventeenth-century kinsmen, they were not quite of that ilk. Yet, through those very pedigrees, through fashionable houses, through political ambition and through sociability, they aspired. One of the first balls which Lewis recalled attending as a teenager was given by Viscountess Galway at her house on Hill Street in Mayfair in the 1770s, and other letters are peppered with references to elite acquaintances.[89] In 1783, Lewis wrote out a list of all the acquaintances she had in London, arranged by street, circling out from her own home on Great Ormond Street.[90] Listed within this social catalogue were Lady Anne Barnard, who famously chronicled her journey to the Cape and was also an accomplished artist, Mary Delany, the famed bluestocking and artist, as well as society figures like Lady Pelham, Lady Stapleton and the Almack's *Female Coterie* co-founder, Miss Lloyd. Lewis astutely used the watercolours to connect herself to the cultural capital of elite London society. Her depiction of 'the court dress of the year 1787' (Figure 3.29) is perhaps the most immediately apparent instance of a sartorial social statement. Her wide court hoop, embroidered and spangled in the slightly more abstract designs of the 1780s, is accompanied by a rust-orange coloured mantua and topped with towering plumes of ostrich feathers. Inherently magnificent, such styles were exclusive to the court and offered a canvas for the 'meaningful signal of political display'.[91] Although the intricacies of Lewis' sartorial messages are, in this instance, lost to time, she nonetheless articulated her membership of court society through her knowledge of this sartorial passport for access.

With her finger on the pulse of elite fashion, Lewis captured some of the key trends and fashionable ensembles of late eighteenth-century society. Lewis used her watercolours to connect herself not only with the broad brush strokes of court dress culture, but also through specific connections to individual socialites, social events and patriotic movements. Lewis' list of fashionable acquaintances included the infamous Seymour Fleming, Lady Worsley (1758–1818). Fleming had been one of the regular company at the York Assembly Rooms for the race week, was part of the Frankland daughters' social circle in Scarborough in 1774, and also appeared on Lewis' list of London acquaintances.[92] Born within a year of one another, the two young women had experienced their early years in fashionable society in Yorkshire side by side. Indeed, it was at the York race week in 1775 that Fleming's future husband, Sir Richard Worsley, publicly declared his intention to marry her.[93] This connection between the two young women, and their membership of the same fashionable circles, was artistically captured by Lewis in the watercolours through her depiction in 1779 of a red riding habit (Figures 3.13 and 3.31).[94] This military-inspired ensemble included a red wool petticoat and jacket, with blue facings at the cuffs and down the front opening. Worn over a white woollen waistcoat and linen habit shirt, the jacket was adorned with gold epaulets. The entire outfit was topped off with a black beaver hat decorated with a plume of black ostrich feathers. The habit depicted by Lewis is almost an exact mirror of the attire

Figure 3.31 *Detail of Ann Frankland Lewis, 1779 (Figure 3.13). Los Angeles County Museum of Art, www.lacma.org*

worn by Fleming in her portrait (Figure 3.32), painted by Joshua Reynolds in 1779, the same year as the Lewis watercolour.[95]

With one hand set confidently on her hip and the other grasping her riding whip, Reynolds' portrait of Fleming depicts a woman at the height of fashion. An adaptation of the uniform of her husband's regiment, the daring red riding habit was part of a major, but brief, fashion trend, which lasted from 1778 until the early 1780s. The trend was spearheaded by Lewis and Fleming's contemporary, the notorious leader of fashion, Georgiana Cavendish, Duchess of Devonshire (1757–1806) who, in 1778, appeared 'at the head of the beauteous Amazons of Coxheath, who are all dressed *en militaire*'.[96] Coxheath was one of two campsites set up in 1778 following France's intervention in the American War of Independence which, while initially established for military training, was swiftly transformed into an elite playground of patriotism. The feminized redcoat riding habit donned by Cavendish, Fleming and, potentially, Lewis became recognized as the uniform of the fashionable women who socialized at Coxheath, and it received a vicious response from the press and satirists alike.[97] A vast departure from the supposed feminine virtue embodied in the act of watercolour painting, the lascivious, gender-disrupting and politicized connotations of this outfit were explicit and public.[98] The appearance of these

Figure 3.32 *Joshua Reynolds,* Seymour, Lady Worsley, *1779. Courtesy of Harewood House.*

momentary and socially significant trends in Lewis' watercolours does vital work to dislodge a superficial narrative of the performance of feminine virtue. As crucibles for fashionable self-reflection, the watercolours reflected back at Lewis a complex picture of her association with cultural modes and moments as she orbited an elite social world. The image resonates with patriotic verve and the chic modishness of the fashionable trend-setters that surrounded the ensemble's original creation.

The fashionable trends surrounding British patriotism can be found elsewhere in Lewis' watercolours. Her 1789 watercolour, captioned 'the Windsor Uniform – worn at the ball at Windsor given on the King's recovery' (Figure 3.34), offers posterity the only visual record of the titular Windsor uniform for women. George III had suffered through a lengthy period of illness in 1788, culminating in the 1788– 1789 regency crisis. When the King's position had looked dire, many courtiers had declared their loyalty to the Prince of Wales and his drive to implement an official regency. With the King restored to good health, loyalty to the recovered monarch was feverishly brandished. Frances Burney noted the sense of national relief with wonder and remarked that 'the preparations of festive loyalty were universal … not a Child could we meet, that had not a Bandeau round its Head, Cap, or Hat of "God Save the King"'.[99] Even women who had previously brandished their support for the Prince were compelled to

Figure 3.33 An officer in the light infantry, driven by his lady to Cox-Heath, *after John Collett, 1780. Courtesy of the Lewis Walpole Library, Yale University.*

Dress of the Year: Watercolours 97

Figure 3.34 *Ann Frankland Lewis,* This Windsor Uniform, *1789. This dress perfectly echoes Lady Louisa Stuart's description of the chaperones' ensembles at the Windsor ball. The outfit incorporated a blue nightgown, trimmed with white and gold fringe. The front is decorated with narrow straps edged with scarlet and gold, and a gold girdle with heavy tassels falls to the side. Los Angeles County Museum of Art, www.lacma.org.*

Figure 3.35 Restoration Dresses, *1789. The image is thought to depict women from the Prince of Wales' set, including the Duchess of Devonshire and Lady Archer. Courtesy of the Lewis Walpole Library, Yale University.*

change their colours, and instead adorn themselves with patriotic ribbons (Figure 3.35).[100] In London, the King's recovery was marked with a ball at Windsor at which the men wore the well-established masculine Windsor uniform of a blue hunting coat with a red collar and cuffs along with tight white breeches. While women usually wore their most recent court dress to such occasions, the King's recovery ball demanded something more unique. Lady Louisa Stuart recalled that there were two categories of women's Windsor uniform which were specifically designed for the event:

> The ladies were in the same colours of blue and scarlet and white. The dancers had a Garter blue body trimmed with a scarlet and gold edge, the stomacher white, laced with gold cord, the sleeves white with a *crêpe* festoon on the shoulders, tied up with gold tassels, a scarlet and gold band round the arm. The petticoat was white *crêpe* with a flounce trimmed at the top and bottom with a white and gold fringe, and the same edge of scarlet and gold. There was also a sort of train tied up behind, of *crêpe* with the same ornaments. The chaperones wore a blue nightgown, trimmed with a very broad white and gold fringe, tied up in a festoon on the one side like a robe, with thick gold corn and

vast great tassels, a white petticoat and an apron under the gown, the same as the dancers' petticoats; the gown made with four straps before, edged with scarlet and gold, and a girdle of the same all fasted with diamond (true or false) buckles. All together it had a very magnificent appearance.[101]

This patriotic sea of blue, white, red and gold, which filled the ball room at Windsor, glittered with the expensive evidence of miraculously new-found or re-established loyalty to his majesty. Stuart's description of the chaperones' uniform precisely matches Lewis' watercolour and, as a married woman in her thirties, it is almost certain this is the role Lewis would have fulfilled.

The Windsor uniform watercolour stands out amongst its thirty-one companions. Alongside the riding habit of 1779, it offers one of the only instances where we can say for certain that the garment recorded was a real garment. It existed, it was worn, and it is extremely likely that it was donned by Lewis herself.[102] Similarly, this is the only occurrence when Lewis recorded the details of the garment, its purpose and the place it was worn, and consequently it is the only garment that can be linked with certainty to a specific and identifiable event. This remarkable level of detailed recording marks this garment out as exceptional and reminds us that even as Lewis adopted the annual temporal cycle of fashion news within her own material life writing, that rhythm was not unvarying. Certain years and particular garments carried more weight as biographical signifiers. Precious memories, whether they were personally or socially important, were captured within the paintings. The codified memorialization of specific events, which elsewhere might be recorded by saving a ticket or other souvenir, was channelled into the watercolours themselves.[103]

Selfhood, emotion and the mourning watercolours

Images and objects have the capability to enshrine deep emotional meaning.[104] As liminal artefacts, occupying a space between self-portraits and crafted objects, Lewis' watercolours bring together strands of scholarship on emotions, portraiture and objects. Women's amateur art, and especially their portraits and self-portraits, were innately capable of memorializing selfhood and embodying emotions. When Lewis' mother died in 1808, she divided up a series of twelve portraits of herself, her late husband, and some of her children painted in the 1770s by Henry Walton (1745–1813) between her children and grandchildren as deeply sentimental keepsakes.[105] As Frances Borzello has suggested, women's self-portraits, portraits of friends and family and even depictions of interiors and landscapes can be treated as painted autobiographies.[106] The careful selection of subject and setting, the extended application to the project over time and the creation of narrative through successive snapshots constructed a visual life story. Intertwined with Marcia Pointon's reading of portraits as objects which are 'imaginatively invested', depictions of the emotionally constructed self can be considered crucibles for complex and idiosyncratic portrayals, as is the case with Lewis.[107] As Pointon suggests, women

Figure 3.36 *Ann Frankland Lewis, The Half dress of the year 1790.* This blue silk gown is depicted worn with a richly embroidered white apron. Los Angeles County Museum of Art, www.lacma.org.

Figure 3.37 Ann Frankland Lewis, Morning dress 1791. *The blue gown is worn with a white cotton petticoat and a deep blue sash. The deep net veil is embroidered at the edge. Los Angeles County Museum of Art, www.lacma.org.*

used amateur portraiture as a means of constructing 'a position, a voice, an identity through their own acts of portrayal and delineation'. Turning to objects, and injecting further emotional significance, Jules Prown writes that artefacts, even if they were created as 'fictions', can be seen as a means to 'recreate the experience of deeply felt moments'.[108] Whether or not Lewis herself wore each and every ensemble depicted, she nevertheless imagined them as temporal signifiers of her evolving selfhood and mobilized her brush to encapsulate numerous threads and pinpoints of her life.[109] While the constraints and cultural discourses surrounding watercolour painting as an accomplishment were a constant cultural presence, such rhetoric did not prevent women such as Lewis from imbuing their creative activities with powerful personal meaning, emotional value and self-reflection.

Personal feeling is intensely present throughout Lewis' watercolours, whether they capture youthful exuberance, social ambition or moments of grief, and can be felt to undulate through the images. They act as material signifiers and, to borrow Prown's phrasing, 'events' in Lewis' personal history.[110] While she felt no need to record births or marriages, the emotional intensity of death repeatedly appears. Just as loss and death dominated the documentary remnants of Lewis' life in the 1790s and 1800s, so too did it govern her watercolours of these years. Of the seventeen watercolours painted in these two decades, eight contain evidence for mourning. In some images, this is confined to a black trim of reverence and respect, in others it is the complete deep black of full mourning. The material and commercial practices surrounding death were increasingly prevalent in the late eighteenth century, and the sartorial visibility and portrayal of grief were established and codified.[111] As demonstrated by Johnson's mourning garments in Chapter 2, black was expected to be worn following the death of family members and public figures such as royalty. When aligned with the familial losses experienced by Lewis, almost all of the watercolour depictions of mourning garb coincide with significant moments of grief.

The first firm appearance of mourning in the watercolours was in 1784 (Figure 3.25), the year that Lewis' father died. The discreet black ribbon trim around the hat and along the front of the gown may have been added to an existing garment or, equally possible but no less significant, a fictional marker of this significant event. Later incidents, however, are more intense, and depict full mourning. In 1794 (Figure 3.40), Lewis painted a pitch-black robe over a muslin gown, and bordered the image not with the soft pastels of the proceeding nineteen watercolours, but with a strong, dark green-black. Captioned as the fashion for May 1794, Lewis painted this image less than six months after the death of her 15-year-old daughter Ann in December 1793. In 1797, Lewis expressed the loss of her husband through a depiction of a woman and child in mourning (Figure 3.44), and this is echoed again in the half-mourning depicted the following year (Figure 3.45). Other examples connect with the death of her sister Charlotte and niece Amelia in 1800 (Figure 3.47) and her sister Katherine in 1806 (Figure 3.52), while the undated watercolour (probably 1792, Figure 3.38) potentially links to the public mourning following Sir Joshua Reynolds' death that year.[112] The black mourning pelisse depicted in 1804 does not appear to connect to a family death but may well have related to the passing of a now

Figure 3.38 *Ann Frankland Lewis, untitled watercolour, probably 1792. More so than in any of her other watercolours, Lewis mimics the engraved effect seen in printed fashion plates. Los Angeles County Museum of Art, www.lacma.org.*

Figure 3.39 *Ann Frankland Lewis, 1793. This white cotton dress has a deep boarder of whitework embroidery at the hem. Los Angeles County Museum of Art, www.lacma.org.*

Figure 3.40 *Ann Frankland Lewis, May 1794. The black mourning robe in this watercolour is accessorized with a bright teal turban and shoes. Los Angeles County Museum of Art, www.lacma.org.*

unidentifiable friend. All these images, which I classify as Lewis' mourning watercolours, blend together the tropes of mourning dress seen in contemporary fashion plates, the commercial and material cultures of grief, and creative responses to emotional turmoil.

Both *Gallerie des Modes* and the *Gallery of Fashion* had included mourning garments amongst their plates in the 1790s, and these garments would become a regular feature of fashion periodicals in the nineteenth century, especially at moments of national mourning. When Princess Charlotte, the only legitimate daughter of the Prince Regent, died in 1817, *Le Belle Assemblée*, the *Lady's Monthly Museum* and the *Repository of Arts* all devoted their fashion pages to mourning dress for the late and publicly beloved princess. In the same year that Lewis' husband died, the *Gallery of Fashion* also contained a mourning dress plate (Figure 3.41). The sartorial prescription of what grief looked like incorporated 'black craped feathers', 'black satin' and 'black net'. Mourning was very much a performative act, and black dress was a uniform for moments of prescribed mourning. Transference from full to half mourning played into the same temporal model that the fashion plate constructed and such images acted as a memorializing record of moments of national or familial grief. With time and fashion side by side, the life cycle was ordered through dress. Lewis' inclusion of these mourning watercolours certainly conforms to this broader culture of public and material signification. Cultures of remembrance and collective modes of reminiscence were key to material modes of mourning.[113] However, Lewis' combined act of not only, presumably, wearing mourning and acknowledging the temporal rhythms of the custom, but also creatively responding to grief moves the watercolours beyond biographical markers, and transforms them into the materialized emotional events described by Prown.

As a material memorialization, the 1797 watercolour is especially striking. Most notably, this is the only watercolour in which more than a single figure is depicted. If we allow that the watercolours are indeed self-representations and that the adult figure is Lewis herself, it follows that the young girl represents Lewis' only surviving daughter, Louisa. The image is prophetic. Seventeen-year-old Thomas Frankland was away at Christ Church, Oxford, and Lewis and Louisa spent the next thirteen years by themselves, travelling between London, Cheltenham and the houses of friends. As a representation of widowhood, Lewis conforms to visual models of mourning.[114] She displays herself as a sombre but dignified widow and, with one arm protectively steadying her oblivious and innocent daughter, as a mother and guardian to her fatherless child. Such motifs of mourning motherhood were popularized through the commercial culture of mourning rings and hair jewellery and in mourning needlework.[115] These creative responses to emotive events were widespread on both sides of the Atlantic. The technique of printing on satin, as used to decorate the muffs and work boxes discussed earlier in this chapter (Figures 3.25, 3.26 and 3.27) was also vital to textile mourning culture. Such prints on textiles often formed the outline for stitched expressions of grief. Angelica Kauffman's artworks, most notably *Fame at the Tomb of Shakespeare*, were especially popular as a model for these embroidered scenes.[116] These material manifestations of emotion were part of a commercialized and standardized method of

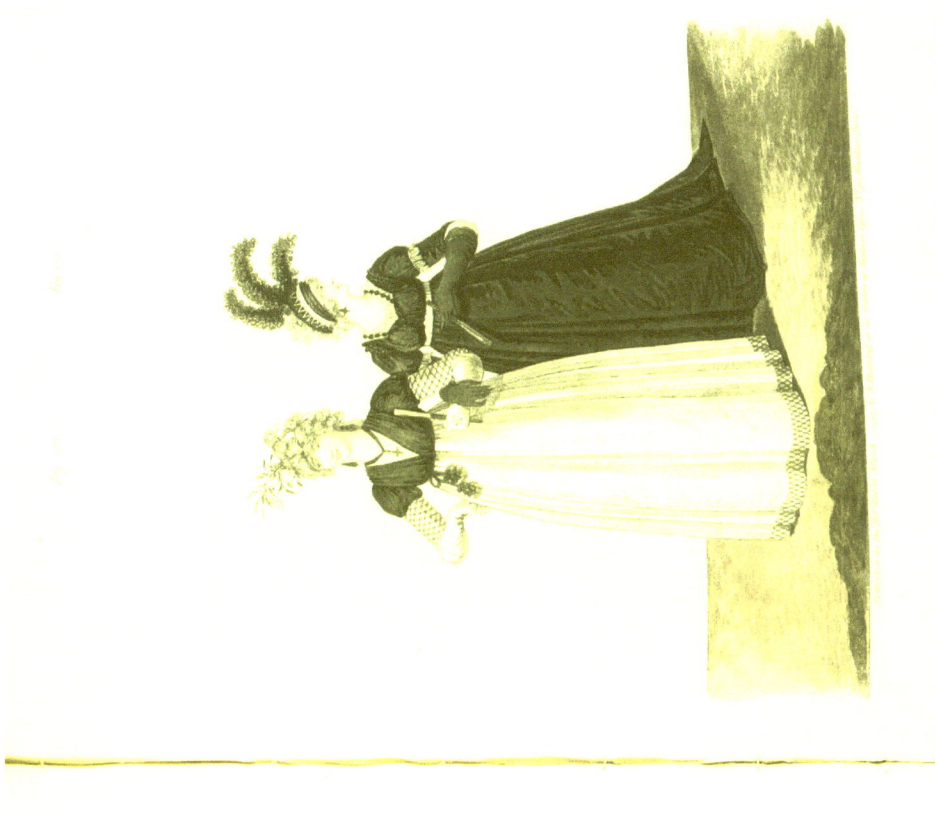

Figure 3.41 *Mourning Dresses, Gallery of Fashion, March 1797. Published by Nicholas Heideloff. Courtesy of the British Library.*

Figure 3.42 Ann Frankland Lewis, Morning dress 1795. The teal colour favoured in 1794 continues to be used in this image, accompanying a simple white cotton dress and coral pink shoes. Los Angeles County Museum of Art, www.lacma.org.

Figure 3.43 *Ann Frankland Lewis, 1796. This is the first watercolour where the figure is not wearing hair powder. Los Angeles County Museum of Art, www.lacma.org.*

Figure 3.44 *Ann Frankland Lewis, 1797. The year of John Lewis' death is marked with this poignant image of a mother and daughter in mourning. Los Angeles County Museum of Art, www.lacma.org.*

Dress of the Year: Watercolours 111

Figure 3.45 *Ann Frankland Lewis, 1798. Dressed in partial mourning, it is possible that from this point onwards Lewis depicts her surviving daughter, Louisa. The uncovered hair and youthful features make this especially likely. Los Angeles County Museum of Art, www.lacma.org.*

Figure 3.46 *Ann Frankland Lewis, 1799. This bright blue gown is trimmed with embroidered or woven bands. Los Angeles County Museum of Art, www.lacma.org.*

Figure 3.47 Ann Frankland Lewis, Morning dress December 1800. *This black pelisse was probably worn for mourning. Los Angeles County Museum of Art, www.lacma.org.*

performing loss through manual creativity. Yet, as codified as these modes of emotional expression appear, the hours of dedicated stitching reveal the intense emotion channelled into culturally managed outlets. Although they often followed standardized compositions, their inscriptions and idiosyncratic adaptations personalized their emotional content. They regularly depicted specific family members, and displayed the family left to grieve standing around the deceased relative's memorial.[117]

A mourning sampler from around 1800, made using the same technique of stitching onto a printed or painted base, depicts a composition which is arrestingly similar to Lewis' 1797 watercolour.[118] The two women, sadly unidentified, gaze out at the viewer, their position on the upholstered bench presented as an inverse mirror of Lewis' own arrangement. Such fancywork stitched compositions were often the work of school girls, and used as a means of mediating early encounters will loss and mourning.[119] With painted faces and stitched garments and landscape, the piece is part of the popular movement in needlework painting propagated by Mary Linwood (1755–1845).[120] In Linwood's artworks, brushstrokes were rendered by stitches, as she captured famous faces of the day with the movements of her needle. Published only months after John Lewis' death, Lucy Aikin celebrated the popularity of Linwood's remarkable technique 'that bids the picture live' in a poem in the *Monthly Museum*.[121] Similar scenes were also, though less commonly, rendered through pencils and paints, as visual languages spread across artistic mediums.[122] Lewis' watercolour was undoubtedly an amalgamation of varied influences, and attests to the shared and interwoven languages of needlework, print and paint. Her life-long interest in the print culture of the fashion plate continued, but it meshed with new modes of sartorial representation and creative self-reflection. While creative cultures of mourning were usually expressed through stitching, Lewis subtly embraced and assimilated these motifs into her own existing artistic practice.

The reflexivity of Lewis' engagement with merged cultures of consumption and craft spills through all of her watercolours. Each image was a crafted representation of her sartorial consumption, which in turn incorporated her own practices of textile making and the influence of commercialized fashion and artistic culture. Lewis' making and buying were merged almost to a point at which they cannot be untangled. The deep-seated influence of commercial cultures of fashion and artistic creation resonate in every image, while the compositional and temporal model of the fashion plate dominated the structuring of the images. As a material diary, the watercolours chronometrically negotiated how Lewis conceived of the passing of time. To return to Prown's conceptualization of material artefacts as 'events', Lewis' practice embodies this notion quite literally. Largely absent from the archival record, the sociable, fashionable and emotional rhythms of Lewis' life play out and fluctuate across the watercolours with each passing year. A patriotic ball, a society trend, a personal loss, and countless other now indecipherable moments were captured by Lewis' brush. Her father, husband and son may dominate her story in the archival breadcrumbs of her life, but through this sartorial biography Lewis memorialized her material life for posterity.

Figure 3.48 *Ann Frankland Lewis, 1801. The white gown is accessorized with a gold pendant. Los Angeles County Museum of Art, www.lacma.org.*

Figure 3.49 *Ann Frankland Lewis, 1802. Either beaded or embroidered, this dress was for evening wear. Los Angeles County Museum of Art, www.lacma.org.*

Figure 3.50 *Ann Frankland Lewis, 1803. The table echoes those depicted in the fashion plates of* La Belle Assemblée *and* Repostory of Arts. *The small fan also seems to be the same as that depicted in 1802. Los Angeles County Museum of Art, www.lacma.org.*

Figure 3.51 *Ann Frankland Lewis, Morning dress 1804. This massive fur muff is depicted with a black pelisse bordered with a deep lace flounce. Los Angeles County Museum of Art, www.lacma.org.*

Figure 3.52 *Ann Frankland Lewis, March 1806. More deep lace flounces adorn this cape. Los Angeles County Museum of Art, www.lacma.org.*

Figure 3.53 *Ann Frankland Lewis,* Morning dress January 1807. *Lewis' final watercolour depicts a brown day dress with a striking coral trim. It would not be long until Louisa, Lewis' last remaining daughter, would die. Los Angeles County Museum of Art, www.lacma.org.*

4

Adorned in silk: Dressed prints

Sabine Winn's written legacy is vast. Her letters, bills, recipe books, notes and domestic records have been carefully preserved, and continue to be held in archival unity. While the lives of Johnson, Lewis and, to an even greater extent, Powell require reassembly from a fractured and incomplete jigsaw, Winn's archive stands comparatively intact.[1] Her life as the wife of Sir Rowland Winn (fifth baronet, 1739–1785) in rural Yorkshire is vividly recounted in her paper archive, and previous studies of these sources have offered insights into her roles as architectural patron, household manager and luxury consumer.[2] Rich written archival evidence does not, however, preclude her from a study of her material life, nor does it make such a study any less pertinent. Instead, Winn offers a vital example of how material approaches can alter familiar biographies.[3] In privileging the letters and other texts produced by Winn over her material outputs, crucial outlets for the expression of Winn's identity and selfhood remain untapped. A holistic approach to Winn's material and written records exposes fresh and vibrant layers within her story, which reveal her to have been a skilled maker as well as an avid consumer.

Winn was not the author of a single consistent and unified material narrative. Her life was, however, peppered with interactions with artefacts which were consistently imbued with intense biographical, emotional, cultural and social meaning. More than any of the other women in this book, Winn's practices demonstrate how pervasive material life-writing practices were. Captured in vignettes of making, Winn's material production was fused with her emotional and personal lives. Winn's most substantial surviving material activity centred on the application of fabric to printed images (Figure 4.1). Variably referred to as 'dressed prints', 'adorned prints', 'modified prints' and 'decorated prints', the exercise of cutting out portions of purchased engravings and attaching pieces of fabric to the reverse was niche, but by no means unique. Sixteen prints dressed by Winn remain in the collection of the National Trust. Sitting at the juncture between her Francophile consumption and her conversance in production skills, the dressed prints provide a dynamic and crucial intervention in prevalent narratives around the material activities of women of the country house elites.[4]

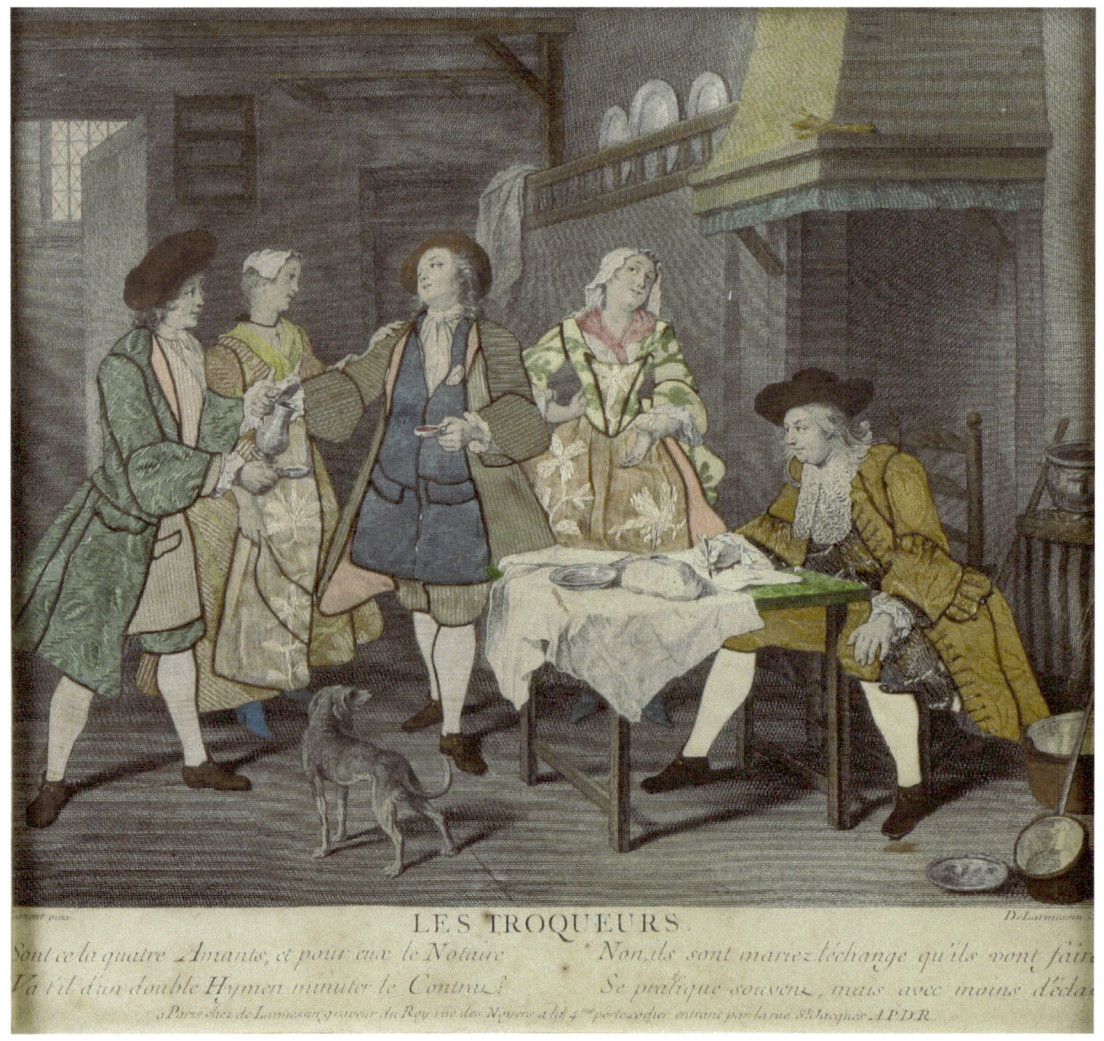

Figure 4.1 *Nicolas Larmessin IV,* Les Troqueurs, *after Nicolas Lancret, dressed by Sabine Winn, 1761–1765, NT 960084.2. Copyright National Trust.*

Sabine Winn (1734–1798)

The preservation of a multitude of letters to and from Sabine Winn and her relations has meant that she and her home, Nostell, have provided ample fodder for historians of art, architecture and consumption.[5] Biographical treatments of Sabine Winn have, however, tended to commence not with her birth, parents, or early life growing up on the shores of Lake Geneva, but with 1756, the year she met her future husband, Rowland Winn.[6] This is, in part, an inevitable consequence of this moment coinciding with her first appearance in the Winn family archive.[7] Yet we must recognize that Sabine Winn's formative years in Switzerland were fundamental in shaping her social and cultural self, and that she continued to be influenced by her Francophile, Swiss upbringing throughout her life. An abridgment of these foundational years fails to fully acknowledge the impact of her Swissness and dismisses Winn as being simply a foreign other within Anglocentric studies of the English elites.

Sabine Winn spent her first twenty-eight years – equating to over a third of her life – not in Yorkshire, but in Vevey in Switzerland. She was born on 25 March 1734 to Jacques Philippe d'Hervart (1706–1764), Baron de Saint-Légier and Governor of Vevey and his wife, Jeanne Esther Dunz (*c.* 1707–1779), and was their only child to survive into adulthood.[8] Her paternal grandfather, Philibert Herwart (1644–1721), was born in Lyon in France, but had fled to England with his father after the Revocation of the Edict of Nantes.[9] Following the Huguenot diaspora, Philibert found favour at the English court of William III, and became envoy to Geneva, before retiring to Vevey in 1702, although he continued to spend some time in England.[10] Jacques Philippe's sister, Marianne-Ursule Herwart (1699–1749), married the English art collector John Guise in 1723, and the family retained its diplomatic ties to England well into the eighteenth century. Philibert was deeply involved in charitable projects for fellow, and less fortunate, Huguenots in London, and when he died in Southampton in 1721 his funeral was a grand spectacle.[11] Sabine Winn's maternal line was equally pan-European, and connected her with the prolific city architects of Bern and Augsburg, stretching Winn's familial continental ties even deeper into Europe.[12]

As daughter of the Governor, Sabine Winn's life in Vevey would have been opulent and bustling with an ever-changing circle of elite foreign guests. The family was decidedly wealthy, and upon her parents' death Sabine Winn was set to inherit a substantial fortune of £70,000.[13] The company in Vevey regularly consisted of young Englishmen on the grand tour, and the town acted as a crucible for cross-cultural education, which included continental language and customs, as well as art, music and literature.[14] Positioned on the northern shore of Lake Geneva, and in the shadow of Mont Pèlerin, Dent de Lys and Dent de Corjon at the edge of the *préalpes*, Vevey was only eleven miles east of Lausanne and fifty miles south of the Swiss capital of Bern. Far from drawing solid distinctions between the French, Swiss, English and German inhabitants, visitors to and residents of the town actively mixed.[15] One such visitor was Bern resident, Gabriel May (1717–1759). May possessed lands in Huningue, at the juncture of the French, Swiss and German borders, and held an administrative position within the army, but had lived in Bern most of his life. He was nearing 40 when he met and married the vivacious and strong-willed 20-year-old Sabine in 1754. Their marriage on 11 October 1754 was, as Christopher Todd has speculated, probably the result of business connections between May and Jacques Philippe d'Hervart.[16] It was a disastrous match. May was serious, religious and worked relentlessly.[17] His new wife resolutely refused to move to Bern to live with him, as she preferred to stay amongst her young friends in familiar Vevey.[18]

Married less than two years, and still defiantly remaining in Vevey rather than moving to live with her husband, Sabine crossed paths with a dashing young baronet's son from England. Rowland Winn arrived in Vevey on 2 August 1756. Aged just 17, Rowland was a stark contrast to her dull, older husband. Rowland was a gifted musician, who had arranged music for Voltaire, and hugely enjoyed the theatre.[19] His material extravagance was also extreme. In Switzerland, Rowland spent a fortune on clothes, jewellery, furniture, paintings, fresh flowers, personal musicians and horses; all of which aimed to counter his anxiety that 'he was not magnificent enough to be in fine company'.[20] The appeal of this young, luxury-loving Englishman quickly attracted the bored Sabine, and within months of meeting, they embarked on a 'little affair'.[21] Despite Rowland's assurances that 'it was only an amusement', it was generally thought that he was 'a little too explosive in his liking for her'.[22] Rowland was swiftly moved from Vevey to Lausanne in the autumn of 1756, in an attempt to separate him from temptation and the gossip that ensued. The young Swiss woman, however, remained firmly in his thoughts.

Two years later, at the start of 1758, it was clear that Gabriel May was seriously unwell. He suffered from intense headaches and haemorrhoids, and by March 1759 he was dead. May's family furiously blamed Sabine's spousal negligence for his death, and her father-in-law claimed that his son's wife had 'abandoned her husband to languish in this sad fate so that probably, and according to the findings of his friends and acquaintances, these sorrows finally cost him his life'.[23] Upon hearing of Gabriel May's death, and nearly three years after his so-called 'little affair' with the dead man's wife, Rowland lost no time in seeking her out. Merely a month after May's death, Rowland sought to marry the dead man's widow, much to the dismay of Rowland's father. Sir Rowland Winn (the fourth baronet, 1706–1765) raised concerns both about his prospective daughter-in-law's virginity and her foreignness, stating that although she and May had 'but little cohabited, there must have been touch on both sides'.[24] He went on to remind his son that he had been known to gleefully mock French accents, and that his prospective wife was sure to suffer similar indignities when seated at an English dinner table. Rowland's four sisters echoed their father's concerns over communication, and co-wrote a letter to their father which lamented that 'we are afraid we shall be greatly at a loss to keep up a Conversation with her, as you say she knowns nothing of the English Language, & we have forgot the greatest part of our French'.[25] Both the sisters' and the father's statements would prove prophetic. Ignoring his family's concerns, however, Rowland went ahead with the marriage. A lengthy discussion of dowries and

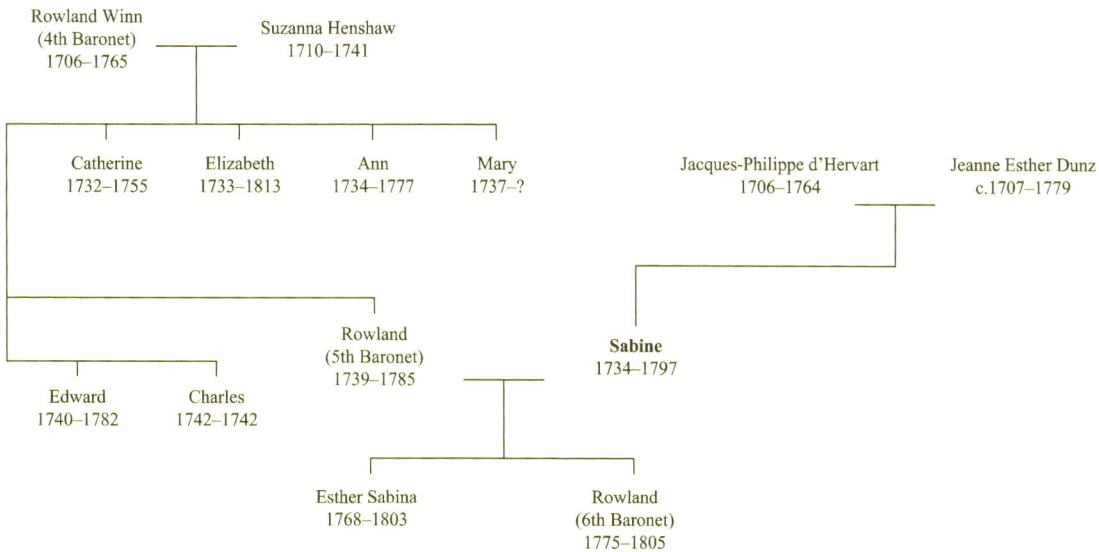

Figure 4.2 *Family tree of the Winn family. Compiled from evidence in the Nostell Archive, WYAS: WYW1352.*

settlements ensued, which would stretch out over two long years, testing the couple's steadfast devotion to one another.[26] The couple finally married in Vevey on 4 December 1761, and swiftly departed for their new life in England.[27] As their boat landed, and Sabine Winn stepped onto English soil for the first time, it is unlikely that she knew that she would never leave England again. While she would never return to her childhood home in Vevey, the influence of her foundational and formative years in Switzerland resonated throughout her life and her making practices.

For the first few years of their marriage, Sabine Winn and her husband Rowland enjoyed the bustling balls and sparkling sociability of London and Bath. They obtained a London house at number 11 St James' Square, which Rowland purchased complete with the previous occupant's furniture and fittings, and they also spent time visiting Rowland's married sisters.[28] Amongst the fashionable French-speakers of London, Sabine Winn tentatively began to make friends in England.[29] But her inability to speak English was already an impediment to sociability. When she met with non-French speakers it was inevitably awkward, and 'they did nothing but laugh at each other'.[30] She fared no better in Yorkshire, where she and Rowland took up residence at Badsworth, about four miles from Nostell.[31] One acquaintance, Catherine Cappe (née Harrison, 1744–1821) dramatically claimed that 'the peace of the [Winn] family' was 'entirely destroyed' by the return of the newlyweds to Yorkshire.[32] The theatricality of this claim is matched in Cappe's lengthy and emotive description of Sabine Winn herself:

> His lady was trifling in her turn of mind, and in her temper, violent and imperious; at once, covetous and extravagant. Her appearance and manner however to strangers was singularly captivating, for

she was very beautiful, and had a great deal of vivacity. When I first saw her, she was habited in a close vestment of pink satin, the colour not more delicate that her own fine complexion; she was tripping lightly along one of the great staircases; and seeing a stranger with one of the ladies of the family, ran up, and accosted us in French, with all the gaitey [sic], ease, and politeness, peculiar to that nation; her fine dark eyes sparkling with a radiance exclusively their own. I had never before seen anything like her, and struck with astonishment, the sudden emotion she excited of surprise and admiration, not wholly unmingled with a sentiment of awe, was probably little inferior to what I should actually have felt, had she been in reality, what at that moment she appeared to be, a being of angelic order.[33]

Emphatic accounts of Sabine Winn's beauty, extravagance and love of novelty recur throughout the archive. Ann Elizabeth Winn, the sister of the fourth baronet, wrote to her brother that her new niece-in-law 'loves variety, & may truly be Cald Lady Restles [sic]'.[34] Sabine Winn's restlessness and disquiet cries out from her own letters; however, they also reveal her tumultuous emotional life. Throughout their marriage, Rowland spent a great deal of time away from his wife. He travelled extensively to pursue a political career, and to carry out other business on his Lincolnshire estates.[35] Alone in Yorkshire, which she denounced as 'one of the most desolate and gloomy corners of the universe', Sabine Winn described herself as 'vegetating like a plant'.[36] Her despair seeps from her letters as she pleads with her husband to return to her. 'The truth is that you love London a good deal more than you do your wife,' she wrote accusingly in 1763.[37]

The couple eventually moved into Nostell itself, following the death of the fourth baronet in 1765. They were determined to make the house their own, and set about implementing a grand refurbishment scheme. They commissioned Robert Adam to drastically transform the existing, outmoded, rococo interiors, which had been completed by James Paine for the fourth baronet, into the newly fashionable neoclassical style.[38] As Kerry Bristol has demonstrated, the furniture of the couple's London house was acquired along with the building to signal perfunctory membership of the London elites; at Nostell, however, the couple imbued their interiors with personal as well as fashionable taste.[39] Their joint portrait captures a moment of hopeful confidence for the couple (Figure 4.3). Depicted together in 1767 in the recently completed library – the first room remodelled by Adam at Nostell – the portrait encapsulated their hopes and aspirations.[40] The fruits of their patronage surround them, including the pedimented bookcases by Adam, paintings by Antonio Zucchi and mahogany furniture by Chippendale.[41] Engineered within the portrait, it is this vision of the Winns, as patrons and arbiters of taste, which has most successfully endured.

As Nostell began to take shape, the couple were still childless. Sabine Winn had believed that she might have been pregnant in 1763, but her hopes were wretchedly dashed.[42] Finally, seven long years after their marriage, Sabine Winn gave birth to her first child, Esther (1768–1803), at the couple's

Figure 4.3 *Hugh Douglas Hamilton,* Sir Rowland Winn and his wife Sabine Winn in the Library at Nostell, *1767. Courtesy of the National Trust.*

London home. Another seven years later, she successfully delivered a second child, little Rowland (sixth baronet, 1775–1805). After the birth of her son, she stopped travelling to London, and remained at Nostell to care for her two children.[43] Young Rowland was certainly the favoured child, and his mother routinely collected locks of the small boy's hair, placing it in diligently labelled packets.[44] This practice of capturing a material relic of the child at regular intervals as he grew is, in itself, a form of material biography. Hair, an intensely emotive item in the eighteenth century, was transformed by Winn into a temporal marker, and a means of chronicling her young son's development.[45] In stark contrast, Esther was perceived by her parents as a 'difficult child', although her own archive demonstrates that she was accomplished as an artist and musician.[46]

Life at Nostell changed dramatically on 20 February 1785, when the fifth baronet unexpectedly died. He had been on his way to London when, as the obituary columns in newspapers and periodicals reported, he 'died suddenly … in the prime of his life' at Retford.[47] Cappe recorded that Rowland's mind was 'torn by the most violent, conflicting passions, and at length, he died wretchedly at an inn'.[48] Although often cited as a carriage accident by biographers, no contemporary account of the cause of death exists.[49] Widowed for a second time, Sabine Winn was intensely and inconsolably devastated. She isolated herself and her children at Nostell, shutting her doors to visitors. Sequestered away from the world, Sabine Winn refused to allow Esther to visit her aunt in London, or for little Rowland to be sent to a suitable school following the death of his tutor. The fifth baronet's sisters banded together, and in 1791 instigated Chancery proceedings against their sister-in-law in order to ensure their nephew's education.[50] Sabine refused to cooperate until the daunting threat of a prison sentence loomed. Two years later, 25-year-old Esther, who had dutifully cared for her ailing mother since the age of 17, eloped to Manchester with the Nostell baker, John Williamson. Isolated in gloomy, lonely, half-built Nostell, with only her demanding mother and little brother for company, Esther had never been able to sample the delights of the London season nor cultivate friendships and connections amongst her peers. Her elopement, however, caused her to become fully estranged from her mother, never to reconcile.[51]

Mountains of unpaid bills and Nostell's incomplete interiors haunted Sabine Winn throughout her final years. The family's solicitor, Shepley Watson, regularly corresponded with the aging and ailing Sabine Winn, advising her on rents, estate management and her ever-present debts.[52] Entering her sixtieth year of age with only her young son for company, her health deteriorated quickly. By the 1790s, the captivating and lively young bride, whom Cappe recalled 'tripping lightly' along the staircases of Nostell, was obese, and suffered so much with either gout or arthritis that in 1798 she had 'so far lost the use of her limbs, as to be obliged to be lifted by two people in and out of bed'.[53] In February 1798 she suffered from a fever, and was prescribed 'James's powders' by Pontefract doctor, Thomas Oxley.[54] It seems, however, that she refused this treatment, and the powders survive preserved and unopened along with the letter.[55] A few months later, on 16 September 1798, Sabine Winn died at

Nostell and was buried in the vault of the estate church. Her 23-year-old son did not see fit to inform his sister or the rest of the Winn family.[56]

This short biographical account of Sabine Winn's life abbreviates many of the myriad details retained within the colossal paper archive. Disputes with tradespeople, arguments between husband and wife and wider family disputes – primarily about money – have here received only a superficial and condensed retelling. There are over 500 boxes of papers in the family archive, amounting to thousands of sheets, and their contents delineate details of a life worthy of a dramatic tragedy.[57] It would be possible to indulge in endless delicious details of the family menagerie, the children's education or the couple's courtship, but the core themes prevalent in the paper archive – luxury consumption, family disputes, country house management and architectural patronage – would remain the same. These papers have been proffered by Todd as evidence of Sabine Winn as a 'Swiss milady' who was 'insecure in a foreign land'.[58] She did undoubtedly struggle with life in rural Yorkshire, but her Swiss roots and continental connections should not be read as obstructive and limiting. While her sisters-in-law and Yorkshire neighbours may have sometimes treated Sabine Winn as a foreign 'other', historical accounts of her life must not follow suit. Winn's material life offers crucial evidence of how continental culture, material literacy and emotional struggles intersected and were united through making. However extensive the written paper archive of an individual may be, their material traces can still provide invaluable nuance and bring vital new understanding.

Paper textiles, dress and the dressed print

The semiotic divide between a paper and a material archive is, of course, fundamentally misleading. Text and textile, paper and fabric: these materials were profoundly interconnected.[59] Paper can be found stitched inside stays, hats and other garments as an interfacing or stiffener, and paper was itself composed of rags and scraps of fabric.[60] The same core fibres composed both materials, and the relationship between text and textile was culturally ubiquitous. The portrayal of *Une Vendeuse des Images* by Martin Engelbrecht (1684–1756) underlines this close connection between printed images and garments (Figure 4.4). One of a series produced by Engelbrecht for an album of prints entitled *Métiers*, the image depicts a print seller subsumed by her wares.[61] Her petticoat, transformed into the canvas for a collaged concoction of prints, peaks out in flashes of scarlet between the fluttering sheets. The prints are transmuted into an overdress, carefully arranged in layers composed to echo tiered flounces. As a garment, the prints take on characteristics and styles which play upon the connections between their foundational shared fibres.

Engelbrecht positioned prints as a figurative fabric, but within the practice of dressing prints, this connection between textile and paper was literal. Dressed prints, like those constructed by Winn, used

Figure 4.4 Une Vendeuse des Images *from Martin Engelbrecht's* Métiers, *1730. Courtesy of Kunstbibliothek, Staatliche Museen zu Berlin.*

pieces of fabric attached to the print to extend the symbiosis between paper and textile even further. Pasted together, fabric and print jostle for primacy within each adorned image, and merge the compositional work of the artist, engraver or etcher with the texture and colour injected by the dresser. Chloe Wigston Smith has reflected upon the 'hybrid' paper-fabric nature of these artefacts.[62] While the print provides the underpinning, genre-specific visual structures, the application and layering of varied textiles added a 'dynamic sense of depth'.[63] Plush velvets, detailed brocades, soft silk twills and intricate lace were deployed to build up an overarching sense of sartorial richness. In Chapter 3, the synergy between printed fashion plates and Ann Frankland Lewis' watercolours demonstrated that genteel women makers were conversant in the forms and visual language of printed images, and that they interacted with them in active and diverse ways. Prints were copied and mimicked, cut out and repurposed. The dressing of prints with snippets of fabric demonstrates that this engagement with print, and the connections between print and dress, stretched even deeper. Through dressed prints, the silks, wools, cottons and linens used to construct full-sized, wearable garments were reunited with their representational print and paper forms.

The techniques adopted by Winn have received limited scholarly attention, although numerous examples of the practice do exist in museum collections throughout Europe and America.[64] The method was inherited from fifteenth-century religious *spickelbilder*, which originated in northern Europe, Germany and Italy, and regained popularity in the late seventeenth century.[65] None of the terminology routinely used to refer to prints with fabrics attached offers a wholly satisfactory means of encapsulating the process of cutting and sticking used to create them, and there was no identifiable contemporary term for the technique. Alice Dolan has suggested that 'adorned print' rather than 'dressed print' is an appropriate moniker for these print and textile fusions.[66] Dolan rightly cites that 'dressed' can be misleading in light of the process of production used, as fabrics were not placed on top of the image, and so did not literally dress the paper bodies beneath.[67] Instead, the print was precisely cut along the edges of the figures' garments, with care taken to preserve distinctive features, such as accessories or the positioning of a hand. Carefully pasted or stitched together, fabric was then cut and composed to create garments to fill the resultant void and attached to the reverse of the print. A heavy paper or card was then stuck to the reverse. This ingenious method meant that the sharply defined paper outline obscured the cut edge of the fabric and hid any unsightly fraying.

The range of alternative terms for this process is not compelling. 'Embellished' and 'decorated' imply a superficial process of surface ornamentation, while 'modified' conjures up the impression that the composition itself has been markedly altered. 'Adorned' remains as an appropriate candidate, in spite of the contentious implication that the image is inherently improved by the application of fabric. However, I would also reinstate 'dressed' as a viable contender. Unlike later nineteenth-century tinsel pictures, the fabric additions to these prints focus almost exclusively on the clothes, and not on background features or props.[68] Throughout Winn's sixteen images, she demonstrated an intimate

Figure 4.5 *Antoine Trouvain, Mademoiselle d'Armagnac en Robe de Chambre, 1695.* Courtesy of the Bibliothèque nationale de France.

knowledge of sartorial conventions and the appropriate textiles for different garments, and this sartorial knowledge and material literacy is consistent across the genre. While the fabrics do not 'dress' a paper body, the maker does, in essence, dress the figure represented within the image with a full outfit of clothes. Knowledge of garment shapes and structures, the hand and behaviours of different fabrics and the textiles appropriate for different items of apparel were routinely displayed. Throughout this chapter, both 'dressed' and 'adorned' will be used, with an eye to the respective connotations.

The origins of the practice of dressing prints is firmly continental.[69] David Pullins has associated dressed prints with the popular French practice of producing '*découpure à la mode*', essentially an early form of decoupage which was highly fashionable in the first decades of the eighteenth century.[70] *Découpure*, Pullins argues, was an elite social marker, which involved cutting out prints and pasting them onto furniture or other small items, before covering the completed article in varnish. Contemporary writers framed *découpure* as an avid craze across France, claiming that precious prints had to be hidden away, or else they would surely be dismembered with scissors at the hands of an eager maker.[71] Archival sources fail to provide an explicit connection between the two practices, but the practical semblance between the techniques needed – cutting, pasting and composition – and the dating of many dressed prints to the 1690s–1730s seems to imply analogy between *découpure* and dressed prints.[72]

Most early dressed prints depict single, full-length figures dressed in contemporary fashions, and are often images of specific, named individuals. One such early dressed print depicts Mademoiselle d'Armagnac, also known as Charlotte of Lorraine (1678–1757, Figure 4.5).[73] The print of this French aristocrat was cut along the edges of her robe, carefully leaving the tassels unscathed, as well as retaining a thin sliver of paper on the skirt, used to distinguish the fold of her train. Comparison with the uncut print reveals that the impression of a stomacher and petticoat were additions, and that, in the original, the gown is closed at the centre front. This shift from the closed-fronted mantuas of 1690s fashions to the predominant stomacher styles of the 1710s reveals incongruence between the date of the print and the date of dressing. More importantly, it demonstrates the role that sartorial knowledge played in shaping the decisions makers made when dressing prints. Print dressers did not faithfully follow all the printed details. They applied their own stylistic choices and updated garments to follow changes in fashion. The fabric chosen to dress d'Armagnac was a twill wool, printed with a red and brown floral design. Combined with the application of watercolour paints to the face, as well as the accessories which survived the knife, the process of dressing the print returned the court beauty to radiant pictorial life. Other celebrated continental figures dominate collections of these early adorned prints, including the Duke of Bourbon (1692–1740), Marie Sophie the Queen of Portugal (1666–1699) and Mademoiselle Subligny (1666–1735).[74]

A striking lacuna exists between these early dressed prints, which date from late seventeenth or early eighteenth-century France, and the re-emergence of the technique alongside broader print collage, tinsel pictures and dressed portrait miniatures at the start of the nineteenth century in England

and America. Only a smattering of examples fills this gap.[75] Alongside Winn's dressed prints, Anna Magdalena Braun's (1734–1791) *trachtenbuch*, or costume book, offers a rare exception to this rule (Figure 4.6).[76] Unlike the watercolours by Lewis, discussed in Chapter 3, Braun's *trachtenbuch* does not represent clothing worn by the artist herself. Instead, Braun recorded the garments worn by a broad social range of men and women in a single year and specific place: Nuremburg in 1773.[77] Yet, like Lewis, Braun mimicked the compositional style of the print, including the full-length single figure view, the proportions and dimensions of the border, and the inclusion of a caption. Adopting the conventions of the dressed print, Braun cut out the silhouette of the garment's shape, and composed the clothing out of fabric, braids and lace, before pasting it to the reverse of her watercolours. Details like hands, fans and even a pocket watch were added in paper. Braun demonstrated a remarkable knowledge of garment construction and textiles, and her captions are specific in identifying the garments worn. This sartorial knowledge extended to the materiality and materials of dress. In some images, for instance, sheer cotton gauze was layered over solid silks to create aprons, imitating the material qualities of the garments she depicted.[78]

A resurgence in the popularity of dressed prints occurred around the turn of the nineteenth century in England. Some examples from this renaissance in dressed prints replicate the early eighteenth-century techniques with precision. An 1820 engraving of Queen Caroline, wife of the newly crowned George IV, faithfully mimicked the practice (Figure 4.7).[79] The queen's paper garments were cut away, leaving tiny slivers of paper to act as outlines and details. A russet silk velvet and white silk satin were then used to fill in the dress, shawl and hat. The fabrics were cut very close to the outlines of the garments, their raw edges covered by only a few millimetres of paper. The print was then backed with a firm card, which completely enclosed the fabric in a paper sandwich. Not only did this process reproduce the practical techniques used in early eighteenth-century France, but also the elite cultural resonances of the subjects chosen.[80] Like the French, Portuguese and German royalty, aristocrats and popular figures favoured in early dressed prints, the subject of this print was also royal, continental and a popular personality in the press. In the 1820s and 1720s alike, the act of dressing acted as a form of elite signifier, pinpointing the subject as being of notable public interest.[81]

The dressed prints of early nineteenth-century England were, however, considerably more diverse than their continental predecessors, both in terms of their subject matter and workmanship. The prints dressed by Fanny Austen Knight (1793–1882), the niece of novelist Jane Austen, lack the high degree of technical skill displayed in many other examples, but retain the key defining characteristics of the practice (Figure 4.8). The cutting and fabric choices were crude compared with the handiwork of Winn or the numerous anonymously dressed prints. The young, unskilled hand of the maker is exemplified by the chunks of uncut paper which surround the hands and the long, angular knife movements. Knight's dressed prints were not individual artworks, intended to be displayed and admired on a wall.[82] Instead, Knight used the fashion plates which were bound into her pocket books,

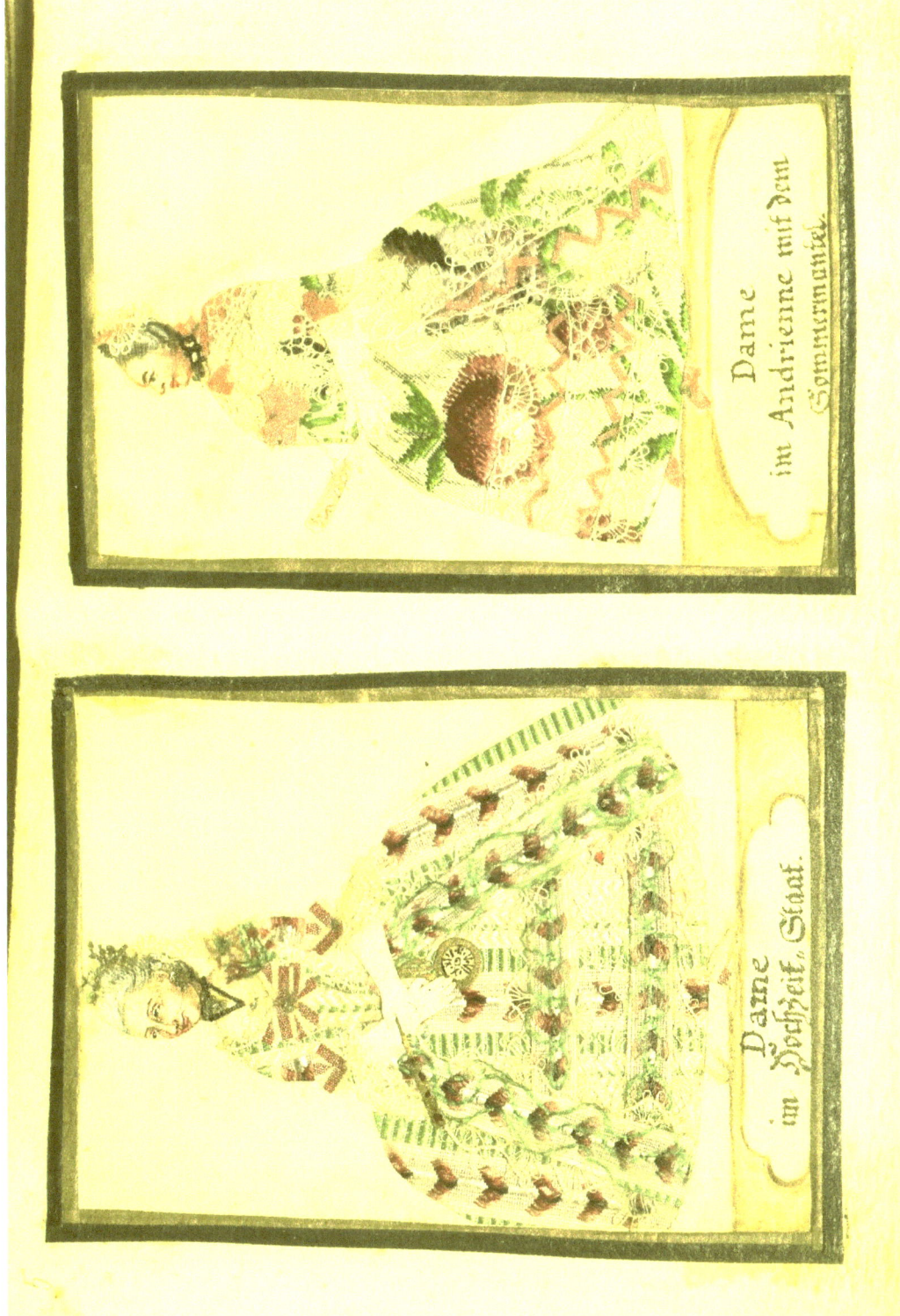

Figure 4.6 *Anna Magdelena Braun, Trachtenbuch, 1773. Courtesy of the Germanishes Nationalmuseum.*

Figure 4.7 R. Page, Caroline, Queen of England, *1820. Private collection.*

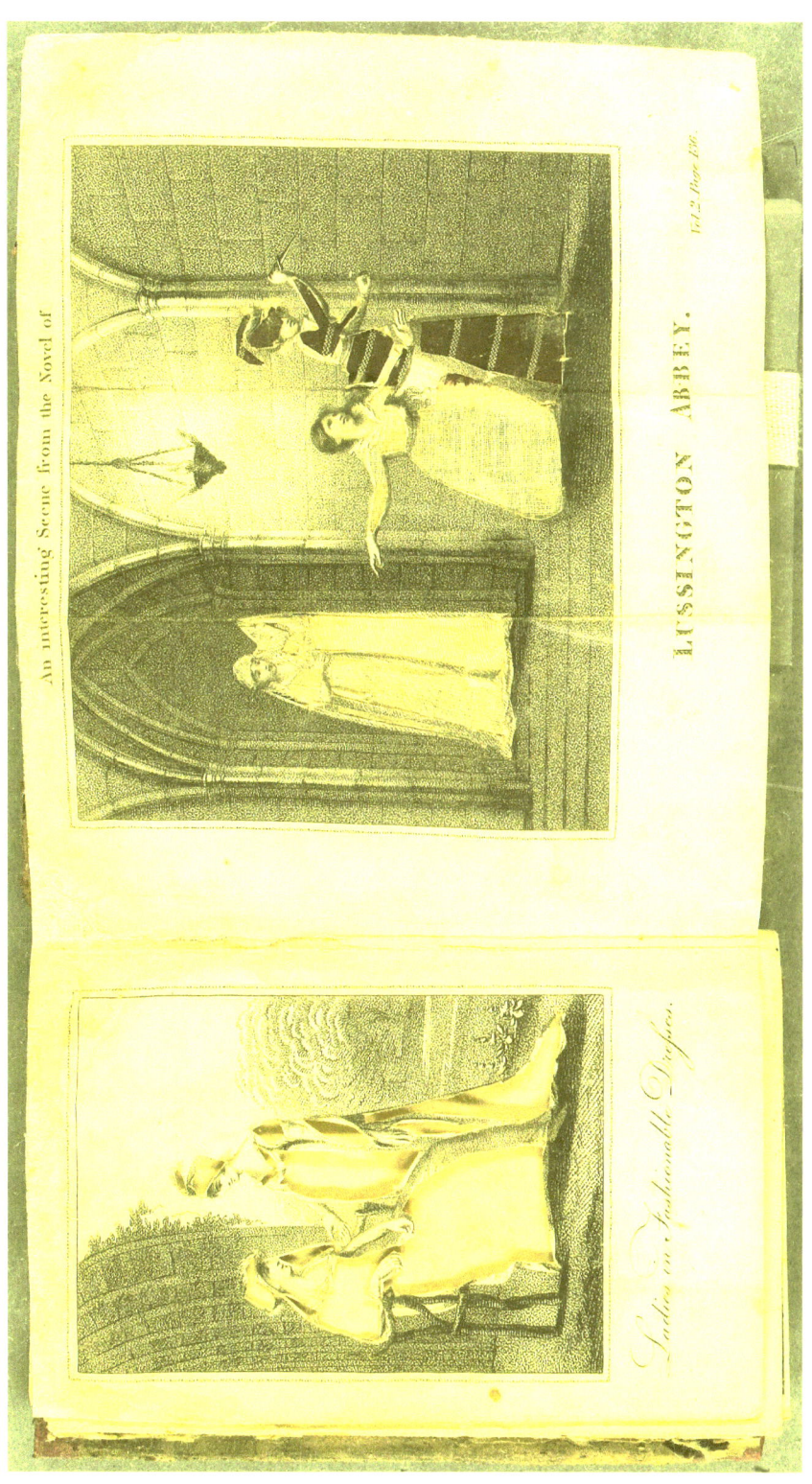

Figure 4.8 'Ladies in Fashionable Dresses' and 'An Interesting Scene from the Novel of Lussington Abbey', from the Ladies Complete Pocket Book, 1805. Courtesy of Kent Archive Service.

extending the connection between dress and the dressed print.[83] From the age of 11 in 1804, to the age of 79 in 1872, Knight routinely purchased and maintained annual pocket books.[84] Knight was gifted her first, the 1804 *Ladies Complete Pocket Book*, as a Christmas gift from her mother, and alongside early entries in the accounts pages for ribbons and sweets, Knight exploited her creativity to engage in an adolescent experiment in making.[85] As was the custom, the 1804 and 1805 pocket books each contained a fashion plate and an engraving illustrating a scene form a novel, and it was these plates that Knight adorned, while keeping them firmly bound into the little volumes. In retaining the integrity of each volume as a whole, Knight perpetuated the connections between her act of print adornment, and the ribbons and other textiles that she recorded purchasing within the accounting pages. The alignment between this creative practice and the self-reflective nature of pocket book accounting and memorandum pages extends the material, temporal and economic bonds between the dressed print and material life-writing – a connection pre-empted in Winn's own dressed prints.

Knight abandoned her dressed prints as she entered her teenage years, but other late-eighteenth- and early-nineteenth-century women adopted and adapted the technique. The most striking repurposing of the technique was undertaken by the American portrait miniaturist Mary Way (1769–1833).[86] Way's composite portraits consisted of a fabric background, which was usually black, onto which she placed a head and hair completed in watercolour on paper. The garments were then constructed from layers of fabric, and interlocked with the painted head, to create a three-dimensional 'dressed portrait miniature'.[87] Way's attentive use of appropriate fabrics – sheer cottons for shirt flounces, caps and aprons and silk for waistcoats, gowns and accessories – continued the resonance between dressed image and dressed person. Way's dressed portraits signal a sea change in the incorporation of fabric into prints, and a turn towards layered collage, rather than cut and recessed fabrics. As the nineteenth century progressed, tinsel pictures, mixed-media collage, and three-dimensional dioramas continued the legacy of the dressed print.[88] As a material strategy, the merging of printed paper scenes with tactile textiles provided an opportunity to express a multidimensional and multimedia material literacy. Knowledge of the material properties of paper, the multiple different fibres and weaves of the fabrics, and the behaviours of the pastes used to adhere the pieces together was required. This practical skill required a broad familiarity with the visual language of print and the sartorial rules and customs of dress.

Sabine Winn's dressed prints

The makers of the majority of eighteenth-century dressed prints remain anonymous, their names, status and lives lost to time. Not only do Winn's dressed prints fill the chronological void in the history of the technique, they also offer an unprecedented opportunity to contextualize the practice of print dressing within the landscape of an individual's emotional, creative and biographical life. The process of intricately cutting the print, designing and composing the replacement garments, and pasting them back into the print was both highly skilled and tremendously time consuming. The decision to engage in such creative activity was not born of passive idleness. It is difficult to imagine that Winn's valued and framed set of sixteen dressed prints represents her first foray into the technique. Winn's prints display a high level of precision and skill, and she undoubtedly spent innumerable hours learning, perfecting and practising the craft. Throughout the preserved sixteen prints, Winn's personal connection to her making shines through.

Winn's knowledge and skill as a maker introduce vital nuances to her current historiographical position as an avid consumer, hungry for the latest Adam interiors, Chippendale furniture, small dogs and fashionable silks. Within Winn's paper archive, there is scattered evidence of her engagement in amateur making. Early in her marriage, her new brother-in-law, George Allanson Winn, praised her as 'a young lady so agreeable and so accomplished'.[89] There is also evidence of her engagement with needlework. A hand-drawn pattern for embroidered lappets has survived in her paper archive, and a bill from Chippendale lists a tambour frame for Lady Winn.[90] Her sisters-in-law had also praised her accomplishments, associating them with her Swiss upbringing: 'We admire the Ladies in Switzerland's manner of spending their time, the generallity [sic] of them must make most nottable [sic] Wives.'[91] To be 'notable', in the eighteenth century, referred to engagement in industrious domestic activity.[92] The interweaving of Winn's Swissness and her making abilities was not only the product of national stereotyping, but a theme which feeds through her material archive. Although a narrative autobiography is absent from these objects, they nonetheless act as autobiographical crucibles into which Winn deposited key emotional, cultural and personal meaning. As Winn demonstrates, material lives could be recorded as vignettes, as well as through a systematic and routine chronicle.

The prints Winn dressed were part of a series, colloquially known as the *Suite de Larmessin*, which illustrated Jean de la Fontaine's (1621–1695) *Fables*, a copy of which survives in the Nostell library.[93] The 239 fables were primarily retellings of the work of Aesop, Babrius and Phaedrus in French free verse, and included time-honoured favourites *The Tortoise and the Hare* and *The Fox and The Crow*. Humorous reflections on the foibles of human nature, the fables were a cornerstone of French literary culture.[94] Copies of the *Fables* were by no means an uncommon addition to eighteenth-century English libraries, and editions proliferate across collections at Wimpole Hall, Plas Newydd, Febrigg Hall, Ickworth Hall, A La Ronde, Uppark House and Kedleston Hall. Further evidence of the fables' cultural reverberations in England can be found in the library at Woburn Abbey, designed by Henry Holland (1745–1806), which contains reliefs of the fables above the doors, as well as the chimneypieces at Blickling Hall and Uppark, which depict similar scenes.[95] The eighteenth-century printed illustrations are, however, far rarer in English collections.[96] The *Suite de Larmessin* prints were first advertised in a 1733 issue of *Mercure de France* and continued to be released over the next decade.[97] The *Suite de*

Larmessin anticipated the widespread popularity of the fables in visual and material culture in the nineteenth and twentieth centuries, but their French cultural capital was firmly established.

Winn received the prints as a gift from Rowland at some point between their marriage in 1761 and their acquisition of Nostell and the baronetcy in 1765. On the reverse of every dressed print, in Winn's own hand, is the carefully written inscription: '*Monsieur Rowland Winn ma donné le tableau Sabine Winn née d'Herwart*' (Figure 4.9).[98] *Le tableau*, meaning 'the picture' in this instance, referred to the unaltered print. Sitting in the quiet darkness of the picture store at Nostell today, these prints are little-known and rarely seen.[99] Yet this inscription, fondly repeated sixteen times across the collection of dressed prints, captures a moment of intense emotion. Newly arrived in England, Winn's first four years of married life with Rowland were emotionally turbulent. Although they spent much of their time in London, Winn also often found herself alone, living in a borrowed house in the middle of the unfamiliar Yorkshire countryside. Two years into their marriage, on one of Rowland's many trips away, Winn wrote to him that 'I cannot sleep, nor eat, which are the only pleasures as you know that can be relished at Badsworth.'[100] Winn's feelings of abandonment are explicit in her letters during this period, and the prints were likely a material means by which Rowland could make amends for his absence and provide his new wife with objects which offered a comforting tie to her continental roots.

Risqué in their subject matter, most of the prints selected by Rowland centre on the themes of love and sex, and were symbols of the humour and sexual intimacy between husband and wife. In *Les Rémois* (Figure 4.10), for instance, the couple depicted are caught in an amorous embrace, the man grasping at the woman's partially exposed breast. Similarly, *Le Fleuve Scamandre* (Figure 4.16) portrays a young woman undressed, sitting on the bank of the river in which she has just bathed. Her thighs exposed, she dries her wet flesh, unaware that she is being watched. *Le Gascon Puni* (Figure 4.18) continues these erotic themes. Dressed as a woman, a man has attempted to infiltrate the bed of a young woman who, bosom exposed, leaps from the bed having realized his deceit. Perhaps most suggestive of all, *La Jument de Compere Pierre* (Figure 4.20) illustrates the tale of a priest who lusts after a peasant's wife and promises her pitiable husband that he has the power to transform her into a mare to work the fields. Conveniently, in order to accomplish this, the priest must see her naked. The tip of the priest's finger sits teasingly on the wife's nipple, while the oblivious husband looks on, engrossed. As a gift from husband to wife, these suggestive and erotic prints reflect a continuation of the playful and passionate dynamic which characterized the couple's courtship.

Rowland's choice of these French figurative prints was, therefore, not haphazard or arbitrary. *Suite de Larmessin* directly connected Winn to the Francophile, Swiss culture she had left behind her in Vevey. Familiar stories told visually, with captions in her own language, must have provided Winn with a comforting lifeline to her much-loved continental roots. As her father-in-law bemoaned, Winn had made little effort to learn English, could not converse easily with her English acquaintances, and took no pleasure in the onerous task of language-learning.[101] Illustrations of Fontaine's *Fables* – stories

Figure 4.9 *Reverse side of one of Sabine Winn's dressed prints, 1761–1765, NT 960084.2. Copyright National Trust.*

Figure 4.10 *Nicolas Larmessin,* Les Rémois, *after Nicolas Lancret, dressed by Sabine Winn, 1761–1765, NT 960084.3. Copyright National Trust.*

Figure 4.11 Nicolas Larmessin, Les Oyes de Frere Philippe, *after Nicolas Lancret, dressed by Sabine Winn, 1761–1765, NT 960084.4. Copyright National Trust.*

Figure 4.12 Nicolas Larmessin, Frere Luce, *after Nicolas Vleugels, dressed by Sabine Winn, 1761–1765, NT 960084.5. Copyright National Trust.*

Figure 4.13 *Pierre Filloeul,* La Matrone d'Ephes, *after Jean-Baptist Pater, dressed by Sabine Winn, 1761–1765, NT 960084.6. Copyright National Trust.*

Figure 4.14 *Nicolas Larmessin,* La Faucon, *after Nicolas Lancret, dressed by Sabine Winn, 1761–1765, NT 960084.7. Copyright National Trust.*

Figure 4.15 *Pierre Filloeul, Le Glouton, after Jean-Baptist Pater, dressed by Sabine Winn, 1761–1765,* NT 960084.8. Copyright National Trust.

Figure 4.16 *Nicolas Larmessin,* Le Fleuve Scamandre, *after François Boucher, dressed by Sabine Winn, 1761–1765,* NT 960084.9. Copyright National Trust.

Adorned in Silk: Dressed Prints 147

Figure 4.17 *Pierre Filleul,* Le Coccu Battu et Content, *dressed by Sabine Winn, 1761–1765, NT 960084.10. Copyright National Trust.*

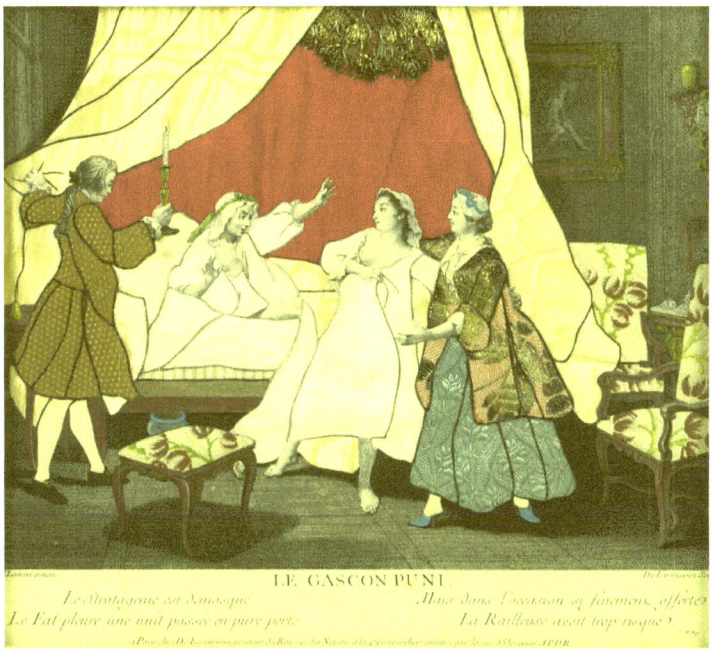

Figure 4.18 *Nicolas Larmessin,* Le Gascon Puni, *after Nicolas Lancret, dressed by Sabine Winn, 1761–1765, NT 960084.11. Copyright National Trust.*

Figure 4.19 Nicolas Larmessin, Les Deux Amis, *after Nicolas Lancret, dressed by Sabine Winn, 1761–1765, NT 960084.12. Copyright National Trust.*

Figure 4.20 Nicolas Larmessin, La Jument de Compere Pierre, *after Nicolas Vleughels, dressed by Sabine Winn, 1761–1765, NT 960084.13. Copyright National Trust.*

Figure 4.21 *Nicolas Larmessin,* Les Aveux Indiscrets, *after Jean-Baptiste Pater, dressed by Sabine Winn, 1761–1765, NT 960084.14. Copyright National Trust.*

Figure 4.22 *Nicolas Larmessin,* La Servante Justifiee, *after Nicolas Lancret, dressed by Sabine Winn, 1761–1765, NT 960084.15. Copyright National Trust.*

Figure 4.23 *Nicolas Larmessin IV,* Nicaise, *after Nicolas Lancret, dressed by Sabine Winn, 1761–1765, NT 960084.16. Copyright National Trust.*

which were culturally French but fashionable and popular in England – were a shrewd choice by Rowland as his new wife attempted to settle into her adopted nation. The prints were probably purchased in London, where print sellers such as Seyffert and Strange advertised the *Fables* as 'now arrived from Paris' complete with '*magnifique estampes*'.[102] The Frenchness of both the prints and Winn was inescapable. Once dressed, the prints embodied a formative moment in Winn's new life in England, and demonstrate the power of paper and textiles to capture moments of biographical importance.

Winn's letters from Rowland reveal that the prints were far from the only gifts he sent his wife, and he frequently acted as a proxy shopper when he travelled to London.[103] Aside from the usual commissions for clothing and books, Rowland also sourced small dogs – the smaller the better – and flocks of exotic birds, which fluttered free around their Yorkshire home. Given the superfluity of gifts sent to Winn by her husband, it is remarkable that she pinpointed this set of prints as a site of intense and extended material engagement. Like Rowland's choice of the prints, this decision was also deliberate. Examples of less visually successful dressed prints, like those by Knight, underline how skilled print dressing was as a material practice, and how much practice and dedication were required in order to become proficient. In contrast to Knight, Winn's dressed prints are exemplary in the exact cutting, the precise placement of fabrics and the minute strands of print which were retained to provide contours and delineation. Each black line across the fabrics is a tiny sliver of the print, diligently left in place. Winn's capabilities must, therefore, have been established prior to Rowland's selection of these prints as a gift, and perhaps he even envisioned what his accomplished wife might achieve with them. As supported by the work of Dolan and Pullins, there are no identifiably English examples of this practice prior to Winn's dressed prints. As an exclusively continental practice prior to the mid-eighteenth century, the dressed prints seamlessly fuse Winn's Frenchness, her proxy-consumption and her making skill. The emotional resonance of handicraft thrums through the dressed prints.[104] They embody Winn's sense of self at a pivotal and determinative moment in her transformation from Swiss heiress to Yorkshire baronet's wife.

Winn's treatment of these prints exposes not only her material skill with paper and a knife, but also her knowledge of fabrics, fashions and the materiality of textiles. Her comprehension of fashion and dress penetrated her making. Consistently across all sixteen dressed prints, attention was paid to the direction of the weave, the quality of a textile and the behaviour and movement of garments represented. In *Nicaise* (Figure 4.23) Winn made use of both the front and reverse of the green figured silk to give the impression of a loosely draped blanket. In *Les Deux Amis* (Figure 4.19) the woman's dress is not cut in a single block, but in sections which sensitively mimic the undulating folds of the gown's skirt. *Le Gascon Puni* (Figure 4.18) again demonstrates this insightful material literacy through the different qualities of plain linen Winn selected for the nightgowns, bedsheets and two mattresses: a fine, tightly woven linen for the garments, and three rougher, loosely woven linens for the bed textiles. Impressively, Winn even cut out each individual element of the brown coat in this image. Highlighted by the raised spot in the weave, it is clear that the sleeves and cuffs in particular were cut with the direction of the weave in mind. This understanding of cut and fabric grain goes beyond passing familiarity and indicates a precise knowledge of how the materiality of a textile informed how it was cut and sewn. Social status and the legibility of appearances are also maintained in Winn's choice of fabrics, and are most explicitly decipherable in the choice of drab, brown and plain textiles for priests and monks (Figures 4.11, 4.12 and 4.20).[105] The synergy between Winn's knowledge of how people are dressed and how to dress prints is palpable.

Winn's own embroidery also appears across the dressed prints. While the tambour frame and embroidery patterns in the archive offer convincing evidence of Winn's engagement with needlework, the prints provide unassailable proof of her skill at this material activity. Across the prints, buttons and buttonholes have been worked with tiny stitches and French knots. This is most visibly evident on the pink waistcoat in *Les Deux Amis* (Figure 4.19), which is adorned with twenty-eight buttonholes, and again in *Le Coccu Battu et Content* (Figure 4.17). An embroidered muslin also appears repeatedly across the prints.[106] Stitched with a floral motif which out-scales the garments in the prints, the quality of workmanship in this textile makes it highly likely that it was Winn's own handiwork. Neither is this fabric alone in repeatedly appearing across the prints. Almost all of the fabrics were reused multiple times in different compositions, with textiles like the pink brocaded silk woven with silver thread in *Le Faucon* (Figure 4.14) appearing numerous times as petticoats, jackets and linings (see Figures 4.7, 4.22 and 4.23).

Given the range and type of textiles which appear in the prints, it is highly likely that the prints were dressed in snippets of Winn's own garments. Silk brocades and damasks were probably once gowns, while the fine linen shifts may have been cut from Winn's own undergarments. The embroidered cotton, in particular, appears to have been cut down from a larger white-worked garment. Perhaps Winn once wore it as a full-sized version of the aprons it represents within the prints.[107] Winn's consumption of textiles is recorded in her correspondence with London and Yorkshire tradespeople.[108] Preserved in the archive, hundreds of fabric samples, known as 'patterns', record Winn's taste for novelty and diversity.[109] The infinite variety of textiles, and the letters which contained them, acted as an epistolary microcosm of the shop counter. Ribbons with charming shoe silhouette motifs, others woven with straw, silks both figured and plain, innumerable printed calicos and a plethora of translucent gauzes were sent to tempt Winn into a purchase. Although the letters and samples are dated to the 1780s, there is congruence between the sartorial habits they display and the dressed prints of the 1760s. A prevailing concern within the letters was Winn's desire for French goods, even when classified as contraband, and she singled out retailers willing to deal in illegal imports. In 1783, milliner Ann Charlton bemoaned that French gloves were 'to [sic] dangerous a thing to deal in', but that she had French gauze with the selvedge removed, so that 'we may run the risk of keeping it in the house'.[110] Winn also purchased a French chemise robe, 'newer and prettier than any other dress'.[111] Even in the secluded depths of Yorkshire, owning and wearing the latest French fashions was a constant concern, two decades after she had last left Vevey. The Frenchness captured in the dressed print pre-empted Winn's lifelong use of material goods to retain links to her cultural heritage.

As composite reflections of Winn's own sartorial choices, the dressed prints' status as emotional objects is enhanced. The prints 'accrue meaning through layering', as they fuse cultural and sartorial significance.[112] Assuming that the textiles were indeed cut from Winn's discarded clothing, or were offcuts from the making process, Winn had bodily, haptic and intimate recollections attached to each textile. Memories of choosing, making and wearing garments are, quite literally, embedded within the prints. Perhaps some were brought with her from Vevey, and held memories of her Swiss childhood, while others may have been part of her wedding trousseau. Much like the emotive status bestowed upon quilts, the dressed prints memorialized Winn's sartorial history.[113] Ellen Weeton (1776–1849), writing to her daughter in 1824, enclosed a piece of patchwork 'out of an old Quilt I made above 20 years ago … The Hexagon in the middle was a shred of our best bed hangings; they were Chintz, from the East Indies, which my father brought home with him from one his voyages'.[114] Familial memories endured for decades and down the generations through textiles. Although Winn's dressed prints are devoid of the explanatory annotations or chronological ordering of records like Johnson's album, makers deposited autobiographical markers within such objects which were decipherable to their eyes only.[115] Our need to speculate is irrelevant; to Winn these memories and meanings were implicit. Unexplained and incomprehensible to strangers, this biographical information was private, secret and personal.

The transformative procedure of combining printed images and snippets of fabric from garments into the dressed print speaks to eighteenth-century cultures of reuse and remaking.[116] Objects, and fabrics in particular, were regularly reused and passed on, altered and adapted.[117] Pin holes, stains, wear and damage endured on objects as scars of their past experiences and can be read for biographical information about the objects themselves. While objects could possess agency of their own, recycling was also an operative process, in which the maker acted as an author of the object's biography. That things could contain a cultural biography is recognized.[118] That the biography of an object and the biography of an individual could intersect and merge in organic and dynamic ways is less established. Winn's dressed prints reveal how complex and interconnected such stories can be. The textiles, the prints and Winn herself all imbued the dressed prints with individual biographical elements, which were compounded together within each object. These stories should not be unpicked and separated. They feed into each other through webs of connections and immutable links.

A comparison of one of Winn's dressed prints with the unalerted print and the original painting reveals the layers of making, meaning and materiality which carried this biographical information. *La Servante Justifiee* (Figures 4.22, 4.24 and 4.25) illustrates the tale of a master who seduces his servant in a garden.[119] When he realizes that his dalliance was observed by a neighbour, he invites his wife into the garden, and engages amorously with her. When the neighbour repeats what she observed to the wife, the latter reassures her that it was she who had been in the garden with her husband, and that the servant was entirely innocent. Side by side, the three iterations of this scene tell a remarkable tale of their own. Winn not only dressed the print but added colour through a loosely applied watercolour wash over the foliage and flowers. The urn, partly concealed by a tree branch in the original painting, was also ornamented in watercolours in a vibrant blue – a colour which reappears frequently throughout the dressed prints and was clearly a favourite of Winn's.[120] When Adam and Chippendale were commissioned to work on Nostell, Winn's dressing room was transformed into a blue paradise, complete with 'blew Veriture paper' and 'blue Moreen window curtains'.[121] According to chalk inscriptions on the reverse of the dressed prints, this is also the room in which they were once hung, probably during Winn's lifetime.[122] This consistent and harmonious use of blue, even when applied in incongruous patterns to the classical vase, infuses the image with personal taste.

The comparison also divulges how the treatment of the clothing in the dressed prints was not always faithful to the original compositions. It is an intriguing coincidence that Winn chose to dress the woman in yellow, mirroring Lancret's painting. While the petticoat (in yellow ribbed silk), lining (in green silk), and underpetticoat (in white linen) are clearly retained and delineated in Winn's dressed print, the jacket and petticoat combination of the original painting have transmogrified into

Figure 4.24 *Nicolas Larmessin,* La Servante Justifiee, *after Nicolas Lancret, 1743, RP-P-1968-150. Courtesy of the Rijksmuseum.*

a gown. This could be read as a failure in Winn's material literacy or, more convincingly, as an act of artistic agency. In dressing the print, Winn joins Lancret and Larmessin as a third artist, each in turn transforming the image a little further with every interaction. As a form of disconnected collaboration, Winn's reconfiguration of the garments reflects her own artistic voice. Her choices make other elements of the image, such as the distinctions between the master and servant, more evidently apparent. While the maid is simply but prettily dressed in a plain silk, her employer is bedecked in elaborate, glistening silk brocade. The scattered pink roses on her apron, which is made from the embroidered muslin, have also shifted. While the lower rose has been cut away, a replacement has been ingeniously fashioned from what would have been the swirl of the printed hem. While the overall composition is always retained, similar idiosyncratic alterations occur throughout the dressed prints. Just as full-sized garments could be altered and adapted by successive owners, so too could their miniature representations.

Figure 4.25 Nicolas Lancret, La Servante Justifiée, 1743, 2004.85. Courtesy of the Metropolitan Museum of Art.

Print and making at Nostell

Winn's dressed prints were one example from a diverse body of making activities that occurred at Nostell in the eighteenth century, which centred on print.[123] Synthesis between miniature and full-sized, print and making is perhaps most explicit in one of Nostell's prize pieces: the dolls' house. The house was initially created for Winn's mother-in-law, Suzannah Henshaw (1710–1742) and her younger sister Katherine (1714–1741), who began the never-ending process of fitting and re-fitting the interior decorations during the 1730s.[124] The mirrors above the fireplaces, over-door insert paintings and the dominance of heavy red velvet in the suite of state rooms mirror the archival evidence of Nostell's own decorative schemes in the 1730s and 1740s. Here, perhaps, we catch a glimpse of Nostell as Winn first encountered it upon entering Yorkshire in 1761: luxurious, sumptuous and dark. As with all dolls' houses, however, they were not created to act as static relics. They were played with, redesigned and refashioned.[125] Dolls' houses had strong links to matrilineal genealogy and were usually passed from mother to daughter. Given the strained dynamics of the Winn family, it is perhaps surprising that Winn herself saw fit to physically and materially engage with the family dolls' house.[126] Yet evidence survives in print: cut, composed and pasted onto the walls of the miniature house. Just as Winn and Rowland took their 1765 inheritance of the real Nostell as a queue to radically redesign the interiors, Winn also took the miniature Nostell into her own hands.

Winn's influence can be seen in two rooms in the house: the red velvet bedroom and the yellow drawing room. The red velvet bedroom, perhaps more than any other room in the dolls' house, conjures up the atmosphere of Nostell in the mid-eighteenth century. Plush, rich and opulent, the room encapsulates the 'Crimson Flock Paper ... and ... Silk Damask' recalled by Dorothy Richardson on her visit to the real Nostell in 1761.[127] While the furniture is contemporary to this mid-century dating, there is one incongruous feature. On the left-hand wall hang two 'portraits' of a fashionably dressed man and woman. Cut from engravings into an oval portrait-like shape, these images have been mounted onto gold embossed paper, intended to imitate an elaborate giltwood slip, and framed with folded paper backed with stamped velvet. The printed engravings from which these images have been cut date from the 1770s: at least thirty years after Henshaw's death, and squarely in the middle of Winn's residence at Nostell. Dressed *à la turque*, the same style of dress favoured by Winn in her 1767 joint portrait with her husband (Figure 4.3), the woman dons the quintessential towering fashionable hairstyle of the 1770s. The print was cut from 'Histories of the *tête-à-tête* annexed' in the August 1773 issue of the *Town and Country Magazine*, and is of Anne Frédérique Heinel (1753–1808), a French dancer at the Paris opera.[128] Her male companion also comes from a *tête-à-tête* from *Town and Country*, this time from April 1776, and is the unnamed lover of Lady Falmouth (1707–1786).[129] An opera-dancer and a clandestine lover, the subjects of these prints hark back to the risqué subject matter enjoyed by Winn and Rowland in the dressed prints. Combined with the French connection via the Parisian dancer, the creative engagement with print and the date, these additions to the dolls' house were undoubtedly created by Winn.

If we travel through the tiny wooden door and into the next miniature room, Winn's continued influence is evident. The walls of the yellow drawing room (Figure 4.26) are swathed in print.[130] An inverse of the dressed prints, it is the background that has been cut away, leaving an array of birds, foliage and figures, which have then been coloured with watercolours, pasted to the walls of the tiny room and varnished over. Winn's creation is a decoupage room. Print rooms, in which printed images were pasted directly to the walls were popular in the late eighteenth century across Britain and Ireland.[131] These rooms, however, were adorned with whole prints, perhaps complemented by cut-out swags and boarders. The yellow drawing room in the dolls' house merges the print room aesthetic with the technique of decoupage, in which individual elements of prints – such as birds, trees and figures – were cut out and repurposed to decorate other objects.[132] Cut from their original works, the tiny Lilliputian elements were reconfigured into new scenes. Just as birds twittered and flew around Winn's real-life Nostell, here they sweep and dive across the scaled-down walls. By the turn of the century, the application of this technique to the interior walls of dolls' houses was culturally established. Published in 1803, Jane West's *A Tale of the Times* included the line 'I have many unatoned sins … worse than tearing up his best Vigil to paper my baby-house'.[133]

Given the intricate detail and superlative skill displayed by Winn in the dressed prints, it is certain that the cutting and manipulation of print was a genre of handicraft in which she was well versed. The complex process was described in a 1760 manual:

> The several Objects you intend for Use must be neatly cut round with Scisars, or the small Point of a Knife; those Figures must be brush'd over on the Back with strong Gum-water, or thin Paste, made by boiling Flour in Water: then take the Objects singly, and with a Pair of small Pliers, fix them on the Place intended, being careful to let no Figure seem tumbling … and when properly plac'd, lay over your Prints a Piece of clean Paper, and with your Hand gently press them even, and when dry … then proceed to varnish … at least seven Times, tho' if you varnish it Twelve it will be still better.[134]

While the final stage – varnishing – is not part of the print-dressing process, the similarities between the two procedures are otherwise compelling. Winn's authorship of the yellow drawing room is further supported by the prints selected. On one of the pastoral scenes it is possible to distinguish the signature of Pierre Mariette (1694–1774), a Parisian publisher and engraver. In the library at Nostell, Mariette's work is represented by a pair of volumes entitled *Recueil d'Estampes* which contain over one hundred plates by Mariette.[135] In French throughout, and dating from the 1760s, these tomes of prints resonate with Winn's tastes and interests. The japanned style, achieved with French prints, continues this correlation between developments in the dolls' house, and renovations to the full-size Nostell. Echoing this aesthetic, in 1771 Winn and Rowland commissioned a suite of furniture 'very neatley Japan'd

Figure 4.26 *The yellow drawing room of the Nostell dolls' house, NT 959710. Copyright National Trust.*

green and Gold', which was to sit in the alcove bed chamber, newly papered in Chinese wallpaper.[136] In contrast to the heavy, languid aesthetic of 1730s Nostell, Chippendale and Adam's schemes brought light, bright delicacy into the interiors. The same can certainly be said of Winn's contributions to the dolls' house. Upon becoming mistresses of Nostell in 1765, Winn mobilized her arsenal of print-related making skills to claim both the dolls' and full-sized Nostell as her new home.

The processes and practices of making doll house interiors, embroideries, decoupage and dressed prints were not separate, and it is at our peril that we divorce them within scholarship. Not only did they share core techniques and methods, their materials, materiality and motivations were also conjoined. As material medleys of memories, the dressed prints invoked an individual sartorial biography. They charted a personal history of garments, in which textiles were as legible as text. They invoked the comfort of cultural familiarity, and embodied emotional meaning as a gift from husband to wife. Through these emotional objects, Winn's consumption and making are folded together. An avid consumer of French prints, rustling silks, small animals and furniture she may have been, but these acts of procurement informed, shaped and contributed to her manifold practices as a maker. As chatelaines of vast country houses, it is easy to see elite wives as wealthy acquirers who were hungry for ever more consumer goods. In the case of Winn, this is compounded by her status as a foreign outsider, whose consumption was readily commented upon by apprehensive family and acquaintances. Yet Winn's consumer and producer activities were symbiotic and cooperative. Busily pouring over her prints, scissors sharp and ready to snip away at the paper, Winn was able to channel her emotional, consumer and maker selves into these dressed prints.

5
Fashions in miniature: Dolls

Miniature and mimetic, imaginative and instructive, fashionable ideals and tactile toys, dolls are imbued with multiple meanings. Dolls proliferated in the toy shops, literature and visual culture of the eighteenth century, and were evidence of what John Harold Plumb has termed the 'invention of childhood'.[1] While young girls played with their diminutive, silent playmates, their mamas and aunts admired fashion dolls, newly imported from Paris, in the windows of modish mantuamakers.[2] Yet these divisions – between the adult and the child, and between the vehicle of fashionable consumption and the vessel for playful learning and instruction – are artificial. At a material level, it is often impossible to distinguish between these two classifications. Dolls which had once been fashion dolls may have been passed on to children and transfigured into toys, while toy dolls often played an integral role in the sartorial education of their owners. Many of the dolls which survive within museum collections are, therefore, ambiguous and secretive about their origins. Yet, while these dolls may be mute and their eyes glassy and lifeless, the tiny stitches used to construct them hold a myriad of stories about their makers, owners and users.

Dolls, perhaps more than any of the other forms of material production considered in this book, embody the fluidity between categories of the consumer and the maker. So often, scholars have discussed dolls only in terms of their consumption, either as pedagogical tools and toys, or as disseminators of new styles.[3] Yet dolls were also vital instruments in the cultivation of material literacy.[4] Women and girls designed and made garments for their dolls, enacting in miniature the techniques required to make fashionable garments. Far from crude and rough impressions of dress, this miniature clothing demonstrates intimate and technical knowledge of the behaviours of textiles and sewing construction techniques. Fabric choices, patterning and cut, and a plethora of stitches are showcased in these tiny garments. Dolls acted in a practical role as a didactic tool for the development of this material knowledge.

Like Winn's dressed prints, dolls could also function as a site of personal sartorial memorialization. Between the age of 13 in 1754 and her death at the age of 60 in 1801, Laetitia Powell carefully dressed at least twelve dolls which, together, tell her personal and material story.[5] Begun in childhood, but continued throughout adulthood, these dolls acted as a sartorial biography. Akin to the annotations in Johnson's album, Lewis' 'dress of the year' captions or the fashion plate descriptions in periodicals, notes tacked to the hems of the dolls' petticoats reveal the date they were stitched and proffer a description of each doll's outfit. These snippets of information reveal that these garments were not generic specimens or imaginative fancies. Instead, they were often miniature versions of Powell's own garments. This life-narrative through fashion, layered with the development and improvement of Powell's own skill as a maker, can be read across the twelve dolls. Through these dolls, the dynamics of making and buying dress were intricately entwined with biography. Dolls, these examples show, could be conduits for a wealth of personal and sartorial information.

Laetitia Powell (1741–1801)

No paper archive of Laetitia Powell's life survives. We can only speculate about where her letters and accounts might be; perhaps they are stashed in a descendant's attic, or maybe they were burnt into nothingness long ago. No words from her pen remain in the historical record. Her sixty years of life has been reduced to a series of birth, marriage and death announcements in newspapers and parish registers, a passing mention in a privately published family pedigree and the genealogical accounts of her grandson, Robert Baden-Powell (1857–1941), the founder of the Boy Scout Movement.[6] Like Lewis, it is only through the success and fame of her male descendants that Powell's name has perpetuated in the historical record at all: as mother, grandmother and great-grandmother.[7] Her identity beyond her maternal function is absent. Her dolls, however, proffer an opportunity to rescue her from this historical oblivion. Like many eighteenth-century women, her material remnants are clearer, stronger and more forthright that any of the written words which sparsely tell her tale.

The perfunctory details of her life, however meagre, nonetheless offer necessary context. Laetitia Powell was part of an extensive creative and commercial family of London merchants, whose exceptional success placed her on a financial par with Lewis and Johnson. She was born in London on Christmas Day 1741. Her mother, Laetitia Kipling (1715–1784) was the daughter of a London draper, who inherited property in Kingsland, Shoreditch.[8] Her father, John Clark (1716–1762), was a London hat merchant on Bishopsgate Street, at the heart of the City of London. Clark was eminently skilled as a merchant. He had been married in a clandestine Fleet wedding in 1734, but when he died he possessed a fortune of over £15,000.[9] During Laetitia Powell's early years as the daughter of a prosperous merchant in the heart of the city, she would have been surrounded with the splendid silks and sumptuous material goods which filtered through this globally mercantile city. The appeal of an affluent commercial life may well have informed Laetitia Powell's choice of husband. She was married to David Powell, described in the newspaper announcement as 'an eminent Italian Merchant', on 15

August 1761.[10] Her marriage settlement was £5,000, from which she received a 3 percent annuity, and a further third of her father's estate upon his death in 1762.[11] Laetitia Powell's new husband was even more successful than her father. After an apprenticeship to a merchant in his youth, in 1760 David Powell went into partnership with his brother Thomas, with the firm's capital a healthy £6,000.[12] Six years into trading, the capital increased to £9,000. Although most records are ambiguous about the types of goods Powell traded in, his description in the marriage announcement as an 'Italian merchant' implies that he was dealing in fashion accessories such as hosiery, millinery, ribbons and other trinkets. Laetitia Powell's wealth originated firmly from sartorial trade. These formative years led her, no doubt, to be conscious of the ever-changing pulse of fashion retail in the capital, and financially equipped her to participate in fashionable sartorial consumption.

The couple lived between a house in Hommerton and a city-centre property at Little St Helen's, which also contained some of David Powell's business premises. They quickly started a family, and Laetitia Powell was almost continually pregnant between the ages of 20 and 36. The couple had fourteen children, although tragically four did not survive into adulthood (Figure 5.1). An oil painting of the young family is within the private collection of the family. Painted in 1771, it depicts David Powell playing trap-bat (a version of cricket) with his brood of children, while Laetitia Powell sits and watches, her latest baby on her knee.[13] The little baby, presumably Edward who was born in 1770, would tragically die within the year. This prolific progeny of children would go on to continue the family's rise to wealth and prominence. The couple's eldest son, John Clark (1763–1847) would become Governor of the London Assurance Company.[14] The younger David (1764–1832) became a Justice of the Peace and lived at Bench House in Loughton, Essex. He died when he was struck by lightning while walking on his estate, and the incident was reported in the papers in gory detail.[15] Baden (1767–1844) became a

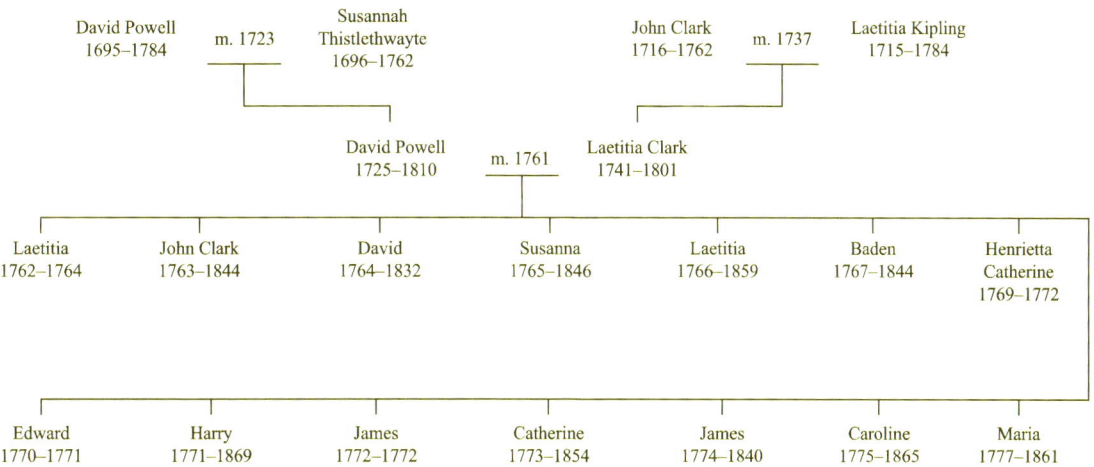

Figure 5.1 *Family tree of the Powell family. Compiled from evidence in Edgar Powell's 1891 Pedigree.*

wine merchant, his son a preeminent theologian, and his grandson would become the founder of the Boy Scout movement. James (1774–1840), also a wine merchant, took over the famous Whitefriars Glassworks in 1834.[16] Like their mother, biographical information about the Powell daughters is less forthcoming. Beyond their marriages, all of which were to vicars and churchmen, their lives have remained archivally silent.

The large Powell family's success continued in later life. In 1774 David Powell purchased a country estate at Reynold's Place, Horton Kirby, Kent, and in the succeeding years he would purchase further property at Swanscombe, also in Kent.[17] By the time of David Powell's death in 1810, he was able to leave his children property in Horton Kirby, Farningham and Swanscombe in Kent, as well as Gracechurch Street, Fenchurch Street, Star Alley and Eastcheap in London and three houses in Hommerton. He also left a fortune of £90,000 to his surviving children.[18] Laetitia Powell, however, had already predeceased him. She died on 27 April 1801 at her son Harry's (1771–1869) rectory at East Hordon in Essex. An inscription in the family bible recalls that she had been ill for many months. On that final day, she was struck with a fit of apoplexy at ten in the morning, before finally passing away at midnight.[19]

A pencil sketch of Laetitia Powell from her later years depicts her in fashionable garments of the late 1790s.[20] Tiny frills at her cuffs, a meticulously positioned fichu, and a strikingly fashionable cap echo the sartorial choices made in her dolls. Caught mid-stitch, her hands clasp a piece of fabric that she has partially embroidered. This depiction of Laetitia Powell, armed with a needle and thread, is eminently appropriate as a pictorial epigraph. Not one of the archival sources which survives was penned by Laetitia Powell. When we restrict our historical enquiry to words, it is her father, husband, sons, newspapermen and official scribes that tell her story. Yet Laetitia Powell's portrait hints at where we should really look to find her voice. It is her needle which she mobilized to tell her story. Stitches and seams, laces and ruffles, miniaturized into the dolls, represented to Laetitia Powell a form of material temporal stability. Through these diminutive depictions of dress, she could chronicle her own life. While paper records preserve her legacy as a wife and mother, textiles and wax secured her story beyond maternity and motherhood, and present Laetitia Powell as a maker.

The Powell dolls

The intimate details of Powell's life may not survive through traditional paper records, but the sartorial snapshots captured in the dolls offer an alternative and rich route into her life. They illuminate her development as a consumer, chronicle her engagement with fashion, record her developing skills as a maker and hold clues about the influence of broader print and material culture upon Powell's own material practices. Her twelve surviving dolls in the Victoria and Albert Museum span Powell's childhood and adolescence, her marriage and motherhood, and later years as a comfortably wealthy woman. They were constructed between 1754 and 1792, with further dolls added to the collection by her descendants.[21] As Powell transitioned between each stage of her life, her dolls captured her evolving tastes, priorities and skills. Although by no means uniform in their presentation style, they explicitly present a chronological narrative of a material life in microcosm, from the ages of 13 to 51. Through each tiny stitch, ruffle and hem Powell charted the process by which she acquired and developed her material literacy as a maker of clothing, from the unskilled and crude experimentation of her teens, to her perfect wedding gown in miniature at the age of 20, and on to the skilled creations of adulthood. The dolls captured Powell's lifecycle through both her making and her consumption, and underline the dynamic and symbiotic relationship between stitching, shopping for and wearing clothes.

Powell's earliest surviving doll dates to 1754 (Figure 5.2), when she was 13 and lived at her father's house in London, at the centre of the capital's bustling mercantile culture.[22] It is small and rudimentary,

Figure 5.2 *Laetitia Powell,* Fashionable Full Dress for Young Lady, *1754, W.183-1919. Powell's earliest surviving doll is rudimentary and makeshift compared to her later creations. Copyright Victoria and Albert Museum, London.*

standing at barely 20 centimetres tall. The doll's wax head is framed by a halo of little metal pins, which probably once attached a cap or headdress to her now bare scalp. Under her skirts, her wax upper body transmutes into a wooden peg leg. She wears a stiff paper petticoat, which acts as her panier, holding out the wide skirts.[23] Over this makeshift paper dress support sits a glazed cotton petticoat, stitched with gigantic, loose stitches, placed over half an inch apart. Like all the dolls, a handwritten note is pinned to the petticoat. On this doll, it reads 'Fashionable Full Dress for Young Lady, 1754'.[24] Over the petticoat the doll dons a gown of white silk woven with a small rosebud pattern, and a stomacher of blue silk woven with a circle repeat. The gown is haphazardly trimmed with braids of pink silk and silver. A pair of leading strings, a symbol of childhood and a staple element of girls' clothing in the eighteenth century, hang down from the back of the doll.[25] Powell's earliest surviving creation, made on the cusp of her teen years, was swiftly followed in 1755, 1757 and 1758 by further, small, child-like dolls, complete with leading strings and out of proportion bodies.[26]

These childhood dolls were vessels for intersecting and dynamic material meanings and explorations. The wide court paniers of some of Powell's childhood dolls indicate that these earliest experiments in doll-dressing were not precise imitations of Powell's own clothing. Instead, they offer an amalgam of adult's and child's clothing which was the product of Powell's imagination and, as such, can be read as an autobiographical reflection of Powell's interior life. The leading strings found on these early dolls were exclusively a feature of children's dress. The wide court skirts, however, were only worn by adults. In life-sized clothing, the two were not combined. Here, mimicry and make-believe sit side by side. These hybrid features are not unique to Powell's dolls, as numerous other toy dolls from the period demonstrate.[27] As Ariane Fennetaux has outlined, dolls could play a 'subversive role' in the hands of a child.[28] In a miniature world controlled by the child, the rules, systems and procedures of the adult world were challenged, manipulated, questioned and explored.[29] Doll dressing was not a simple process of copying and replicating adults' garments, but a creative means through which children explored sartorial rubrics. Through these childhood dolls, Powell manufactured hybrid adult-children, which captured her evolving knowledge of how people dressed. The dolls acted simultaneously as miniature versions of the adult she would become, and a temporary substitute for the child she would mother in the future.

Beyond explorations of selfhood and identity, the dolls also acted in a practical role as a means of needlework training. A comparison between the 1754 doll and Powell's fifth, sixth and seventh dolls, all made in 1759 at the age of 18, demonstrates the radical improvement in Powell's skills as a maker over these five years.[30] The fifth doll (Figure 5.3), like its 1754 predecessor, has a wax head. However instead of a crude peg leg, she instead has a full cloth body, complete with silk-wrapped legs, imitating silk stockings. Unlike the earlier dolls, whose layers of underwear were perfunctory, the 1759 doll was clothed in all the necessary layers, from the shift outwards.[31] Over her neatly stitched linen shift, the

Figure 5.3 *Laetitia Powell,* Fashionable Full Dress for Spring 1759, *W.183:4-1919. Powell's fifth doll mimics court styles and demonstrates Powell's playful exploration of sartorial rules. Copyright Victoria and Albert Museum, London.*

doll wears an underpetticoat, a full court hoop made of linen and shaped with canes, and a further petticoat. The final layer is a court mantua in striped silk, embellished with blonde lace. As with the other childhood dolls, it is highly unlikely that this was a miniature version of Powell's own garments. As the daughter of a London merchant, however successful, a court garment is unlikely to have been within this 18-year-old's wardrobe remit. The incongruity of a striped silk for a court mantua provides further evidence that this was not a full-sized garment in miniature, but another hybrid. The fabric was likely to have come from one of Powell's own garments, but the style was imagined. Through these experimentations, Powell had refined her sewing skills. From the tiny and exceptionally neat robings at the front of the gown to the impeccably even hem, the doll is superbly made.

On the doll's petticoat sits its little paper label, which reads 'fashionable full Dress for spring 1759'. The phrasing of the label, like the 1754 doll, echoes the captions of pocket book fashion plates, which were so influential in shaping Johnson's and Lewis' material outputs.[32] This is repeated on Powell's seventh doll, also from 1759, whose note reads 'fashionable undress for spring 1759'. This mirrored phrasing places these dolls as a pair, presenting undress and full dress for the same year. Like Lewis' watercolours, the Powell dolls acted as a creative response to the consumed printed image, and the finished doll closely resembles contemporary fashion plates (Figure 5.4). Powell's doll embodies the two-dimensional print in three-dimensional materiality, with features like the stomacher front,

Figure 5.4 A Lady in the Dress of the Year 1758, *from Barbara Johnson's Album, 1746–1823, T.219-1973. The caption and aesthetic of the pocket book fashion plate is echoed in Powell's dolls. Copyright Victoria and Albert Museum, London.*

engageantes and scalloped trim presented in a strikingly similar fashion. These captions directly reference the cultural sartorial practices of print. Powell's dolls sit at the junction between her developing skills as a maker, her ownership of silks and garments, and her consumption of fashion plates. The paired dolls also recall an infamous anecdote, purported to be the first use of 'Pandora' as a byword for a fashion doll, in which Madeleine de Scudéry, a French seventeenth-century *salonnière*, dressed two dolls in full and undress, whilst discussing contemporary literature.[33] Powell did not imbue the dolls with a single purpose or meaning; they funnelled together disparate aspects of sartorial culture. They are not simply childhood toys or idle outlets for hands at leisure.[34] Instead, these early dolls act as a conduit for her explorative adolescent identity as both a consumer and maker of fashion.

The sixth of Powell's dolls is extremely similar to the fifth, while the seventh, also constructed in 1759, is remarkable for its level of precision and detail.[35] The doll's head has been substituted for a Victorian ceramic replacement, and her eighteenth-century hair and cap unceremoniously deposited on top. In spite of this nineteenth-century indignity, the doll's garments are extraordinary. Like her other 1759 twins, she wears a linen shift and two petticoats underneath her white silk sack-back. The gown and petticoat are a perfect miniature replication of the techniques, patterning, cut and construction of full-sized versions of this style. Although dolls' garments could easily have been sewn permanently onto the doll, the practicalities of wear unheeded, even the fastenings of Powell's dolls – in this case pins – echo the full-sized equivalent. The level of garment-making expertise required to construct a gown like this must not be underestimated. The gown and petticoat were assembled with extreme care, each seam turned in to enclose the raw edges. Her petticoat, trimmed with pinked and ruched strips of matching silk, mimics the fashionable styles of the period. Similarly, the engageantes, which are pulled up into minute gathers at the elbow, are perfect miniature replicas of this fashionable cuff treatment. The doll's garments are a model of precision. The only tell-tale sign that this garment is homemade from scraps and offcuts of fabric is the appearance of the fabric's selvedge on the ruched trim and around the neck bindings. This minor blemish, however, underscores the cleverness of the doll's construction. With a precious, limited supply of silk, Powell needed to employ the same economy of cutting and ingenuity as did contemporary dressmakers.

Powell's eighth doll, constructed in 1761, is undoubtedly the most significant of the set (Figure 5.5). It is a miniature sartorial self-representation, and is undoubtedly the doll most explicitly bound to

Figure 5.5 *Laetitia Powell,* Mrs Powell's Wedding Suit, *1761, W.183:7-1919. Made from a fragment of silk from Powell's own wedding gown, the doll acts as a sartorial self-portrait. Copyright Victoria and Albert Museum, London.*

Powell's biography. The note tacked to the petticoat, which reads 'Mrs Powell wedding suit 1761' unambiguously identifies the doll as a sartorial representation of Powell on her wedding day on 15 August 1761.[36] The creative process behind the construction of this doll is sadly lost to us. It could have been an experiment in design, with which Powell pondered and deliberated, before finalizing the choices for her final wedding gown. Most likely, as per the family story, it was constructed from the offcuts of her actual wedding gown as a diminutive replica.[37] This doll acts as a sartorial form of portrait in miniature. As Marcia Pointon has demonstrated, the portrait miniature was overwhelmingly popular in eighteenth-century England.[38] Pointon has described miniatures as 'ambulant portraits' which, when attached to clothing and jewellery, were compact and wearable, much like Lewis' 'satin prints'.[39] Within the social economy of portraiture, the miniature functioned as affective, personal and intimate. Powell's doll inverts and collapses Pointon's model of the portrait miniature as a wearable item, and instead embodies the portrait miniature through small-scale replica clothing. The emotive and subjective aspects of the portrait miniature are carried across to the doll and are entwined with what Susan Stewart has described as the 'hermetic world' of the dolls' house.[40] Powell's wedding doll is a sartorial, self-representational and sentimental time capsule.

Dolls have an innate ability to stop time and capture a moment in perpetuity. The nostalgia of the perfect, complete miniature world offers an opportunity to resist and escape the unpredictability and chaos of the full-sized world. Through a doll, it is possible to capture a time, a day or a moment in material permanence. Powell's wedding doll embodies this desire to halt, record and possess a moment of time, and to infuse an object with the emotional and personal resonances of that occasion.[41] The doll acts as a trigger for a memory, a stimulus for sensory remembrance and an external memorial of an event. While the wedding gown actually worn by Powell may have been cut up and repurposed, updated and re-worn, the doll remained constant. As 'taxonomies of sentimental value' such objects act as 'companions to our emotional lives' which aid in the navigation of the relationship between the self, others and the material world.[42] Powell's wedding doll is a miniature self which embodies a moment of cultural, social, economic and personal significance for its maker. The transition from daughter to wife was a key moment of material transformation, best exemplified by the wedding trousseau. This burst of consumption of the paraphernalia required for wedded life materialized marriage. While preparing for her marriage to a local Yorkshire clergyman, Elizabeth Woodhouse, the daughter of a successful York haberdasher, spent a vast amount of money on new clothes.[43] Within one month she purchased four aprons, a common gown, a muslinet gown, a dimity petticoat, six night shifts, and a black beaver hat, among sundry other item required of her as a wife-to-be. As Amanda Vickery has demonstrated, new wives collated numerous objects required to set up home in the months before marriage.[44] Practices of material culture and consumption marked this biographical milestone. Powell's wedding suit, captured in the doll, was the sartorial marker of that liminal moment between singledom and marriage, and is a prime example of the broader cultural work done by clothing as a signifier of biographical transition.

The doll itself was expertly dressed. The doll has a wax head, glass eyes and a stuffed body, with a carefully styled wig of human hair.[45] Like the 1759 dolls, she wears a shift with a tiny neat hem and an underpetticoat. On top of these, she dons a luxurious quilted petticoat of ivory silk satin. The diamond patterned quilting was executed with painstakingly miniscule running stitches, and the repeat is remarkably regular. The contrast between this expert needlework and the huge, loose stitches of the 1754 doll is palpable. Alongside the continuing development of Powell's ability as a maker, the wedding doll also shows a greater acknowledgement of the doll's miniature status. Unlike the scale of the motifs on the woven fabrics, the quilting has been scaled down to be in proportion with the size of the doll.[46] While this petticoat may have been made from scraps of fabric from a full-sized quilted petticoat, the miniature quilting must have been accomplished specifically for this doll. This tension between the proportionate scale of the quilting and the disproportionate scale of the floral figured design on the silk of the gown reveals two modes of authenticity at play in the dolls. While miniature scale is respected and observed in the quilting, it is the authentic status of the outer silk – the genuine material of the wedding gown – which is prioritized over congruence of scale.

Like the seventh doll, the wedding gown is another sack-back style garment. The ivory figured silk has a floral design typical of the period, and the construction of the gown follows standard practice for the 1760s. The robings at the front of the gown are pinned in place, again echoing typical methods of dressing. The selvedge is ingeniously concealed within the seam allowance along the long edges of the skirt seams, a custom often seen in extant full-sized garments. The petticoat and the front of the gown are trimmed with tiny strips of pinked silk, ruched into a wave pattern and attached with a running stitch in a straight line down the centre, again mirroring standard habits in dressmaking. A silk fly-fringe, made by knotting lengths of silk thread, has also been applied to the front of the skirt and the silk flounce at the cuff. Bobbin lace was fashioned into the engageantes at the cuffs and the fichu around the neck. The cap has a wired brim and is topped with a festoon of tiny silk flowers. The final accessories are a string of beads around the doll's neck, fashioned to imitate pearls, and a poesy of laurel leaves at the bosom. Her outfit is complete and complex, leaving out no detail of the gown worn by Powell at this symbolic and transitional moment.

The years following Powell's wedding see a break in her doll making. The ninth of the dolls was constructed in 1769, eight years after her marriage. The first surviving doll that Powell constructed during this period wears a brunswick (Figure 5.6), the same fashionable travelling garb purchased by Johnson in 1772.[47] Made from a checked silk, which is also remarkably similar to Johnson's blue and white Manchester check for the same garment, the doll perfectly captures the myriad features specific to this particular garment. Popularized by Princess Augusta (1737–1813) upon her marriage to the Duke of Brunswick-Wolfenbütel in 1764, and worn throughout the late 1760s and 1770s, the brunswick constituted a jacket and petticoat combination.[48] The jacket featured the stacked box pleats of the sack-back, along with long sleeves reaching beyond the elbow flounces and down to the wrists,

Figure 5.6 *Laetitia Powell, Doll dressed in a brunswick, 1769, W.183:8-1919. The brunswick was a travelling outfit, popularized by Princess Augusta. Originally a vibrant candy pink, the silk has now faded to a dull blue-grey. The cinched in waist is not original and is the result of Victorian mounting. Copyright Victoria and Albert Museum, London.*

a hood and a false waistcoat or buttoned compere front. Powell's doll retains all these myriad features, unique to this particular style. Bias cut silk imitates stockings on the doll's legs, and her feet are clod in little silk shoes with leather heels. She wears a carefully constructed shift, an underpetticoat and a petticoat of the check silk, all reflecting the same exquisite workmanship as the wedding ensemble. The silk of the brunswick, now faded to a muddy blue-grey, was once the vibrant candy-pink tone still visible between the seams and creases and beneath the hood.

In 1769 Powell was the mother of an ever-growing family, the mistress of a busy household, and the wife of a successful and prosperous businessman. Powell modified and evolved her doll-making practices, adapting to her new roles. As Powell's eldest surviving daughter, Susanna, reached her fourth birthday, it is possible that Powell's doll making transitioned from an autodidactic and private practice to a collaborative bonding and educational exercise with her young daughters. The note on Powell's doll reads 'A Brunswick Dress for Travelling or Morn'g fashionable in 1769'. Like the earlier examples, the terminology of the dolls' notes echoes pocket book fashion plate captions. The tone, however, has subtly shifted. Instead of autodidactic reflections and regurgitations of familiar phrasings, the style is instructive. Here, Powell's voice as an educator, mother and a materially literate woman comes to the forefront. We are confidently informed that this garment was 'fashionable in 1769', a turn of phrase which adds a retrospective and authoritative air to the label. The doll continues to hold temporal power, and acts as a chronometric marker. However, it shifts from being a vessel of personal and emotive remembrance, to a new role as fashion chronicler. The notes on Powell's dolls from her years of motherhood hint at the dolls' use as pedagogical tools, used to instruct her growing brood in the terminology and materiality of dress, much as Powell's early dolls had reflected her own burgeoning material literacy.[49] Yet they also reflect Powell's own changing relationship with fashion. Instead of the hybrid experiments of her youth, or the emotive significance of her wedding gown, Powell instead moved towards creating perfect imitations of fashionable garments in miniature, chronicling and historicizing dress, and positioning herself as a beacon of fashion knowledge.

After a ten-year break, filled with the births of seven further children, the 1780s saw another spate of doll making for Powell. In 1784 and 1785 Powell created her tenth and eleventh dolls, at which time she had five daughters aged between 7 and 19. The dolls from this period hold material evidence of mixed and varied motives, meshing Powell's role as a mother and educator with her continued interest in sartorial chronicling and her own advanced skill as a maker. The 1784 doll (Figure 5.7), clothed in Powell's now-standard underpinnings of a shift and underpetticoat, wears a white linen petticoat and gown, adorned with stripes of printed cotton to mimic borders.[50] Flounces of translucent muslin, with a miniscule rolled hem, trim the petticoat, collar and the front edge of the gown. The ribbon sash at the waist conceals the incredible detail of the bodice construction. Tiny tucks in the linen shape the bodice which, cut in one with the gown's skirt, merge into the skirt's pleats.[51] The detail here is exceptional. It required an expert knowledge of garment construction and an advanced literacy in the modes and methods of dressmaking. The label on this doll reads 'Undress called a Levite 1784'. Writing from London in 1783, Elizabeth Elliot (1764–1847), proffered a description of this briefly fashionable style: 'They wear for morning a white poloneze or a dress they call a Levete, which is a kind of gown and Peticote, with long sleeves made with scarcely any pique in the back, and worn with a sash tyed on the left side. They make these in winter of white dimity, and in summer of Muslin with Chints borders.'[52] This description perfectly matches Powell's doll, including the long sleeves, the sash, and the printed cotton Chintz borders. Powell's doll materializes this brief fashion, which is otherwise lost to time.[53] Powell used both her 'Levite' and 'Brunswick' dolls to capture and memorialize a specific, named, sartorial moment. Much like Lewis' watercolours, whether or not the ensemble depicted was truly owned by Powell, or even based on a real or specific garment, the doll historicized and recorded this brief trend for posterity.

The eleventh doll, constructed one year later in 1785, briefly disrupts this narrative of the sartorial chronicle.[54] The doll's label, devoid of the specialized vocabulary and detail of her predecessors, simply reads '1785'. The doll's dress, which has sadly deteriorated over time leaving much of the silk skirt

Figure 5.7 *Laetitia Powell,* Undress called a Levite, *1784, W.183:9-1919. This doll ingeniously integrates a printed cotton into the design to imitate a border. Copyright Victoria and Albert Museum, London.*

shattered, is made neatly, but lacks the precision and construction knowledge evident in the examples made between 1761 and 1784. The doll has a plain linen petticoat, over which is worn a while silk petticoat and brown silk bodice. A train of white gauze trimmed with brown silk flows down the back of the doll. Sequins, lace and a ruched strip of brown silk adorn the outfit. She wears a miscellany of jumbled styles, recalling the experimental hybrid dolls of Powell's youth. The quality of the sewing also varies enormously. While the cut of the bodice and precise hemming of the skirt are expertly done, the application of the trims is uneven and loose. Here, we see greater evidence of collaboration between mother and children. Perhaps Powell assisted with the basic construction and cutting, while her daughters – now the same age that Powell was when she made her first doll – cooperated to design and decorate their doll. Like Winn, who painted side by side with her own daughter Esther, and Johnson, who began her album as a childhood pedagogical practice, material lives often ran parallel with familial habits and ties. As with written life-writing, the authorship of material life-writing could be collaborative and cooperative across generations.[55] Simultaneously a bonding experience and a didactic exercise in making and dress, the construction of the 1785 doll reflects the amalgam of motivations and memories embedded in material objects.

Powell's final surviving doll was constructed in 1792. Aged 51, Powell's youngest daughter was now 15 years old, and her elder daughters were on the cusp of marriage. The doll (Figure 5.8) is dressed in a cotton petticoat with a woven stripe and deep, whip-gathered flounce at the hem, and wears bright red silk shoes. Over this, she wears a petticoat, jacket and fichu of diaphanous white muslin. She is accessorized with a hat of silk, which has a wide brim stiffened with two layers of paper, decorated with silk flowers. Her head, sadly, is a later replacement. Powell's label reverts to her previous identification method and reads 'fashionable visiting dress 1792'. The quality of the workmanship also returns to Powell's exquisitely high levels of execution. The back of the bodice is carefully patterned, and fans out into the peplum at the centre back. The sleeves are shaped at the elbow, matching 1790s cutting techniques. The frills around the bottom of the jacket, the fichu and the hem of the petticoat are all ornamented with delicate whitework embroidery. Undoubtedly accomplished by Powell, this tiny decorative stitching has been designed in proportion with the doll, miniaturizing popular contemporary motifs. It is a notable feature of all of Powell's adult dolls that she selected fabrics which are appropriate in scale for the dolls. The sympathy between doll and textile creates an illusion that the doll was, quite literally, miniaturized: a shrunken down woman's garments. As a culmination

Figure 5.8 *Laetitia Powell,* Fashionable visiting dress, *1792, W.183:11-1919. Embroidery, possibly by Powell herself, decorates this delicate gown. Copyright Victoria and Albert Museum, London.*

of Powell's life-long making of dolls, this final creation epitomizes the progression of her skill as a maker.

Although Powell's death in 1801 prevented the production of further dolls, her legacy did not die with her. Around thirty-eight additional dolls were constructed by her descendants, who continued Laetitia Powell's doll-making tradition for another century.[56] The last doll was added to the collection in 1911. At some point in the later nineteenth century, supplementary labels were added to all the dolls, simply stating the year that the doll represented. By 1919, when the collection was donated to the Victoria and Albert Museum by Harry Powell (1853–1922), Laetitia Powell's great-grandson, the collection was framed as a series of 'costume dolls'.[57] The complex and layered motivations and meanings with which Powell imbued her dolls were, to some extent, masked by this categorization of the dolls as a simple timeline of 'costume' history. The smattering of furniture, which accompanied the dolls upon donation, was also dislodged from its context. The furniture and the dolls had probably once furnished a now-lost dolls' house, similar to the Nostell dolls' house. Coal scuttles, mirrors, two fireplaces (one for a kitchen with mechanical clockwork spit, the other with a smart overmantel mounding), a firescreen, a dish of cauliflowers and even a miniature monkey once surrounded the dolls, along with a plethora of other dolls' house paraphernalia. This incongruence, between the historicized cavalcade of fashion and the conventional collection and arrangement of doll furniture brings us back full circle, to those first hybrid concoctions of Powell's. Experimental, playful and inharmonious, dolls can never be classified as simple children's playthings.

The symbolism and purpose of Powell's dolls were perpetually renewed throughout her lifetime, and beyond. Although they were constantly in flux, four key overlapping themes and stages of Powell's life narrative can be perceived through the dolls: childhood subversion of sartorial rules, making skill and material literacy, motherhood and collaborative making, and finally, emotional and personal memorialization. The first six dolls, constructed in 1754 to 1759, capture those early years of subversive play, in which mimicry and make-believe sat side by side.[58] The sartorial rules of dress were the subject of experimentation and exploration through these miniature creations, as Powell learnt the material techniques of dress. The second stage, which encompasses the fifth to twelfth dolls, centred on the materialization and application of sartorial terminology and skill. In transforming the fashion plates and descriptions, so prevalent in print culture, into three-dimensional dolls, Powell articulated her literacy in this language of dress, and aped the chronicling and memorializing characteristics of print. Simultaneously, Powell's extremely high level of skill as a maker dominates these dolls, from their tiny hems to their expert patterning. The 1785 doll captures the third theme in a moment of intergenerational collaboration, while the 1769, 1784 and 1792 dolls hint at an authoritative and educational purpose. Finally, Powell's seventh doll, her 1761 wedding suit, explicitly memorialized a biographically, emotionally and personally significant day through a sartorial self-portrait.[59] While the affective resonance of the wedding doll is explicit, similar associations and remembrances were likely attached to all the dolls. Like Winn's dressed prints, each ensemble was likely made from the remnants of textiles from Powell's own garments. Materially captured memories, legible only to her, were perpetuated by these dolls. Fluid and intersecting as many of the uses and motivations behind the Powell dolls were, their significance as a medium for sartorial autobiography abounds. Powell's voice may be silent within the written record, drowned out by her husband and sons, but she told her own life narrative with her needle.

Mimetic dolls and miniature selves

Powell's mobilization of her little army of dolls as vessels for her personal memorialization sat firmly within the broader culture of doll use and ownership in the eighteenth century. Dolls were perceived as little versions of the self, through which women could project their identities and practise social scenarios. The doll's tea party, for instance, far from passive child's play, was an arena for the cultivation of adult social skills.[60] The doll's miniature status meant that these little women were governable and controllable, but they could also reflect back to their owners mirrored aspects of their own selfhood, culture and identity. The compulsion to imitate the doll and for the doll to be crafted to imitate the self does not, however, mean that dolls were socially prescriptive. Mary Wollstonecraft bemoaned that little girls were stuck in an endless cycle of repressive replication, in which they repeated the same restrictive and prescribed tasks as their maternal relations. 'She will imitate her mothers and aunts,' Wollstonecraft wrote in 1792, the same year that Powell dressed her final doll, 'and amuse herself by adorning her lifeless doll.'[61] This mimicry could extend to the woman herself embodying the doll, reduced to a controlled and imprisoned plaything.[62] Yet the rhetorical trope of the eighteenth-century woman as a doll herself, captive and powerless in a patriarchal system, is fundamentally challenged by practices and cultures of doll ownership. Dolls and doll-owning women were not devoid of agency, as Wollstonecraft would have us believe. Instead, dolls could act as vital vehicles through which sartorial modes of identity formation could be negotiated.

The intimate relationship between the doll and the fashion plate, so palpable within Powell's dolls and their labels, is evident throughout eighteenth-century sartorial culture.[63] Powell's dolls materialized fashion plate figures, the engraved features brought to life with wax, silks and trims. As their maker, Powell articulated her knowledge of the materials and methods of garment construction which were tacit within the two-dimensional printed image. Both print and doll, however, present mirrors of the self in miniature, offered up to viewers as exemplars of fashionable dress. Doll and print simulated versions of sartorial selfhood which could be reflexive and self-referential. A fashion plate from the French *Gallerie des Modes* from 1780 depicts a child grasping a doll (Figure 5.9). Child and doll are dressed exactly alike. Both wear a child's back-fasting gown made from silk taffeta, adorned with a

Figure 5.9 *Fashion plate from* Gallerie des Modes, *1780, RP-P-2009-2110. A little girl and her doll are dressed almost identically. Courtesy of the Rijksmuseum.*

gauze ruffle around the hem, along with an apron, also made from gauze. The only difference between the two is the colour, which, applied to the engravings by hand, could vary enormously from print to print. Child, doll and print correlate in this image, and present a united front in the articulation of sartorial style. The doll is a replication of the child: small, innocent, perfect. As mutual material mirrors, doll and owner are both active agents in the collective fashioning of selfhood and material identities.

The *Gallerie des Modes* image reveals tensions and variations between the representational ideal of doll-sized fashion and the practices exemplified by Powell and other young makers. Powell's childhood dolls were experimental. They referenced disparate elements of adult fashion and brought them together in disjointed discord. It was not until Powell's early adult years that she began to create perfect miniature replicas of her own clothing. While this subversive play was not unique to Powell's dolls, it was also not universal. Making doll-sized garments was often framed as a structured educational exercise and, from at least the later eighteenth century, was an integral part of girls' schooling.[64] Miniature manuals, outlining how garments from shirts and caps to knitted stockings should be made, contained tiny samples of completed work.[65] The miniature size of these garments did not classify them as toys to be played with, but as pseudo apprentice pieces, through which girls could learn the methods and techniques required to create full-sized garments. This extended beyond the so-called plain sewing, often found in such manuals, to complete fashionable gowns. Like Powell's brunswick and levite, gowns made by schoolgirls could replicate the intricate details of fashionable dress, from perfect lace insertions to the patterning and cut of complex sleeves.[66]

Dolls provided an ideal arena for the development of sewing skill and were often sold undressed expressly so that they could be clothed by their new owners. In 1787, for instance, a toy warehouse on Cornhill advertised 'all sorts of undressed dolls in wood or wax'.[67] Jean-Jacques Rousseau's principles of girls' education, although controversial and challenged by generations of feminists, outlined the relationship between dolls and sewing:

> The doll is the girl's special plaything; this shows her instinctive bent towards her life's work . . . Here is a little girl busy all day with her doll; she is always changing its clothes, dressing and undressing it, trying new combinations of trimmings well or ill matched; her fingers are clumsy, her taste is crude, but there is no mistaking her bent . . . What the little girl most clearly desires is to dress her doll, to make its bows, its tippets, its sashes, and its tuckers . . . Here is a motive for her earliest lessons, they are not tasks prescribed but favours bestowed. Little girls always dislike learning to read and write, but they are always ready to learn to sew.[68]

Tinged with gendered stereotypes as Rousseau's claims may be, the premise that dolls were utilized by girls as a means of developing sewing skills is substantiated by women's own accounts of their sewing. Anne Hicks (1749–1774), the daughter of Gloucestershire baronet, dressed her doll in a full brocade gown.[69] In 1824, 9-year-old Mary Stock was sent fragments of ribbon and textiles by her mother, expressly intended to be made into dolls' garments.[70] In the early nineteenth century, Betsy Nutt made her friend's doll 'such a pretty frock and petticoat'.[71] Some of the dolls which populate Winn's Nostell dolls' house also appear to wear homemade garments.[72] This miniature making was not performative, but practical. It was an opportunity to practise the core stitching skills required of all adult women, whether princess or pauper.

Dolls were a crucial educational tool for eighteenth-century children, and they recurred throughout the didactic literature and commercialized toys of the period. Dolls provided a focus for the development of empathy and responsibility, but they also offered a tool through which children were taught about materials, materiality and the world of goods. Dorothy Kilner (1755–1836), in her 1802 *The Doll's Spelling Book*, dedicated the volume to 'every Doll's Mama' and encouraged her readers to be 'anxious for the welfare of your dear little families, whether they are composed of Wax, Wood, Leather or Rag'.[73] Consisting of conversational dialogues between a child and her anthropomorphized doll, the book depicts the child playing at the role of mother, and teaching her doll the very same lessons she is herself in the process of learning.[74]

Mam-ma   Come, my dear doll, though you can not talk, I will make-be-lieve that you can. So come, my child, sit in my lap, and tell me if you know what you are made of?

Doll   I am made of paper.

Mam-ma   Oh you sil-ly thing! Do you not know bet-ter than that? You are made of wood.[75]

As with Powell's childhood dolls, mimicry and make-believe were joined in pedagogical unity. This combination was also pervasive in the commercial culture around childhood which ballooned in the latter part of the century. Educational kits for dolls, like the 1815 'doll's casket', were sold by the London publisher John Marshall (1756–1824). Marshall had published children's literature by Kilner, as well as her contemporaries Ellenor Fenn (1743–1813), also known as Mrs Teachwell, and Sarah Trimmer (1741–1810). Sets of teaching aids, such as Fenn's *Set of Toys, for Enabling Ladies to Instill the Rudiments of Spelling, Reading, Grammar, and Arithmetic* (1785), had set a precedent for the sale of teaching materials.[76] The 'doll's casket' amalgamated such educational aids with the maternal dynamics presented by Kilner, in which the child played as mother and the doll played as child. The casket consisted of a small wooden box, painted with a scene depicting a girl giving a lesson to her doll.[77] The lid of the box slid open to reveal a set of the same teaching aids produced for children, but in miniature. This included prints of animals and landscapes, an alphabet, a world map and disciplinary aids.[78] This highly gendered, didactic play encouraged girls to re-enact and project the fundamental experiences which built up their own identities onto their dolls. In so doing, the doll's status as an externalized, mirrored materialization of the self was reinforced.

The fantastical projection of the self onto the doll was certainly not the sole province of children, as Powell's dolls amply demonstrate. Women continued to indulge in dolls and dolls' houses in adulthood, and dressed, collected for and admired their miniature worlds. Neither was the commercialization of the doll purely aimed at children.[79] Fashion dolls, used to disseminate and advertise adult women's fashion between Paris and London, held the same mimetic qualities and also functioned as material educators. The fashion doll has become ubiquitous in narratives of fashion history, propelled into the limelight by McKendrick's 1983 declaration of its commercial power.[80] Yet, as Julie Park has decried, scholars still know surprisingly little about the materiality and practices which surrounded the so-called fashion doll: where and how they were made, how they were displayed and circulated, who viewed them and when.[81] Their size is a particularly ambiguous issue. While some extant fashion dolls follow the proportions of dolls classified as playthings, others are life size.[82] The life size fashion dolls held a function akin to the mannequin, as their movable limbs allowed potential consumers to pose and play with garments on a substitute body.[83] Newspaper advertisements from as late as 1800 announced that women might inspect the ensembles 'by a trial on themselves', a novelty in a fashion marketplace that focussed on the bespoke.[84] At first glance, these commercial fashion disseminators, regular in scale and following homogenous fashion rather than an individual's clothing, seem to be a far cry from Powell's personal, miniature and ramshackle collection of dolls. Yet core characteristics were shared. With both, it was the garments, rather than the facial features, which were the focus. Silks and cottons, lace and braid commanded the key communicative work done by these dolls. Temporality, too, took centre stage. While the fashion dolls disseminated fleeting styles, and Powell's dolls memorialized ensembles, both placed a time-watch on fashion. The temporality of dress, and its capability to historicize and materialize time, from an epoch to a single day, is captured in eternal stillness through these dolls.

Dolls as sartorial social narrators

The historicized memorialization and sartorial education practised through dolls were unified in dolls' roles as social narrators. As pedagogical tools, dolls could act as moralizers and social commentators. Nowhere is this more evident than in the commercially produced paper dolls manufactured to accompany didactic children's books in the early years of the nineteenth century. These little doll figures, which appeared as both boys and girls, were accompanied by interchangeable paper clothes, which corresponded with the scenes of the accompanying story. The 'brand of instruction and delight' favoured in these publications married the mimetic qualities of the doll with self-regulation and discipline, echoing and commercializing the pedagogical methods and tools Jane Johnson produced in the 1730s.[85] Crucially, they also placed the doll within a structured narrative, and explicitly used dress as a means of articulating change over time. The doll embodied broader social concerns over the legibility of appearances and defined sartorial modes of distinction and social difference. These little paper people, with their changeable outfits and swappable headgear, may appear ephemeral and frivolous. Yet, through these miniature paper dolls, children enacted fundamental social lessons, and came to understand how dress could reflect a life story.

The London publishers, Samuel and Joseph Fuller, were prolific as producers of these paper doll books. They commenced trading together in 1808, and in 1810 published *The History of Little Fanny* (Figure 5.10). At a cost of five shillings, the book was expensive, but its popularity meant that it ran to several editions within its first two years of publication. The book came in a little cardboard sleeve, which contained the story, told in verse, Fanny's little paper head, and a series of seven outfits which aligned with each episode of the story. The tale commences with the eponymous Fanny as a wealthy, spoilt and 'idle' girl, who, ironically, is chiefly occupied playing with her doll. For the first stage of Fanny's story, she is 'dressed in a white frock, and pink sash, with a doll in her arms'.[86] Next, Fanny desires to go to the park to show off her finery, and is dressed in a 'great coat, muff, and bonnet, ready to go out' (5). Mama, however, says no, and the distraught Fanny runs away with her maid. Alas, abandoned by her distracted maid, Fanny finds herself lost and alone, her fancy clothes stolen from her. Fanny's fall from grace sees her wear 'a red cloak, with a hat in her hand, begging for bread' (7). Not one to be cast down for long, little Fanny finds work as an errand girl, and is quickly promoted from carrying smelly fish to eggs and milk in her little basket (11). As luck would have it, little lost Fanny's hard work and diligence pay off when her next errand takes her back to her mother's house and Fanny is 'restored to [her] mother's love' (14). Finally, we find Fanny 'restored to her former station,

Figure 5.10 The History of Little Fanny, *1810, Briggs Collection of Educational Literature, PZ6.H4. Courtesy of the University of Nottingham Special Collections.*

modestly dressed in a coloured frock, with a book in her hand' (15). This story of the naughty girl redeemed, popular amongst comparable contemporary literature, is materialized through the paper dolls. The narrative of Fanny's adventures with the dolls, enacted by the reader, positioned the reader as complicit in the creation of a 'theatre from the materials of society'.[87] Dolls, here, are personifications of a moralistic narrative tale but, much like Powell's dolls, it is dress which tells this biographical story.

Numerous published paper doll tales were sold, following in the footsteps of Fanny's commercial success.[88] Publications like Rudolph Ackermann's *The New Doll, or Grandmama's Gift* (1826) even used the doll format to promote the sale of further toys in order to enact the activities within the book.[89] The women and girls who purchased and read these tales were far from passive consumers. Instead, they produced creative responses and replications of the paper doll story, penning tales and painting dolls of their own. One of the best examples of this, *The History of Miss Wildfire*, was written and made in 1832 by Anne Sanders Wilson for her younger sister Mary.[90] The narrative is extremely similar to *The History of Little Fanny*. Miss Wildfire begins her tale as a fashion-loving, self-indulgent woman, the apple of her benevolent father's eye. Her father's untimely death, however, plunges her into debt and misery. She descends through the social strata, temporarily finding work as a milkmaid, before being dismissed and forced onto the street. She briefly joins a band of gypsies, before meeting a group of Quakers, who teach her to make lace and be humble. She finds marital happiness with a 'precise, demure, upright' Quaker lad, and learns that the sin of pride is 'most unfit for Woman'.[91] Sixteen hand-painted paper dolls and two heads accompany this tale of religious redemption. Their fashions range from fashion-plate-like depictions of garments at the height of fashion in 1832, to the plain clothes and red cloak of Miss Wildfire's days as a servant, and finally to her outfits as a Quaker lace-maker and modest married woman. This biography through clothes told a socially instructive tale which echoed *The History of Little Fanny* in its moralizing tone. Its status as a homemade replication of a commercial product, however, underlines the centrality of making to women's personal responses to these works. Echoing fashion dolls and toy dolls, there was no hard line between commercially produced and homemade paper dolls.

The flurry of popularity enjoyed by the paper doll from the 1810s onwards was the culmination of sporadic interest in the genre over the proceeding decades.[92] Commercially produced paper fashion dolls had enjoyed a burst of popularity in the 1790s.[93] Johann Ludwig Stahl's (1759–1835) German-made *La Poupée anglaise, a diverse modes* (1790) depicted a fashionable woman in profile, wearing pink stays, shoes and an underpetticoat. This paper woman was accompanied by four interchangeable petticoats, two open robes, a closed redingote and a pierrot jacket, as well as eight different hats.[94] This collection was not a moralizing tale and possessed no ethical overtones. These assemblages of dolls were more akin to the fashion plate. They furnished their owners with the ability to test out and experiment with fashion, proffering a sartorial kaleidoscope of possibilities. These dolls were haptic treasures to be touched and played with; and were creative rather than prescriptive. A similar set was published by the London bookseller John Wallis (1750s–1818) in 1791, this time with both a man's and a woman's head and nine assorted outfits, which were drawn to represent miscellaneous social roles.[95] Through the change of an outfit, the same face could be a soldier or a sailor, an aristocrat or a servant. This set pre-empted the legibility of appearances, so important in *The History of Little Fanny*, and used paper clothes to demonstrate the transformative role of dress. Clothes made the paper man. Home-produced examples also flourished throughout this period. The Burton sisters, Eliza (1786–1877), Jane (1792–1879), Octavia (1796–1837) and Jessy (1804–1844) were the daughters of preeminent property developer James Burton (1761–1837). In 1806 they collaboratively produced a set of their own paper dolls. These dolls had carefully hand-painted faces, white muslin dresses, pantaloons and blue sashes.[96] At once creative and commercial, moralizing and modish, the paper doll had as many meanings as it had outfits.[97]

In 1787, 14-year-old Harriet Johnson (1773–1821) began her own extensive paper doll project. Working in watercolour, she painted a little doll on thick paper, furnishing her with blue stays, a shift and white petticoat, her hair perfectly coiffured. Johnson created a varied array of nine outfits for her doll, and wrote a description and number on the reverse of each, mimicking Powell's customary notes. Number one, for instance, was described as a 'morning jacket' of white muslin, while number eight was an elaborate 'court dress', with a contrasting bodice, fluffy lace engageantes, fur trim and a gargantuan be-feathered cap (Figure 5.11).[98] Other outfits include a blue redingote with shiny metal buttons, a soft blue day gown and a striking black and pink *robe à la Turque*. These watercolour sartorial representations mirror Lewis' 'dress of the year' watercolours, and the court dress in particular possesses numerous similarities to Lewis' own 1787 court gown (Figure 3.29), from the contrasting bodice to the poesy of flowers at the bosom. Around each of the ensembles, little tabs were cut from the paper, which could be folded and wrapped around the paper doll, holding the garments in place. The little hats, which accompanied seven of the outfits, were fashioned with small, precisely made cuts, which allowed them to be slotted over the doll's voluminous fashionable hair.

This little paper lady, with her highly fashionable wardrobe, was none other than a paper queen, painted to represent outfits worn by Queen Charlotte (1744–1818).[99] Rather than imaginative flights of fancy, or garments which reflected a broad variety of social roles, this was the comprehensive wardrobe of a monarch. It is unclear whether the outfits worn by Johnson's personal paper queen were drawn from direct sight but, living in London and with family ties to fashionable parliamentary circles, it is likely Johnson caught occasional glimpses of her royal muse. Johnson's lionization of elite fashions transferred the memetic properties of the paper doll from the self to a celebrated figure and transformed that idolized figure into a possessable object. As an exemplar for British womanhood, Queen Charlotte was an icon of feminine productivity and a figurehead for patriotism and textile production.[100] These sartorial dolls built upon the Queen's reputation as a champion of women as makers and positioned Johnson within a broader culture of feminine productivity.

Fashions in Miniature: Dolls

Figure 5.11 *Harriet Johnson's paper doll, 1787, 1995.123/10a-b. Johnson created nine different outfits for her paper doll in 1787, purported to be copied from garments worn by Queen Charlotte. Photo © Historic Royal Palaces/Robin Forster/Bridgeman Images.*

Figure 5.12 *Letter from Harriet Johnson to her sister Maria, 1802, BOD: MS. Don. c. 195, fol. 87. The accompanying text reads: 'Mrs Duff & the Miss Manners's way of wearing a veil at Publick breakfasts &c'. Courtesy of the Bodleian Library, University of Oxford.*

Johnson was the daughter of land-owning vicar Robert Augustus Johnson (1745–1779) and the aristocratically connected Anna Rebecca Craven (1745–1816). She was also, coincidentally, the niece of Barbara Johnson, whose album is the subject of Chapter 2 in this book. Johnson's diligent and detailed recording of aristocratic fashions was not confined to her dolls. By 1802, Johnson was the wife of John Hamilton Dalrymple (1771–1853), an aristocratic member of parliament. As the wife of an MP, Johnson spent a great deal of her time amongst the political and fashionable elites of London. She took to drawing the sartorial likenesses of acquaintances and used watercolour paintings to illustrate her letters to her unmarried sister, Maria.[101] The letters include depictions of society ladies, including Lady Ann Wyndham (1772–1832), Maria Molyneux, Countess of Sefton (1769–1851), Mary Caroline Duff (1775–1805) and Laura Manners (1780–1834). The content of the letters focussed on veils and turbans, and Johnson recounted in explicit detail how these women tied and pinned their headdresses and the occasions on which each style was worn. Like her royal paper doll, Johnson used her paintbrush and paper to position herself within a specific fashionable social stratum. These styles, as she noted in her letters to her sister, were to be mimicked and copied, adapted and worn. For Johnson, Powell and the abundance of other women whose doll making this chapter has touched upon, dress was not a frivolous amusement and making was not an occupation for idle hands. It was an integral part of how these women negotiated and navigated their social and cultural worlds. Replicated in miniature, dress offered a microcosmic version of the self and of society.

Whether composed of wood, wax or paper, dolls were charged with reflective, didactic and constructive powers. They defined and expressed contradictory perspectives: sartorial distinction, creativity, individuality and fashionable homogeneity. Dolls have been read as transitional, binary objects; seen either as 'child's plaything' or 'adult's possession'.[102] The dolls made by Powell and her contemporaries, however, reveal the fluid and variable motivations behind the act of dressing a doll. Perhaps most prominent amongst these incentives was the doll's temporal abilities. Dolls operated as chroniclers who preserved for posterity a sartorial moment, whether that belonged to a celebrated queen, a fictional little girl or the daughter of a London merchant. Frozen in time, each silent, inert doll represented a brief moment in perpetuity through tiny garments, either painted or stitched. The clothing of these dolls broadly reflected how lives were lived through material practices; however, they also animated an interior life. Every fragment cut from a well-worn garment and refashioned into a doll's gown, petticoat or hat preserved and immortalized personal and otherwise unrecorded memories. Steeped with biographical, emotional and personal meaning, dolls could be miniature memorials of the self.

6
Conclusion: Material afterlives

Anyone who has undertaken a project to make an object is aware of the time, preparation, persistence and diligence required to complete it. To clothe a single doll, paint one watercolour or dress an individual print requires hours of assiduous patience. It is not a task carried out on a whim, or a flight of creative fancy. It takes dedication, creativity and manual skill. Nevertheless, Barbara Johnson, Ann Frankland Lewis, Sabine Winn and Laetitia Powell persisted. Year upon year, they returned to their acts of making, be it in repeated replication of the same practice or, as with Winn's dressed prints and print-adorned doll house, adaptations and reapplications of related skills in evolving formats. Between them, 170 years of Georgian women's lives were recorded, ordered and materialized through acts of making. Imbued with meaning, emotion and cultural resonances, each of these material lives was intensely biographical and personal. Supported by a comprehensive study of both material and manuscript sources, this book has demonstrated that objects – fabrics, watercolours, prints and dolls – could chronicle the pitfalls and pleasures, hardships and happiness of life.

This book has come full circle, from Barbara Johnson's first 'flower'd calico long sack' in 1746, to her niece Harriet Johnson's sartorial watercolours in 1802, via a multitude of creative women in between.[1] This familial connection represents the joined-up nature of material life writing: the women who undertook it, its themes and preoccupations and its modes and mediums. Connections and associations have been prevalent throughout this book, reflective of the symbiotic and reciprocal flow of practices and ideas which coursed through eighteenth-century culture. Perhaps the most ubiquitous of these was the negotiation of selfhood and identity. The primacy of the 'self' connects this superfluity of creative endeavours with Dror Wahrman's notion of the 'modern regime of selfhood', which emerged in the eighteenth century.[2] Born with 'a core of selfhood subject to a continual maturational development', eighteenth century men and women turned towards individuality and interiority.[3] In this fluid world of identity and idiosyncrasy, a clear definition of a coherent self was not necessarily forthcoming. As forms of life-writing, the material archives explored in this book offered a means by which that lucid selfhood could be identified and defined in relation to a broader cultural context. Like diaries and journals, these 'constructs of the self … are produced through social, historical, and cultural factors; and the "self" both positions itself in the discourses available to it, and is produced by them'.[4] These material lives sat at the nexus of a vast web of concepts and practices, and were constructed as forms of cultural compass, positioning the heterogeny of the individual within the homogeny of society.

The management and memorialization of selfhood are recurrent themes throughout the creative practices of Johnson, Lewis, Winn and Powell. These twin motivations echo the multiple audiences for whom these records were created. As tools for self-management – of money, consumption and emotions – they were personal and private. Johnson's album was an implement of individual financial as well as sartorial regulation, while Winn's dressed prints contained now-lost intimate affective meaning and were cloistered away in her private domestic space. At the same time, as materialized records of self-management, they invited the inspection of others, and held their makers accountable. Johnson's mother peered over her daughter's shoulder as she made her first album entries, and Lewis' watercolours reflected her social successes and participation in major events and trends. The audiences for these records widen further when we consider their memorializing attributes. Lewis' watercolours and Powell's dolls alike honoured and remembered momentous biographical moments from weddings to deaths. As souvenirs of precious memories, mementos of lost loved ones and tokens of times past, these objects contained an 'emotional charge' and provided an external channel for 'conceptualising and processing emotions'.[5] These objects were meaningful and momentous to their owners. The tendency for cross-generational collaboration and familial continuation of related practices was also commonplace. Johnson's nieces entered further fashion plates into her album and developed their own means of sartorial chronicling.[6] Lewis' brothers and nieces were also gifted with artistic talents and interests. Winn and her daughter engaged in creative practice side by side, and her granddaughter went on make fantastical feathered collages.[7] Finally, and perhaps most impressive of all, members of the Powell family still dressed dolls over a century after Powell's death. These material methods had lives of their own and persisted across the generations. The performative nature of the creative methods adopted by these women puts them at risk of accusations of artifice. It would be easy to suggest that Lewis simply enacted the codified structures of mourning culture, or that Johnson only played at the rationalization and moderation of her consumption without it actually impacting upon her purchases in any way. Yet such readings are reductive. The performative elements of these rituals of recording were central to the memorializing qualities of the created objects. They were strategies for image making and recitals of selfhood.[8] But that does not make them artificial, or any less affective and authentic. The veracity of their contents is only as questionable as any written autobiography.

The temporal resonance of these activities was profound. Each individual brush stroke, stitch and snip was a chronometric marker, which captured for posterity one moment within a lifetime. At a time when the English were concerned with 'a national operation of self-dating' which contributed to 'national self-making', self and time stood side-by-side.[9] The self of the present could only be defined in relation to the self of the past, and 'historicism's hegemony' was especially prevalent in commerce and fashion.[10] The temporality of the fashion plate, in particular, had a profound influence on the material life-writing of these women. Johnson mobilized the dated fashion plate as part of the chronological markers of her album, while Lewis' annual sequence of watercolours mimicked the yearly rhythm of pocket book fashion plate production. Lewis' repeated caption for her watercolours and the standard moniker for pocket book fashion plates, 'dress of the year', could easily have been the title for this book. For all four of these women, the passing of days, months and years was mapped against fashion. Time was measured through dress, and garments assigned their own chronometric signature.

The limited lifespan assigned to dress through the fashion press venerated print as a sartorial timekeeper. Print was a fundamental presence within and influence upon all four of the material practices studied in this book. However, the ways in which print exacted that influence are not as they might first appear. As discussed in Chapter 3, fashion plates have regularly received more credit than is due as practical disseminators of fashion.[11] They are not cited as a sartorial source by eighteenth-century women, and the information contained within a two-dimensional printed image is profoundly limited in terms of materiality and instruction. Through Johnson, Lewis, Winn and Powell, however, we see that print influenced sartorial practices in other ways. Print, and in particular the pocket book fashion plate, was pervasive as a creative influence. For Johnson, they proffered a source of up-to-date sartorial terminology and resonated with the self-regulatory ethos of the pocket book genre. Lewis imitated their compositional style and the phrasing of their captions, as did Powell in her dolls. Taking the influence of print to its extreme, Winn physically cut, pasted and composed with fragments of prints, turning them into something new.

These women all consumed print, in one form or another. As producers, however, they made creative interventions which disrupt straightforward narratives of consumption. Prints were 'altered and adorned'; they were painted, cut out, stuck to other objects, had other objects stuck to them and copied in ink and watercolour.[12] One of the core purposes of this book has been to demonstrate that the ascendancy of the 'consumer society' of the eighteenth century does not mean that genteel consumers did not understand how things were made.[13] In the eighteenth-century press, genteel women were branded as passive consumers, and victims of an increasingly cunning retail world.[14] Women's consumption was smeared as a 'Source of great Corruptions', which took them away from productive pursuits, household management and the care of children.[15] The material archives of these four women make two fundamental interventions in this narrative. First, that consumer goods were not purchased and preserved. Prints, garments, books and dolls were manipulated and altered, remade and reused after the point of purchase.[16] The commercial marketplace fuelled domestic production.[17] Second, these domestic making activities were vibrant acts of agency. Far from passive consumers in an overwhelming world of goods, these women mobilized their making skills to negotiate and manage their consumption.

All four of these archives take this symbiotic relationship between production and consumption even further. As historians, we have a tendency to classify and order; we divide and group in order to make sense of a messy past. Yet these material archives defy traditional modes of classification. They existed outside of neat categorizations of either production or consumption and blurred the boundaries of this division. Whether album, watercolour, dressed print or doll, these material archives were all crafted representations of consumption: they reflected and recorded the acquisition of goods through material interventions. The connections, networks and cooperative influence revealed through these objects reflect holistic cultural practices. They merged production with consumption, making with buying and self with society. Inevitably, the negotiation of interiority and selfhood transformed the individual into the anchor within a swirling sea of socially defined and prescribed activities.

So many of the dominant narratives, both in the eighteenth century and in scholarship, have been defined by elite white men. Historical methodologies which privilege the written word – and usually specific, codified and formalized forms – constrict what, and who, is prioritized. Women's voices are so often silent in the archive. While the works of exceptional women or rare survivors have formed the basis for vital foundational work, thousands of women remain forgotten.[18] These four women were privileged in innumerable ways: they were white, educated and socially and financially advantaged. Undoubtedly, this has contributed to the preservation, recovery and excavation of their material lives. But the methodological possibilities opened up by the material life-writing model proffer opportunities which benefit more people than white, middling sort women.[19] It opens up possibilities for fresh approaches to marginalized voices throughout history. When pens are silent, needles, brushes, glue and scissors tell innumerable tales.

The products of this assortment of creative implements could be subversive and political, impassioned and emotive.[20] They could record achievement and success, but they could also offer outlets for trauma and grief. A sampler stitched by Elizabeth Parker (1813–1889) in the 1830s resonates with autobiographical and meditative self-reflection.[21] Stitched in red silk upon a large rectangle of linen, this sampler quite literally records Parker's life narrative in prose.[22] We learn that Parker was born into a large family, with eleven brothers and sisters, and aged 13 she entered service as a nursery maid. A year later, she left to become housemaid to the vile 'Lieut G' where 'they treated me with cruelty too horrible to mention for trying to avoid the wicked design of my master I was thrown down stairs'. Distraught and traumatized, Parker contemplated 'that great sin of selfdestruction', but found comfort and strength in the words of 'that worthy Gentleman Dr W'. Repeatedly throughout the 1,722 words of the sampler, Parker remarks on her own silence. She feels a moral mandate to remain mute and has not told her friends or family about her experiences. The sampler is her place of affective, confessional outpouring. Maureen Daly Goggin has framed the sampler as a 'text/ile' which made use of 'alternative rhetorical techniques' to create a 'discursive space in which to cope with debilitating struggles'.²³ Parker could not contemplate conveying her tale in spoken words or pen and ink, but silk and linen brought comfort and an outlet for her tale.

In her sampler, Parker proclaimed: 'ah the dead forgotten lie'. Her pessimism, however, was not shared by many of her fellow women makers and consumers. The phrase 'when this you see, remember me' was frequently repeated on samplers and love tokens throughout the eighteenth and early nineteenth centuries.²⁴ Writing to Margaret Cavendish, the Duchess of Portland (1715–1785), renowned bluestocking Elizabeth Montague (1718–1800) recalled a visit to the Northfleet Fair in the 1740s at which there 'were nymphs and swains buying garters with amorous posies; some only with the humble request "when this you see, remember me"'.²⁵ Purchased or made, objects carried memories and recalled biographical moments. The memorializing authority of objects imbued them with immense cultural power. While letters and diaries might have been burnt or struck out, objects were perpetual and granted material immortality. From the tiniest fragments, like the tokens left with the babies at the London Foundling Hospital, to the comprehensive material lives amassed by Johnson, Lewis, Winn and Powell, objects recall the lives of the dead.²⁶ Each object studied in this book is a material echo of a life. Long dead and buried these women may be, but within each fragment of fabric and paper they endure.²⁷ Their stories, told in stitches and brushstrokes, will not be expunged from history. The objects they made are their material remains; they are the things left behind. The person, their memories, emotions, thoughts and ideas may fade, but objects offer an eternal material afterlife.

Glossary of sartorial terms

Brunswick a jacket and petticoat combination, fashionable in the late 1760s and 1770s. The jacket often had a hood, false or separate waistcoat with button closure, and long sleeves.

Coat either an abbreviation of petticoat or a child's back-closing dress.

Compere front a false stomacher front attached to the gown and fastened using buttons.

Dishabille a casual, everyday form of dress. From the French, *déshabillé*, meaning partly clothed.

Engageantes embroidered muslin or lace ruffles worn at the cuff.

Fichu a white cotton shawl, usually made of embroidered muslin, worn around the neck.

Fly-fringe an embellishment made from knotted silk filament thread.

Levite a casual gown with a pointed collar, reveres and sash around the waist.

Lustring alternatively spelt lutestring, a fine, glossy silk with a lustrous finish.

Negligée also known as *robe à la française* or sack-back gown, this style of garment is identified by its stacked box pleats at the centre back. It was worn with a stomacher and petticoat.

Nightgown also known as a *robe à l'anglaise*, this style of gown was close fitted at the back and worn with a stomacher and petticoat.

Pelisse popular in the early nineteenth century, this was a coat-like garment.

Robings also known as robins, these were broad flat strips which ran around the neck and down the front of the bodice. They sometimes extended down the front of an open-fronted gown.

Round-gown this transitional style was closed at the front, in contrast to the negligée or nightgown, which opened to expose the petticoat beneath.

Sack-back see negligée.

Sarsanet a soft, lightweight, plain weave silk.

Satin a smooth, glossy weave created by the weft floating over three or four warp threads at a time.

Selvedge the 'self-finished' edge of a woven fabric. There are no raw edges along the selvedge.

Stuff a general term for woven fabrics. Stuffs were usually wool but could also be linen or cotton blends.

Taffety a crisp, smooth, plain-woven silk with a slight sheen.

Notes

Chapter 1

1 Rebecca Elisabeth Connor, *Women, Accounting and Narrative: Keeping Books in Eighteenth-Century England* (London: Routledge, 2004); Amanda Vickery, 'His and Hers: Gender, Consumption and Household Accounting in Eighteenth-Century England', *Past & Present* 1 (2006): 12–38; Alexandra Shepard, *Accounting for Oneself: Worth, Status, and the Social Order in Early Modern England* (Oxford: Oxford University Press, 2015).

2 Amanda Vickery's work on the genteel women of eighteenth-century Yorkshire and Lancashire set the precedent for studies in this vein. See Vickery, *The Gentleman's Daughter* (London: Yale University Press, 1998).

3 There is a large body of literary work on the autobiography. See, for example, Patricia Ann Mayer Spacks, *Imagining a Self: Autobiography and Novel in Eighteenth-Century England* (Cambridge, MA: Harvard University Press, 1976); Felicity Nussbaum, *The Autobiographical Subject: Gender and Ideology in Eighteenth-Century England* (London: Johns Hopkins University Press, 1989).

4 The surnames used in this book reflect how each of these women styled themselves during their most productive periods.

5 I use Vickery's definition of genteel throughout this book. See Vickery, *The Gentleman's Daughter*, 13.

6 David S. Landes, *The Unbound Prometheus: Technological Change and Industrial Development in Western Europe from 1750 to the Present* (Cambridge: Cambridge University Press, 1969); Neil McKendrick, John Brewer, and John Harold Plumb, *The Birth of a Consumer Society: The Commercialization of Eighteenth-Century England* (Bloomington: Indiana University Press, 1982); John Brewer and Roy Porter, eds., *Consumption and the World of Goods* (London: Routledge, 1993); Ben Fine and Ellen Leopold, 'Consumerism and the Industrial Revolution', *Social History* 15, no. 2 (1990): 151–79.

7 Historical material culture methodologies and approaches have been detailed in Karen Harvey, ed., *History and Material Culture* (London: Routledge, 2009); Hannah Greig, Jane Hamlett, and Leonie Hannan, eds., *Gender and Material Culture in Britain since 1600* (London: Palgrave, 2016); Leonie Hannan and Sarah Longair, eds., *History Through Material Culture* (Manchester: Manchester University Press, 2017).

8 James Deetz, *In Small Things Forgotten: The Archaeology of Early American Life* (New York: Anchor Books, 1977).

9 Barbara Burman and Ariane Fennetaux, *The Pocket: A Hidden History of Women's Lives, 1660–1900* (London: Yale University Press, 2019), 18; Giorgio Riello, *Cotton: The Fabric That Made the Modern World* (Cambridge: Cambridge University Press, 2013), 13.

10 For work on material culture and empire, see Margot C. Finn and Kate Smith, eds., *The East India Company at Home, 1757–1857* (London: UCL Press, 2018); for work on material culture and the emotions, see Stephanie

Downes, Sally Holloway, and Sarah Randles, eds., *Feeling Things: Objects and Emotions through History* (Oxford: Oxford University Press, 2018).

11 Kate Smith and Leonie Hannan, 'Return and Repetition: Methods for Material Culture Studies', *The Journal of Interdisciplinary History* 48, no. 1 (2017): 1–17.

12 Jules David Prown, 'Mind in Matter: An Introduction to Material Culture Theory and Method', *Winterthur Portfolio* 17, no. 1 (1982): 1–19, 7.

13 Igor Kopytoff, 'The Cultural Biography of Things: Commoditization as Process', in *The Social Life of Things: Commodities in Cultural Perspective*, ed. Arjun Appadurai (Cambridge: Cambridge University Press, 1986), 64–92; see also Ariane Fennetaux, Amélie Junqua, and Sophie Vasset, eds., *The Afterlife of Used Things: Recycling in the Long Eighteenth Century* (London: Routledge, 2015); Karin Dannehl, 'Object Biographies: From Production to Consumption', in *History and Material Culture*, ed. Karen Harvey (Abingdon: Routledge, 2009), 123–38.

14 Paula Byrne, *The Real Jane Austen: A Life in Small Things* (London: Harper Press, 2013).

15 Neil MacGregor, *A History of the World in 100 Objects* (London: Allen Lane, 2010).

16 In history, an exception would be Leonie Hannan et al., '"A View from Old Age": Women's Lives as Narrated Through Objects', *Life Writing* 16, no. 1 (2019): 51–67. Quilts have also been read from this perspective. See, for example, Janet Floyd, 'Back into Memory Land? Quilts and the Problem of History', *Women's Studies* 37, no. 1 (2007): 38–56; Mara Witzling, 'Quilt Language: Towards a Poetics of Quilting', *Women's History Review* 18, no. 4 (2009): 619–37. Literary scholars, on the other hand, have embraced this notion. See Julie Park, *The Self and It: Novel Objects in Eighteenth-Century England* (Stanford: Stanford University Press, 2010); Jennifer Van Horn, *The Power of Objects in Eighteenth-Century British America* (Chapel Hill, NC: University of North Carolina Press, 2017) .

17 Kate Strasdin, *Inside the Royal Wardrobe: A Dress History of Queen Alexandra* (London: Bloomsbury, 2017).

18 Philippe Lejeune, *Le Pacte Autobiographique* (Paris: Seuil, 1975), 14.

19 Felicity Nussbaum, *The Autobiographical Subject: Gender and Ideology in Eighteenth-Century England* (Baltimore: Johns Hopkins University Press, 1989), 4.

20 Amy Culley, *British Women's Life Writing, 1760–1840: Friendship, Community, and Collaboration* (London: Palgrave, 2014), 2.

21 Michael Mascuch, *The Origins of the Individualist Self: Autobiography and Self-Identity in England, 1591–1791* (Cambridge: Polity Press, 1997), 7.

22 Ulinka Rublack, 'The First Book of Fashion', in *The First Book of Fashion: The Books of Clothes of Matthäus & Veit Konrad Schwarz of Augsburg*, ed. Ulinka Rublack and Maria Hayward (London: Bloomsbury, 2015), 1–26. It is worth noting that Schwarz commissioned these watercolours and did not himself engage in making.

23 For more on the scrapbook, see Ellen Gruber Garvey, *Writing with Scissors: American Scrapbooks from the Civil War to the Harlem Renaissance* (Oxford: Oxford University Press, 2012); Louise Williams, '"To Amuse for an Hour"? Materiality, Femininity and Performance in the Scrapbook of Lady Maxwell'. *Scottish Archives* 19 (2013): 106–18; for more on social media and fashion, see Wendy Bendoni, *Social Media for Fashion Marketing: Storytelling in a Digital World* (London: Bloomsbury, 2017).

24 Nussbaum, *The Autobiographical Subject*, xi.

25 For work on women's life writing and imagined communities, see Cynthia Anne Huff, ed., *Women's Life Writing and Imagined Communities* (London: Routledge, 2005); Daniel Cook and Amy Culley, eds., *Women's Life Writing, 1700–1850* (London: Palgrave, 2012); Culley, *British Women's Life Writing, 1760–1840*.

26 For Johnson's niece's album, see Northampton Archives: ZB0702/02. For the Powell dolls, see VAM: W.183:13-1919 – W.183:18-1919.

27 For an extensive study on proxy shopping, see Miles Lambert, '"Sent from Town": Commissioning Clothing in Britain During the Long Eighteenth Century', *Costume* 43, no. 1 (2009): 66–84.

28 Nussbaum, *The Autobiographical Subject*, xiii.

29 Rozsika Parker, *The Subversive Stitch: Embroidery and the Making of the Feminine* (London: I B Tauris, 2010).

30 Vickery, *The Gentleman's Daughter*, 150; Ann Bermingham, *Learning to Draw: Studies in the Cultural History of a Polite and Useful Art* (London: Yale University Press, 2000); Amanda Vickery, 'The Theory and Practice of Female Accomplishment', in *Mrs Delany and Her Circle*, ed. Mark Laird and Alicia Weisberg-Roberts (London: Yale University Press, 2009), 94–109.

31 See, in particular Maureen Daly Goggin and Beth Fowkes Tobin, eds., *Women and Things, 1750–1950* (Aldershot: Ashgate, 2009).

32 For more on material literacy, see Serena Dyer and Chloe Wigston Smith, eds., *Material Literacy in Eighteenth-Century Britain: A Nation of Makers* (London: Bloomsbury, 2020).

33 A notable exception here would be the pin, which was integral to the wearing of clothes and not just their making. For more on sewing tools, see Mary Carolyn Beaudry, *Findings: The Material Culture of Needlework and Sewing* (London: Yale University Press, 2006).

34 Elizabeth Kowaleski-Wallace, *Consuming Subjects: Women, Shopping, and Business in the Eighteenth Century* (New York: Columbia University Press, 1997), 73–108; Cindy McCreery, *The Satirical Gaze: Prints of Women in Late Eighteenth-Century England* (Oxford: Oxford University Press, 2004), 139.

35 Harriet Guest, *Small Change: Women, Learning, Patriotism, 1750–1810* (Chicago: University of Chicago Press, 2000), 79.

36 Thorstein Veblen, *Theory of the Leisure Class* (London: George Allen and Unwin, 1925), 54.

37 *The Gentleman's Magazine* (London: F. Jeffries, 1731), 389.

38 Helen Berry, 'Polite Consumption: Shopping in Eighteenth-Century England', *Transactions of the Royal Historical Society* 6, no. 12 (2002): 375–94.

39 Kate Smith, 'Sensing Design and Workmanship: The Haptic Skills of Shoppers in Eighteenth-Century London', *Journal of Design History* 25 (2012): 1–10.

40 YCA: Munby Papers, Acc. 54.19.

41 NA: RG 4, Piece Number: 3138.

42 Louisa Stuart, *Gleanings from an Old Portfolio, 1785–1799*, ed. Godfrey Clark, vol. 2 (Edinburgh: D. Douglas, 1895), 169.

43 James Beresford, *The Miseries of Human Life* (London: William Miller, 1806), 263.

44 For work which examines eighteenth-century masculinities, see Karen Harvey, *The Little Republic: Masculinity and Domestic Authority in Eighteenth-Century Britain* (Oxford: Oxford University Press, 2012); Matthew McCormack, 'Boots, Material Culture and Georgian Masculinities', *Social History* 42, no. 4 (2017): 307–1022; for work on men and consumption, see Margot Finn, 'Men's Things: Masculine Possession in the Consumer Revolution', *Social History* 25, no. 2 (2000): 133–55.

45 WYAS: WYW1352/3/4/6/3.

46 Karen Harvey, 'Craftsmen in Common: Objects, Skills and Masculinity in the Eighteenth and Nineteenth Centuries', in *Gender and Material Culture in Britain since 1600*, ed. Hannah Greig, Jane Hamlett, and Leonie Hannan (London: Palgrave, 2016), 68–89; Sally Holloway, *The Game of Love in Georgian England: Courtship, Emotions, and Material Culture* (Oxford: Oxford University Press, 2019), 79.

47 Peter McNeil, *Pretty Gentlemen: Macaroni Men and the Eighteenth-Century Fashion World* (London: Yale University Press, 2018).

48 See, for example Lindsay Boynton and Nicholas Goodison, 'Thomas Chippendale at Nostell Priory', *Furniture History* 4 (1968): 10–61; Christopher Todd, 'A Swiss Milady in Yorkshire: Sabine Winn of Nostell Priory', *Yorkshire Archaeological Journal* 77 (2005): 205–24; Frances Sands, 'Nostell Priory: History of a House, 1730-85' (University of York, 2012).

49 Deetz, *In Small Things Forgotten*, 260.

Chapter 2

1 Abbé d'Ancourt, *The Lady's Preceptor. Or, a Letter to a Young Lady of Distinction upon Politeness* (London: J. Watts, 1743), 59.

2 Richard Campbell, *London Tradesman* (London: T. Gardener, 1747), 198.

3 Alexandra Shepard, *Accounting for Oneself: Worth, Status, and the Social Order in Early Modern England* (Oxford: Oxford University Press, 2015), 2. See also Rebecca Elisabeth Connor, *Women, Accounting and Narrative: Keeping Books in Eighteenth-Century England* (London: Routledge, 2004).

4 Women's consumption has been accessed via account books in work such as Lorna Weatherill, *Consumer Behaviour and Material Culture in Britain, 1660-1760* (London: Routledge, 1996); Amanda Vickery, *The Gentleman's Daughter* (London: Yale University Press, 1998).

5 VAM: T.219-1973, f. 1.

6 This phrasing was used to frame the album in Natalie Rothstein, ed., *Barbara Johnson's Album of Fashions and Fabrics* (London: Thames & Hudson, 1987).

7 The phrasing is borrowed from the title of Shepard, *Accounting for Oneself*.

8 Arlene Leis, 'Displaying Art and Fashion: Ladies' Pocket-Book Imagery in the Paper Collections of Sarah Sophia Banks', *Journal of Art History* 82, no. 3 (2013): 252–71. On collecting, see also Kim Sloan and Andrew M. Burnett, *Enlightenment: Discovering the World in the Eighteenth Century* (London: British Museum Press, 2003); Arthur MacGregor, *Curiosity and Enlightenment: Collectors and Collections from the Sixteenth to the Nineteenth Century* (London: Yale University Press, 2007); Joan Michèle Coutu, *Then and Now: Collecting and Classicism in Eighteenth-Century England* (London: McGill-Queen's University Press, 2015).

9 The album is considered alongside the extensive archival materials of the Johnson family, held in the Bodleian, Northampton Archives and Lincoln Archives, as well as Jane Johnson's pedagogical materials, held in the Lilly Library, Indiana University.

10 The family history is told across numerous family trees and charts. See BOD: MS Don, c. 190, fols. 34–5 and 192, fols. 108–17; LA: JOHNSON/1/3.

11 Witham Hall is now a boarding school, and a feeder school for Eton. Woolsey Johnson was a supporter of the enclosure of the land at Witham-on-the-Hill. See G. E. Mingay, *Parliamentary Enclosure in England: An Introduction to Its Causes, Incidence, and Impact, 1750–1850* (Abingdon: Routledge, 2014), 61.

12 For an 1808 watercolour of the Great House at Olney, see LA: JOHNSON/3/1, f. 4.

13 Susan Whyman, *Pen and the People: English Letter Writers, 1660–1800* (Oxford: Oxford University Press, 2011), 162.

14 BOD: MS Don c 190, f. 21.

15 BOD: MS Don, c. 190, f. 19. This aligns Jane Johnson with the concept of the 'incorporated wife'. See Susanna Rabow-Edling, *Married to the Empire: Three Governors' Wives in Russian America 1829–1864* (Fairbanks: University of Alaska Press, 2015), 174; Hilary Callan and Shirley Ardene, *The Incorporated Wife* (London: Croom Helm, 1984).

16 Whyman, *Pen and the People*, 167.

17 BOD: MS Don. c. 190, f. 15.

18 Frederick died as a child in 1743, but all the other brothers lived into adulthood.

19 For more on the civic and financial independence of single women, see Amy M. Froide, *Never Married: Singlewomen in Early Modern England* (Oxford: Oxford University Press, 2005), 117–53.

20 NA: PROB 11/844/305. This was this equivalent of £175,000 in terms of spending power. Conversion calculated using the National Archives' currency converter, http://www.nationalarchives.gov.uk/currency-converter.

21 Froide, *Never Married*, 3.

22 See in particular work which relies on household inventories, such as Lorna Weatherill, 'Consumer Behaviour, Textiles and Dress in the Late Seventeenth and Early Eighteenth Centuries', *Textile History* 22, no. 2 (1991): 297–310; Weatherill, *Consumer Behaviour*.

23 For work on the never-married woman, see Judith M. Bennett and Amy M. Froide, eds., *Singlewomen in the European Past, 1250–1800* (Philadelphia: University of Pennsylvania Press, 1999); Froide, *Never Married*; David Hussey and Margaret Ponsonby, *The Single Homemaker and Material Culture in the Long Eighteenth Century* (London and New York: Routledge, 2016).

24 BOD: MS Don. c. 193, f. 11; Jan de Vries 'industrious revolution' model, for instance, does not take single women into account. See *The Industrious Revolution: Consumer Behaviour and the Household Economy, 1650–Present* (Cambridge: Cambridge University Press, 2008).

25 Gertrude Savile, *Secret Comment: The Diaries of Gertrude Savile, 1721–1757*, ed. Alan Saville (Kingsbridge: Kingsbridge History Society, 1997).

26 William Craven, the 6th Baron Craven's son, would be created the 1st Earl of Craven in 1801.

27 Paula R. Backscheider, *Eighteenth-Century Women Poets and Their Poetry: Inventing Agency, Inventing Genre* (Baltimore: Johns Hopkins University Press, 2005), 31.

28 This was common practice for never-married women. See Froide, *Never Married*, 44–86.

29 Johnson's address in Bath was the eminently fashionable 22 Queen's Square. See BOD, MS Don. c. 191, f. 75.

30 Wodhull was spelt interchangeably, sometimes appearing as Woodhull or Woodhall.

31 For work on surrogate kinship, see Froide, *Never Married*, 71.

32 See, for example, Michael Wodhull, *Poems* (London: W. Bower and J. Nichols, 1772).

33 Abraham Swan, *The British Architect* (London, 1750).

34 Natalie Rothstein, 'The Family and the Album', in *Barbara Johnson's Album of Fashions and Fabrics*, ed. Natalie Rothstein (London: Thames & Hudson, 1987), 9–17.

35 NA: PROB 11/1695/80.

36 This is the equivalent of £13,725 in terms of purchasing power. Conversion calculated using the National Archives' currency converter, http://www.nationalarchives.gov.uk/currency-converter.

37 Quoted in Rothstein, 'The Family and the Album', 14.

38 Evelyn Arizpe, Morag Styles, and Shirley Brice Heath, *Reading Lessons from the Eighteenth Century: Mothers, Children and Texts* (Lichfield: Pied Piper Publishing, 2006), 25; Amy M. Froide, *Silent Partners: Women as Public Investors during Britain's Financial Revolution, 1690–1750* (Oxford: Oxford University Press, 2017).

39 BOD: MS Don. c. 193, f. 1.

40 Froide, *Never Married*, 63.

41 LLIU: LMC 1649.

42 Elizabeth Bennis, *The Journal of Elizabeth Bennis, 1749–1779*, ed. Rosemary Raughter (Dublin: Columba Press, 2007); Emma Major, *Madam Britannia: Women, Church, and Nation, 1712–1812* (Oxford: Oxford University Press, 2011); Misty G. Anderson, *Imagining Methodism in Eighteenth-Century Britain: Enthusiasm, Belief, and the Borders of the Self* (Baltimore: Johns Hopkins University Press, 2012).

43 BOD: MS Don. c. 190, ff. 11–12. For examples of Johnson's cut paper work, see BOD: MS Don.c.190, ff. 5–6.

44 BOD: MS Don. c. 190, ff. 11–12.

45 Rabow-Edling, *Married to the Empire*, 174; Callan and Ardene, *The Incorporated Wife*.

46 BOD: MS Don. c. 190, f. 19.

47 LLIU: LMC 1649; Victor Watson, 'Jane Johnson: A Very Pretty Story to Tell Children', in *Opening the Nursery Door: Reading, Writing, and Childhood, 1600–1900*, ed. Mary Hilton, Morag Styles, and Victor Watson (London: Routledge, 1997), 31–46.

48 François Fénelon and George Hickes, *Instructions for the Education of a Daughter Done into English, and Revised by Dr George Hickes* (London: James Reid, 1713).

49 See, for example, VAM: T.360:1-3-1998.

50 Arianne Baggerman, 'The Moral of the Story: Children's Reading and the Catechism of Nature around 1800', in *Making Knowledge in Early Modern Europe: Practices, Objects, and Texts, 1400–1800*, ed. Pamela H. Smith and Benjamin Schmidt (London: University of Chicago Press, 2007), 143–63.

51 LLIU: LMC 1649, Set 5.

52 'Pelf' meaning money, usually gained in a dishonest or dishonourable way.

53 LLIU: LMC, Set 19, no. 4. Michael Lally was a dancer and actor. See *London Daily Post*, 11 April 1743.

54 LLUI: LMC, Set 19, no. 2 and 5. Although the surname of the Earls of Peterborough was Morduant, this does not seem to correlate with a specific member of the family.

55 These books are discussed in Chapter 5.

56 John Locke, *The Works of John Locke*, vol. 8 (London: Rivington, 1824), 199–201.

57 *The Important Pocket Book* (London: John Newbery, 1765), 1.

58 John Newbery, *The Ladies Compleat Pocket Book* (London: John Newbery, 1753), 2. We know that Johnson purchased John Newbery pocket books, as their fashion plates appear pasted into the album.

59 For more on the pocket book, see Jennie Batchelor, 'Fashion and Frugality: Eighteenth-Century Pocket Books for Women', *Studies in Eighteenth Century Culture* 32 (2003): 1–18.

60 Watson, 'Jane Johnson', 32.

61 VAM: T.219-1973, f. 2. Pocket book fashion plates are discussed further in Chapter 3.

62 Barbara Johnson records only fashionable outer garments. She does not include stays, shifts or other smaller items.

63 Madeleine Ginsburg, 'Barbara Johnson and Fashion', in *Barbara Johnson's Album of Fashions and Fabrics*, ed. Natalie Rothstein (London: Thames and Hudson, 1987), 21.

64 LLUI: LMC, Set 19, no. 2 and 5.

65 See, for example, VAM: T.696&A-1913.

66 Clare Rose, *Children's Clothes Since 1750* (London: Batsford, 1989), 35.

67 VAM: T.219-1973, f. 4.

68 Rothstein, 'The Family and the Album', 16.

69 VAM, T.219-1973, f. 7.

70 See, for example, Alice Dolan, 'The Fabric of Life: Time and Textiles in an Eighteenth-Century Plebeian Home', *Home Cultures* 11, no. 3 (2014): 353–74.

71 Amanda Vickery, 'His and Hers: Gender, Consumption and Household Accounting in Eighteenth-Century England', *Past & Present* 1 (2006): 12–38.

72 *Harris's Original British Ladies Complete Pocket Memorandum Book* (London: J. W. Pasham, 1782), 4.

73 On credit, see Margot Finn, *The Character of Credit: Personal Debt in English Culture, 1740–1914* (Cambridge: Cambridge University Press, 2003); Anne L. Murphy, *The Origins of English Financial Markets: Investment and Speculation before the South Sea Bubble* (Cambridge: Cambridge University Press, 2009); Carl Wennerlind, *Casualties of Credit: The English Financial Revolution, 1620–1720* (Cambridge, MA: Harvard University Press, 2011).

74 Finn, *The Character of Credit*, 21.

75 Norfolk Record Office: WLS/LI/12/427. Baron Walsingham was a British peer and politician who served as Groom of the Bedchamber to George III from 1771–1777.

76 West Sussex Record Office: PHA/7558. The Earl was a peer and great patron of the arts. He had numerous mistresses and was rumoured to have over forty illegitimate children.

77 YCA: Acc. 203.

78 Centre for Buckinghamshire Studies: D-X827.

79 BOD: MS Don. c. 193, fol. 9.

80 Whyman, *Pen and the People: English Letter Writers, 1660–1800.*, 172–73.

81 Josiah Hort, *Sixteen Sermons by Josiah, Lord Bishop of Kilmore and Ardagh* (Dublin: George Grierson, 1738), 252.

82 Margot Finn has explored consumer control in relation to middle-class perception of plebeian debt in the nineteenth century in 'Working-Class Women and the Contest for Consumer Control in Victorian County Courts', *Past & Present*, no. 161 (1998): 116–54; see also Shepard, *Accounting for Oneself*, 278.

83 Adam Walker, *A Complete System of Family Book-Keeping* (London: T. Kinnersly, 1758), 4–5.

84 BOD: MS. Don. c. 190, ff. 103–18.

85 BOD: MS. Don. e. 193. Johnson's commonplace book is also discussed in Elspeth Jajdelska, *Speech, Print and Decorum in Britain, 1600–1750: Studies in Social Rank and Communication* (Abindgdon: Routledge, 2016), 184.

86 BOD: MS. Don. e. 194–98.

87 BOD: MS. Don. c. 193, f. 19.

88 Many of these were preserved by later generations of the family. See LA: JOHNSON/3/1.

89 See, for example, BL: Add MS 22257-22262.

90 Anne Sykes' 'dress diary' is in a private collection. For Anne Hayslip's album, see CW: Acc. No. 2016-124 (S). For the Hardy fabric samples, see Dorset County Museum: 1941.7.87. See also Lucy Johnston, 'Clothing in Context: Nineteenth-Century Dress and Textiles in the Thomas Hardy Archive', *Costume* 52, no. 2 (2018): 261–84.

91 See HRP: HRP12857-9; HRP01728-34.

92 Kimberly Chrisman-Campbell, *Fashion Victims: Dress at the Court of Louis XVI and Marie-Antoinette* (London: Yale University Press, 2015), 100–101.

93 On scrapbooks, see Ellen Gruber Garvey, *Writing with Scissors: American Scrapbooks from the Civil War to the Harlem Renaissance* (Oxford: Oxford University Press, 2012); Louise Williams, '"To Amuse for an Hour"? Materiality, Femininity and Performance in the Scrapbook of Lady Maxwell', *Scottish Archives* 19 (2013): 106–18.

94 Beverly Lemire, *Fashion's Favourite: The Cotton Trade and the Consumer in Britain, 1660–1800* (Oxford: Oxford University Press, 1991), 111.

95 Arlene Leis, 'Displaying Art and Fashion'.

96 NA: ZB0702/02.

97 Ulinka Rublack and Maria Hayward, eds., *The First Book of Fashion: The Books of Clothes of Matthäus & Veit Konrad Schwarz of Augsburg* (London: Bloomsbury, 2015).

98 LA: JOHNSON/1/3.

99 Garvey, *Writing with Scissors*, 2.

100 On quilts, see Elaine Hedges, 'The Nineteenth-Century Diarist and Her Quilts', *Feminist Studies* 8, no. 2 (1982): 293–99; Laura Horton, *Mary Black's Family Quilts: Memory and Meaning in Everyday Life* (Columbia: University of South Carolina Press, 2005); Janet Floyd, 'Back into Memory Land? Quilts and the Problem of History', *Women's Studies* 37, no. 1 (2007): 38–56; Mara Witzling, 'Quilt Language: Towards a Poetics of Quilting', *Women's History Review* 18, no. 4 (2009): 619–37.

101 Janet Floyd, 'Back into Memory Land?', 38.

102 John Styles, *The Dress of the People: Everyday Fashion in Eighteenth-Century England* (London: Yale University Press, 2007), 115–19; John Styles, *Threads of Feeling: The London Foundling Hospital's Textile Tokens, 1740–1770* (London: Foundling Museum, 2010); Alice Dolan, 'Touching Linen: Textiles, Emotion and Bodily Intimacy in England C. 1708–1818', *Cultural and Social History* 16, no. 2 (2019): 145–164.

103 BOD: MS. Don. c. 193, f. 13; 191, f. 74.

104 Lemire also notes this shift in Johnson's consumption, see Lemire, *Fashion's Favourite*, 112.

105 Giorgio Riello and Tirthankar Roy, eds., *How India Clothes the World: The World of South Asian Textiles, 1500–1850* (Leiden: BRILL, 2009), 10.

106 Lemire, *Fashion's Favourite*, 97; Beverly Lemire, ed., *The Force of Fashion in Politics and Society* (Farnham: Ashgate, 2010), 78; Giorgio Riello, *Cotton: The Fabric That Made the Modern World* (Cambridge: Cambridge University Press, 2013), 124.

107 Lemire, *Fashion's Favourite*, 112.

108 Quoted in Will Bowden, *Industrial Society in England Towards the End of the Eighteenth Century* (London: Frank Cass, 1965), 115.

109 VAM: T.219-1973, f. 29.

110 BOD: MS. Don. c. 192, f. 93.

111 BOD: MS. Don. c. 191, ff. 120–25 and 192, ff. 1–45.

112 *The Repository of Arts, Literature, Commerce, Manufactures, Fashions, and Politics* (London, 1809), I, 58.

113 For more on Ackermann and the 'patterns of British manufacture', see Serena Dyer, 'Fashioning Consumers: Ackermann's Repository of Arts and the Cultivation of the Female Consumer', in *Women's Periodicals and Print Culture in Britain, 1690–1820s*, ed. Jennie Batchelor and Manushag N. Powell (Edinburgh: Edinburgh University Press, 2018), 474–87. On the inclusion of similar pages in the *Lady's Magazine*, see Chloe Wigston Smith, 'Fast Fashion: Style, Text, and Image in Late Eighteenth-Century Women's Periodicals', in *Women's Periodicals and Print Culture in Britain, 1690–1820s*, ed. Jennie Batchelor and Manushag N. Powell (Edinburgh: Edinburgh University Press, 2018), 440–57.

114 *The Repository of Arts*, I, 58.

115 *The Repository of Arts*, I, 58.

116 For more on the gift, see Linda Zionkowski, *Women and Gift Exchange in Eighteenth-Century Fiction: Richardson, Burney, Austen* (London: Routledge, 2016), 131. For further work on the nature of gift giving, see Alan Schrift, *The Logic of the Gift: Toward an Ethic of Generosity* (London: Routledge, 1997); Marcel Mauss, *The Gift: The Form and Reason for Exchange in Archaic Societies* (Abingdon: Routledge, 2002); C. Klekar, ed., *The Culture of the Gift in Eighteenth-Century England* (London: Palgrave Macmillan, 2009).

117 VAM: T.219-1973, f. 8.

118 BOD: MS Don. c. 192, f. 52.

119 Amanda Vickery, 'Mutton Dressed as Lamb? Fashioning Age in Georgian England', *Journal of British Studies* 52 (2013): 858–86.

120 VAM: T.219-1973, f. 45, 55, 75.

121 For more on regency fashion, see Hilary Davidson, *Dress in the Age of Jane Austen: Regency Fashion* (London: Yale University Press, 2019).

122 On recycling and reuse, see Ariane Fennetaux, Amélie Junqua, and Sophie Vasset, eds., *The Afterlife of Used Things: Recycling in the Long Eighteenth Century* (London: Routledge, 2014).

123 BOD: MS. Don. c. 193, f. 14.

124 BOD: MS. Don. c. 193, f. 30.

125 BOD: MS. Don. c. 193, f. 36.

126 Johnson also occasionally inserted other prints from pocket books, including book illustrations, portraits of significant people and engravings of country houses. Some of the later prints date from after Johnson's death, and were likely added to the album by her nieces.

127 Leis, 'Displaying Art and Fashion', 252.

128 Catherine Hutton, *Reminiscences of a Gentlewoman of the Last Century*, ed. C. H. Beale (Birmingham: Cornish Brothers, 1891), 214. For White's album, see Manchester City Galleries: 1987.29.

129 VAM: T.219-1973, f. 16.

130 For more detail about this style, see Chapter 5.

131 VAM: T.219-1973, f. 11.

132 VAM: T.219-1973, f. 8.

Chapter 3

1 Although there is a single 1759 example of a fashion plate in a periodical, their rise is usually charted from 1770. The development of the periodical press has been charted in Alison Adburgham, *Women in Print: Writing Women and Women's Magazines from the Restoration to the Accession of Victoria* (London: Allen and Unwin, 1972); Katherine Shevelow, *Women and Print Culture: The Construction of Femininity in the Early Periodical* (Abingdon: Routledge, 1989); Margaret Beetham, *A Magazine of Her Own?: Domesticity and Desire in the Women's Magazine, 1800–1914* (Abingdon: Routledge, 1996).

2 Ann Frankland Lewis' father, Admiral Sir Thomas Frankland, had sold her childhood home of Kirby House in Inkpen, Berkshire in 1771. He had inherited the baronetcy, and Thirkleby Hall with it, upon his brother's death in 1768. Lewis became her surname upon marriage. Yorkshire Archaeological Society: DD94, box 2 and box 4.

3 A compere front is a gown with an attached stomacher which is buttoned down the centre, rather than a separate stomacher pinned to the stays and the gown.

4 Engageantes are the lace or embroidered muslin ruffles which are tacked to the ends of sleeves.

5 While there are hints within the paintings that these are self-portraits, there is no conclusive evidence. However, there is clear evidence that the images relate closely to events in Lewis' life. As such, 'self-representation' is used throughout this chapter to describe the watercolours.

6 NLW: Harpton Court Papers, 2373–80, 4068, 4070.

7 The Frankland family's holdings are detailed in Yorkshire Archaeological Society: DD94.

8 John Charnock, *Biographia Navalis: Or, Impartial Memoirs of the Lives and Characters of Officers of the Navy of Great Britain* (London: R. Faulder, 1797), 18.

9 TNA: PRO, ADM 36/525 Chatham, 3395 Scarborough, 4735 York.

10 *Boston Post*, 20 June 1743.

11 Simon Smith, *Slavery, Family, and Gentry Capitalism in the British Atlantic: The World of the Lascelles, 1648–1834* (Cambridge: Cambridge University Press, 2006), 114. Conversion calculated using the National Archives' currency converter, http://www.nationalarchives.gov.uk/currency-converter.

12 Important work is being done to find and tell the stories of enslaved people. See, for example, Marisa J. Fuentes, *Dispossessed Lives: Enslaved Women, Violence, and the Archive* (Philadelphia: University of Pennsylvania Press, 2016).

13 Smith, *Slavery, Family, and Gentry Capitalism in the British Atlantic*, 122.

14 The correspondence of Sir Thomas Frankland and Sir Joseph Banks is held by the Royal Botanic Gardens, Kew, Library and Archives: GB 0068 JBK/1.

15 This information has been compiled from evidence in NLW: Harpton Court Papers and Yorkshire Archaeological Society: DD94, in particular NLW: Harpton Court Papers, 2342.

16 NLW: Harpton Court Papers, 2352–2356.

17 Jane Rendell, *The Pursuit of Pleasure: Gender, Space & Architecture in Regency London* (London: Athlone, 2002), 97.

18 University of Nottingham Archives and Special Collections: Portland (Welbeck) Collection, Pw F 5286; NLW: Harpton Court Papers, C95-97.

19 Ian Haywood, '"A Metropolis in Flames and a Nation in Ruins": The Gordon Riots as Sublime Spectacle', in *The Gordon Riots: Politics, Culture and Insurrection in Late Eighteenth-Century Britain*, ed. Ian Haywood and John Seed (Cambridge: Cambridge University Press, 2012), 117–43.

20 NLW: Harpton Court Papers, C230.

21 NLW: Harpton Court Papers, C337.

22 NLW: Harpton Court Papers, 2546.

23 Ann Frankland Lewis memorialized her mother's passing by sequentially listing all of her mother's children and grandchildren, mimicking and feminizing the family pedigrees which litter the Lewis and Frankland archives. NLW: Harpton Court Papers, 2389, 2390.

24 NLW: Harpton Court Papers, 2364.

25 For more on consumption in this period, see Carolyn Day, *Consumptive Chic: A History of Beauty, Fashion, and Disease* (London: Bloomsbury, 2017).

26 NLW: Harpton Court Papers, C341.

27 David R. Green and Alastair Owens, 'Gentlewomanly Capitalism? Spinsters, Widows, and Wealth Holding in England and Wales, c. 1800–1860', *The Economic History Review* 56, no. 3 (2003): 513.

28 Gloucestershire Archives: P78/1 IN 1/26.

29 Ann Frankland Lewis' grandson Sir George Cornewall Lewis (1806–1863), for instance, was Chancellor of the Exchequer, Home Secretary and a scholar of linguistics.

30 The 1841 census shows that the two independent women also retained one male and three female live-in servants. Class: HO107; Piece: 353; Book: 6; Civil Parish: Cheltenham; County: Gloucestershire; Enumeration District: 12; Folio: 58; Page: 29; Line: 1; GSU roll: 288767.

31 Gloucestershire Archives: P78/4 IN 1/8; NA: PROB 1, piece 1966.

32 Her adoption of the conceit of using '*fecit*' after her name on the watercolours explicitly linked them to the standard modes of print culture.

33 Chloe Wigston Smith, 'Fast Fashion: Style, Text, and Image in Late Eighteenth-Century Women's Periodicals', in *Women's Periodicals and Print Culture in Britain, 1690–1820s*, ed. Jennie Batchelor and Manushag N. Powell (Edinburgh: Edinburgh University Press, 2018), 440–57.

34 *Lady's Magazine* (London, 1773), 199–200.

35 For the extensive literature on fashion plates, see Doris Langley Moore, *Fashion through Fashion Plates, 1771–1970* (London: Ward Lock, 1971); Vyvyan Holland, *Hand Coloured Fashion Plates, 1770–1899* (London: Batsford, 1988); Catherine Flood and Sarah Grant, *Style and Satire: Fashion in Print, 1777–1927* (London: Victoria and Albert Museum, 2014); April Calahan, *Fashion Plates: 150 Years of Style*, ed. Karen Trivette Cannell (London: Yale University Press, 2015).

36 This would not be addressed until Rudolph Ackermann's inclusion of fabric samples in his periodical, *Repository of Arts*, in 1809. The corresponding fashion plates sometimes showed these fabrics made up into garments. See Serena Dyer, 'Fashioning Consumers: Ackermann's *Repository of Arts* and the Cultivation of the Female Consumer', in *Women's Periodicals and Print Culture in Britain, 1690–1820s*, ed. Jennie Batchelor and Manushag N. Powell (Edinburgh: Edinburgh University Press, 2018), 474–87.

37 Timothy Campbell, *Historical Style: Fashion and the New Mode of History, 1740–1830* (Philadelphia: University of Pennsylvania Press, 2016), 63.

38 Similar serialized prints of dress had appeared separately to periodicals and pocket books. For example, John June engraved a series of images depicting the months through fashion in 1749, as did Robert Deighton in 1781. See British Museum: 1850,1109.29-39 and 2010,7081.393-403.

39 Anne Hollander, *Seeing Through Clothes* (Los Angeles: University of California Press, 1993), 311.

40 Felicity Nussbaum, *The Autobiographical Subject: Gender and Ideology in Eighteenth-Century England* (London: Johns Hopkins University Press, 1989), xiii.

41 'Dishabille', meaning the state of being only partly or scantily clothed, was usually used as a term for informal and everyday garments.

42 Calahan, *Fashion Plates*, 6.

43 Due to the change in Lewis' signature from her maiden to married name in 1778, we can be confident that the watercolours were indeed painted during the year they depict.

44 For a reflection on the cross-cultural nature of the fashion plate, see Peter McNeil and Patrik Steorn, 'The Medium of Print and the Rise of Fashion in the West', *Journal of Art History* 82, no. 3 (2013): 135–56.

45 For further discussion, see Lynn Festa, 'Person, Animal, Thing: The 1796 Dog Tax and the Right to Superfluous Things', *Eighteenth-Century Life* 33 (2009): 1–44; Ingrid H. Tague, *Animal Companions: Pets and Social Change in Eighteenth-Century Britain* (Pennsylvania: Pennsylvania State University Press, 2015).

46 MFA: 44.1468 and 44.1587.

47 Calahan, *Fashion Plates*, 32.

48 Susanne Schmid, 'Mary Berry's "Fashionable Friends" (1801) on Stage', *The Wordsworth Circle* 43 (2012): 172–77.

49 The album is now in a private collection, but one scene has been reproduced within Patrick Elliot, *Cut and Paste: 400 Years of Collage* (Edinburgh: National Galleries Scotland, 2019), 59.

50 The original design for this plate by Thomas Uwins was sold by Kerry Taylor Auctions on 17 June 2019, lot 36. It is more delicate in style and treatment than the watercolour in Figure 3.19 and it is painted on a different weight and quality of paper. I am confident it is not by the same hand.

51 Ann Bermingham, *Learning to Draw: Studies in the Cultural History of a Polite and Useful Art* (London: Yale University Press, 2000), 149–55.

52 Examples of crudely coloured fashion plates are widespread. For an especially extensive collection of such images, see Hereford Museum: 9371.

53 Bermingham, *Learning to Draw*, xi.

54 George Brookshaw, *A New Treatise on Flower Painting, or, Every Lady Her Own Drawing Master* (London: Longman, 1816).

55 Amanda Vickery, 'The Theory and Practice of Female Accomplishment', in *Mrs Delany and Her Circle*, ed. Mark Laird and Alicia Weisberg-Roberts (London: Yale University Press, 2009), 94.

56 Bermingham, *Learning to Draw*, 183.

57 Maria Edgeworth and Richard Lovell Edgeworth, *Practical Education* (London, 1798), 182.

58 Beth Fowkes Tobin and Maureen Daly Goggin, 'Introduction: Materializing Women', in *Women & Things, 1750–1950: Gendered Material Strategies*, ed. Maureen Daly Goggin and Beth Fowkes Tobin (Aldershot: Ashgate, 2009), 1–14; Amanda Vickery, *Behind Closed Doors: At Home in Georgian England* (London: Yale University Press, 2009), 231–56.

59 Bermingham, *Learning to Draw*, 197–227; Kim Sloan, *'A Noble Art': Amateur Artists and Drawing Masters, c. 1600–1800* (London: British Museum, 2000); Noel Riley, *The Accomplished Lady: A History of Genteel Pursuits, c. 1660–1860* (Huddersfield: Oblong, 2017), 263–99.

60 Rozsika Parker, *The Subversive Stitch: Embroidery and the Making of the Feminine* (London: I B Tauris, 2010).

61 Bermingham, *Learning to Draw*, 184.

62 Colin Harrison, *John Malchair of Oxford: Artist and Musician* (Oxford: Ashmolean Museum, 1998).

63 The portraits are now held by The Chequers Trust as a private collection.

64 See Beinecke Library, Yale: 11861218.

65 Stephen Lloyd and Kim Sloan, *The Intimate Portrait: Drawings, Miniatures and Pastels from Ramsay to Lawrence* (Edinburgh: National Galleries Scotland, 2008), 176.

66 Sloan, *A Noble Art*, 245–48.

67 Bermingham, *Learning to Draw*, 128.

68 Alexandra Loske, *Colour: A Visual History* (London: Tate Publishing, 2019), 32.

69 Cindy McCreery, *The Satirical Gaze: Prints of Women in Late Eighteenth-Century England* (Oxford: Oxford University Press, 2004), 171.

70 Bermingham, *Learning to Draw*, 127.

71 John Ford, *Ackermann, 1783–1983* (London: Ackermann, 1983), 23.

72 Bermingham, *Learning to Draw*, 183.

73 *La Belle Assemblée* (London, 1812), 100.

74 Ibid., 265.

75 Hannah Robertson, *The Young Ladies School of Arts* (Edinburgh, 1767), vii.

76 For more on knitting for children, see Riley, *The Accomplished Lady*, 186.

77 These items are referred to as 'sattin prints' and 'medallions' in contemporary advertisements. Medallions can refer to either the printed or painted images on silk satin fabric.

78 For an extensive discussion of satin prints, see Elisabeth Gernerd, 'Têtes to Tails: Eighteenth-Century Underwear and Accessories in Britain and Colonial America' (PhD Thesis, University of Edinburgh, 2015), 190–200.

79 See, for example, *Morning Herald and Daily Advertiser*, 14 February 1783. Extensive work has been undertaken by Gernerd to identify advertisements for satin prints. See *Têtes to Tails*, 194. For a trade card mentioning satin prints, see an advertisement for Daniel Orme, who listed 'sattin prints, & medallions' amongst his wares in 1792–97. Yale Center for British Art: Z232.O76. Satin prints could also be used to make accessories such as silk drawstring bags. See VAM: T.44-1948.

80 Examples have been identified in the collection of the Victoria and Albert Museum, the Museum of Fine Arts, Boston, Colonial Williamsburg and the Albany Institute.

81 Gernerd, 'Têtes to Tails', 192–200. For other satin prints intended for items like muffs, see CW: 1958-33–36.

82 CW: 1958-25.

83 John Styles, *The Dress of the People: Everyday Fashion in Eighteenth-Century England* (London: Yale University Press, 2007), 104. For an example of Hope on jewellery, see Royal Museums Greenwich: JEW0204 and JEW0267.

84 I have not been able to identify any work boxes advertised with the satin prints pre-attached.

85 A visually similar image of a woman wearing a large hat can be seen on a satin print which adorns the muff in the 'Winter' print in Robert Sayer' 1785 Four Seasons. BM: 2010,7081.474.

86 Tim Clayton, *The English Print, 1688–1802* (London: Yale University Press, 1997), 246. For a silk print for making an embroidered map, see VAM: T.20-1929.

87 The 'town', which occupied the space between Holbourn and Hyde Park, had developed throughout the eighteenth century. See Hannah Greig, *The Beau Monde: Fashionable Society in Georgian London* (Oxford: Oxford University Press, 2013), 9.

88 In 1798 Lewis did record purchasing a ticket to the exclusive Almack's, implying that she had made it onto the 'list'. NLW: Harpton Court Papers: 2546 f4.

89 NLW: Harpton Court Papers, C345.

90 NLW: Harpton Court Papers, 2517.

91 Hannah Greig, 'Dressing for Court: Sartorial Politics and Fashion News in the Age of Mary Delany', in *Mrs Delany and Her Circle*, ed. Mark Laird and Alicia Weisberg-Roberts (London: Yale University Press, 2009),

80–93, 91. In 1809, on a visit to her sister Mary in Ireland, Lewis felt qualified to pass judgement on the dress worn at the Irish court. She wrote that 'the ladies trimmings, feathers, & finery were chiefly very clumsy & shabby'. NLW: Harpton Court Papers, 2344 f18.

92 NLW: Harpton Court Papers, 2352–2356, 2358, 2517.

93 Hallie Rubenhold, *Lady Worsley's Whim: An Eighteenth-Century Tale of Sex, Scandal and Divorce* (London: Random House, 2011), 24.

94 For a history of the eighteenth-century riding habit, see Cally Blackman, 'Walking Amazons: The Development of the Riding Habit in England during the Eighteenth Century', *Costume* 35, no. 1 (2001): 47–58.

95 The only major differences are the black neck cloth depicted in Lewis' watercolour, and that Lewis painted black rather than ivory shoes.

96 *London Chronicle*, 18 July 1778. Both Fleming and Cavendish are regularly associated with this military style of dress. See McCreery, *The Satirical Gaze*, 165–67.

97 Matthew McCormack, *Embodying the Militia in Georgian England* (Oxford: Oxford University Press, 2015), 66–68.

98 McCreery, *The Satirical Gaze*, 142. See also Linda Colley, *Britons: Forging the Nation, 1707–1837* (London: Yale University Press, 1992), 247–54; .

99 Frances Burney, *Diary and Letters of Madame D'Arblay*, ed. Charlotte Barret (London, 1842), 192.

100 Greig, *The Beau Monde*, 127.

101 Louisa Stuart, *Gleanings from an Old Portfolio, 1785–1799*, ed. Godfrey Clark, vol. 2 (Edinburgh: D. Douglas, 1895), 133.

102 There is no guest list or similar account of all those who attended the ball. However, given that the garment is recorded in such accurate detail, Lewis' connections to parliament and other evidence of her social circle, it is difficult to imagine that she was not present.

103 Lewis did also retain tickets to assemblies on 24 February 1777 and 8 August 1808 that, perhaps, held particular significance to her. See NLW: Harpton Court Papers, 2359.

104 See, for instance, the very varied examples included in Stephanie Downes, Sally Holloway, and Sarah Randles, eds., *Feeling Things: Objects and Emotions through History* (Oxford: Oxford University Press, 2018).

105 NA: PROB 11, piece 1477. I have identified four of these paintings. The portraits of Sir Thomas Frankland (fifth baronet), Sir Thomas Frankland (sixth baronet), Lady Dorothy Frankland (wife of the sixth baronet) and Lady Roche (born Mary Frankland) were sold by auction in the late 1990s. Portraits of Lady Sarah Frankland (wife of the fifth baronet) and those of her daughters Harriet, Dinah, Katharine, Charlotte, William, Roger and Ann Frankland Lewis herself are also mentioned in the will, but I have been unable to trace these.

106 Frances Borzello, *Seeing Ourselves: Women's Self-Portraits* (London: Thames and Hudson, 1998), 22, 121–22.

107 Marcia Pointon, *Strategies for Showing: Women, Possession, and Representation in English Visual Culture 1665–1800* (Oxford: Oxford University Press, 1997), 7.

108 Jules David Prown, 'The Truth of Material Culture', in *American Artifacts: Essays in Material Culture* (East Lansing: Michigan State University Press, 2000), 1–19, 6.

109 For a discussion of fashion and selfhood, see Dror Wahrman, *The Making of the Modern Self: Identity and Culture in Eighteenth-Century England* (London: Yale University Press, 2004), 59–69, 318.

110 Prown, 'The Truth of Material Culture', 6.

111 Lou Taylor, *Mourning Dress: A Costume and Social History* (London: George Allen and Unwin, 1983). For work on the material practices of mourning, see Maureen Daly Goggin and Beth Fowkes Tobin, eds., *Women and the Material Culture of Death* (Aldershot: Ashgate, 2009).

112 My thanks to Seymore Ayers for raising this possible connection. Although this image at first appears to be an engraving, rather than a watercolour, the etched appearance is in fact achieved with pencil. My thanks for Hannah Lyons and Sarah Grant for this identification.

113 For more on cultures of rememberance, see Marcia Pointon, 'Materializing Mourning: Hair, Jewellery, and the Body', in *Material Memories*, ed. Marius Kwint, Jeremy Aynsley, and Christopher Breward (London: Bloomsbury, 1999), 39–71; Susan Stabile, *Memory's Daughters: The Material Culture of Remembrance in Eighteenth-Century America* (London: Cornell University Press, 2018).

114 For visual representations of widowhood, see the essays in Alison Levy, ed., *Widowhood and Visual Culture in Early Modern Europe* (London: Routledge, 2003).

115 For the commercial cultures around mourning, see Fennetaux, 'Fashioning Death/Gendering Sentiment'; for a study of mourning samplers, see Goggin, 'Stitching (in) Death'.

116 For an embroidered example of Kauffman's image, see VAM: 39-1874. For more on the practice of embroidered pictures, see Rosika Desnoyers, *Pictorial Embroidery in England: A Critical History of Needlepainting and Berlin Work* (London: Bloomsbury, 2019), 176.

117 For examples, see Art Institute Chicago: 2008.134; Cooper Hewitt: 1974-100-31; Slater Memorial Museum: 250-E-207.

118 Cooper Hewitt: 1974-72-6.

119 Goggin, 'Stitching (in) Death', 77.

120 For more on Linwood, see Heidi A. Strobel, 'Mary Linwood, Thomas Gainsborough, and the Art of Installation Embroidery', in *Materializing Gender in Eighteenth-Century Europe*, ed. Jennifer G. Germann and Heidi A. Strobel (London: Routledge, 2016), 173–91.

121 Lucy Aikin, 'On Miss Linwood's Admirable Pictures in Needle-work', *Monthly Magazine*, March 1798, 287.

122 See, for example, Mount Vernon: W-3614/A-D.

Chapter 4

1 All of Winn's paper archive, including that of her parents, is held by the West Yorkshire Archive Service, Wakefield, Yorkshire. Many of her material possessions are still in the collection of the National Trust at Nostell Priory, Wakefield, Yorkshire. Supplementary information was also found in Swiss birth and marriage records.

2 Work on the Winns includes Christopher Todd, 'A Swiss Milady in Yorkshire: Sabine Winn of Nostell Priory', *Yorkshire Archaeological Journal* 77 (2005): 205–24; Julie Day, *Elite Women's Household Management: Yorkshire, 1680–1810*, PhD Thesis, University of Leeds, 2007; Frances Sands, *Nostell Priory: History of a House, 1730–85*, PhD Thesis, University of York, 2012; Jane Elizabeth Troughton, *The Role of Music in the Yorkshire Country House, 1770–1850*, PhD Thesis, University of York, 2014; Kerry Bristol, 'A Tale of Two Sales: Sir Rowland Winn and No. 11 St James's Square, London, 1766–1787', *History of Retailing and Consumption* 2, no. 1 (2016): 9–24;

Kerry Bristol, 'Between the Exotic and the Everyday: Sabine Winn at Home 1765–1798', in *A Taste for Luxury in Early Modern Europe Display, Acquisition and Boundaries*, ed. Johanna Ilmakunnas and Jon Stobart (London: Bloomsbury, 2017), 161–78.

3 Kerry Bristol's extensive work on the Winns has examined Sabine Winn's role in the development of Nostell's interiors, as well as Winn's consumption practices. See Bristol, 'Between the Exotic and the Everyday'.

4 Usually confined to discussions of accomplishment, making within the country house has yet to be fully explored. For work on consumption in the country house, see Jon Stobart and Mark Rothery, *Consumption and the Country House* (Oxford: Oxford University Press, 2016).

5 Nostell is now known as Nostell Priory, but this ecclesiastical addition has only been used since the nineteenth century. Occasionally, Nostell also appears as Nostel.

6 See, for example, Todd, 'A Swiss Milady in Yorkshire', 207.

7 Papers relating to Sabine Winn's parents and first marriage are also held at WYAS. They came to Nostell after her parents' deaths.

8 She was baptized on 12 April 1734. The baptism record states that she was born at the end of March. Archives cantolales de Lausanne: Répetoire d'Etat civil, Registre Baptistaire 1722–1766, Eb 132/5, 222. A letter from Mary Winn to her brother Rowland declared 25 March as Sabine Winn's birthday. WYAS: WYW1352/1/1/5/5.

9 Sabine Winn dictated much of her family history to Shepley Watson, Nostell's agent, in 1791. See WYAS: WYW1352/1/1/6/11/5. The family surname is variably spelt Hervart or Herwart. I have followed the spellings generally used by each individual.

10 Further information about the Herwart/Hervart family can be found in Charles Wirz, ed., *Annales de La Société Jean-Jacques Rousseau* (Geneva: Librairie Jullien, 1992), 124.

11 WYAS: WYW1352/1/1/6/11/1, 18 April 1721.

12 Todd, 'A Swiss Milady in Yorkshire', 210. See also WYAS: WYW1352/1/1/7/21.

13 £70,000 was the equivalent of over £7,000,000 in 2017 in terms of spending power. Conversion calculated using the National Archives' currency converter, http://www.nationalarchives.gov.uk/currency-converter.

14 WYAS: WYW1352/1/1/4/27. Rowland's tutor, Isaac Dulon, recounted many details about life in Vevey to Rowland's father back at Nostell. Other English men in the town included Earl Cowper's son, Lord Fordwich. See Hertfordshire Archives: DE/P/F312/141.

15 For more on the grand tour, see Jeremy Black, *The British Abroad: The Grand Tour in the Eighteenth Century* (London: Sutton, 1997).

16 Todd, 'A Swiss Milady in Yorkshire', 207.

17 WYAS: WYW1352/1/1/7/7.

18 WYAS: WYW1352/1/1/6/2.

19 Todd, 'A Swiss Milady in Yorkshire', 206.

20 WYAS: WYW1352/1/4/24/19, May 1758. Translated from the French, '*qu'il n'était pas assez magnifique pour aller dans les compagnies*'.

21 WYAS: WYW1352/1/1/4/27, 19 October 1756. Translated from the French, '*petite affaire*'.

22 Ibid. Translated from the French, '*ce n'était qu'un amusement*' and '*un peu trop fait éclater son gout pour elle*'.

23 WYAS: WYW1352/1/1/7/18, 19 April 1759. Translated from the French, 'aurait abandonné son mari à ce triste sort de languir de sorte que probablement, et suivant le résultat de ses amis et connaissances ces chagrins lui ont à la fin coûté la vie'.

24 WYAS: WYW1352/1/4/3/7, May 1759.

25 WYAS: WYW1352/1/1/4/15, 28 November 1761.

26 WYAS: WYW1352/1/1/7/17.

27 Archives cantolales de Lausanne: Répetoire d'Etat civil, Registre de Mariage, Eb 132/5, no. 5, 111.

28 For a detailed study of the contents of the Winns' London house, see Bristol, 'A Tale of Two Sales'.

29 For example, the Countess of Strathmore and the Countess of Dundonald, who appear amongst her correspondents. See WYAS: WYW1352/1/1/6/18 and WYW1352/1/1/6/4. See also WYW1352/1/4/54/12, an invitation to Sabine Winn from Mrs Wharton.

30 WYAS: WYW1352/1/4/35/5, 19 August 1762.

31 The house was lent to the couple by the Marquis of Rockingham. Rowland was angered that his father did not immediately step aside for him and his new wife to take up residence at Nostell itself. Catherine Cappe, *Memoirs of the Late Mrs Catherine Cappe* (London, 1823), 97.

32 Ibid., 74.

33 Ibid., 75.

34 WYAS: WYW1352/1/4/11/8, 9 December 1763.

35 For more on Rowland Winn's political career and estate management, see Todd, 'A Swiss Milady in Yorkshire', 213.

36 WYAS: WYW1352/1/4/52/171, March 1763. Translated from the French, 'un de coins de l'univers les plus deserts et funestes'. WYAS: WYW1352/1/4/52/172, 1760s. Translated from the French, 'se nommer végéter comme une plante que comme une créature'.

37 WYAS: WYW1352/1/1/5/9, 3 April 1763.

38 For more on the history of Nostell's interiors, see Eileen Harris, *The Genius of Robert Adam: His Interiors* (London: Yale University Press, 2001), 199.

39 Bristol, 'A Tale of Two Sales'; for work on the material culture of the London elites, see Hannah Greig, *The Beau Monde: Fashionable Society in Georgian London* (Oxford: Oxford University Press, 2013).

40 Alastair Laing, 'Sir Rowland and Lady Winn: A Conversation Piece in the Library at Nostell Priory', *Apollo* 152, no. 458 (2000): 14–18.

41 All of these items survive in the Nostell collection. For the bookcases, see NT: NT 960961; for the paintings, see NT 960060, for the table, see NT 959723.

42 WYAS: WYW1352/1/4/11/15, 10 February 1763.

43 For a discussion of the Winn children, see Christopher Todd and Sophie Raikes, 'Love, Rebellion and Redemption: Three Generations of Women at Nostell Priory', in *Maids and Mistresses: Celebrating 300 Years of Woman and the Yorkshire Country House*, ed. Ruth M. Larson (York: Yorkshire Country House Partnership, 2004), 77–88, especially 83.

44 WYAS: WYW1352/1/1/6/13, 1770s.

45 For more on the emotional value of hair, see Sally Holloway, *The Game of Love in Georgian England: Courtship, Emotions, and Material Culture* (Oxford: Oxford University Press, 2019), 81–84.

46 Todd and Raikes, 'Love, Rebellion and Redemption', 93.

47 See, for example, *The Gentleman's Magazine* (London, 1785), 159; *Gazetteer and New Daily Advertiser*, 28 February 1785; *Leeds Intelligencer*, 1 March 1785.

48 Cappe, *Memoirs of the Late Mrs Catherine Cappe*, 158.

49 Todd suggests that the weather was particularly icy, and caused a carriage accident, although there is no archival confirmation of this. See 'A Swiss Milady in Yorkshire', 220. Cappe's account of Rowland Winn's mental state, and the family's dire financial situation, raises suicide as a possibility.

50 WYAS: WYW1352/1/4/25/21, 1790–1792.

51 WYAS: WYW1352/1/4/36/2–8, 10–13, 18, 1790s.

52 WYAS: WYW1352/1/1/4/18/21–30.

53 WYAS: WYW1352/1/4/36/7, 30 August 1797.

54 WYAS: WYW1352/1/1/9/10, February 1798.

55 Sabine Winn's interest in medicine and home remedies may have caused her to distrust 'James' powders', a combination of phosphate of lime and oxide of antimony, the validity of which was widely questioned. See, for example, *The Lady's Monthly Museum* (London, 1799), 408.

56 It was left to Shepley Watson to inform Esther. Watson stated that the illness was short. See WYAS: WYW1352/1/4/39/1, 17 September 1798.

57 The personal papers of the family alone amount to 4,298 items.

58 Todd, 'A Swiss Milady in Yorkshire', 224.

59 Chloe Wigston Smith's chapter on 'Paper Clothes' offers a particularly thorough exploration of this relationship. See *Women, Work and Clothes in the Eighteenth-Century Novel* (Cambridge: Cambridge University Press, 2013), 47–80.

60 Richard Hills, *Papermaking in Britain, 1488–1988* (London: Athlone, 1988).

61 *Métiers* translates as craft, trade or profession.

62 Smith, *Women, Work and Clothes*, 65.

63 Ibid.

64 Aside from Smith, see also Alice Dolan, 'An Adorned Print: Print Culture, Female Leisure and the Dissemination of Fashion in France and England, around 1660–1779', *V&A Online Journal* 3 (2011), http://www.vam.ac.uk/content/journals/research-journal/issue-03/an-adorned-print-print-culture,-female-leisure-and-the-dissemination-of-fashion-in-france-and-england,-c.-1660-1779; David Pullins, 'The State of the Fashion Plate, circa 1727: Historicizing Fashion between 'Dressed Prints and Dezallier's Recueils', in *Prints in Translation, 1450–1750: Image, Materiality, Space*, ed. Suzanne Karr Schmidt and Ed Wouk (London: Routledge, 2017): 136–57; Patrick Elliot, ed., *Cut and Paste: 400 Years of Collage* (Edinburgh: National Galleries Scotland, 2019), 54–55. Examples of dressed prints have been identified in the Bibliothèque Nationale de France, the Morgan Library,

Winterthur Museum, the Museum of Fine Arts, the Museum of London, Victoria and Albert Museum and numerous private collections.

65 See Houghton Library: Typ 630.00.454 and Typ 725.07.299.

66 Alice Dolan, 'An Adorned Print'.

67 In their catalogues, the Morgan Library, New York and the Museum of Fine Arts, Boston use the term 'dressed prints'.

68 Two of Winn's prints include chair backs and bedding which have been 'dressed'. Across the genre this is relatively rare.

69 For an early history of creative interactions with prints, see Suzanne Karr Schmidt, *Altered and Adorned: Using Renaissance Prints in Daily Life* (Chicago: Art Institute of Chicago, 2011).

70 Pullins, 'The State of the Fashion Plate, circa 1727'; see also Sigrid Metken, *Geschnittenes Papier: Eine Geschichte Des Ausschneidens in Europa von 1500 Bis Heute* (Munich: Callwey, 1978); Peter Fuhring, Louis Marchesano, Rémi Mathis, and Vanessa Selbach, eds., *A Kingdom of Images: French Prints in the Age of Louis XIV, 1660–1715* (Los Angeles: Getty Publications, 2015). Decoupage and bricolage became popular in eighteenth-century England. See Ariane Fennetaux, 'Female Crafts: Women and Bricolage in Late Georgian Britain, 1750–1820', in *Women & Things, 1750–1950: Gendered Material Strategies*, ed. Maureen Daly Goggin and Beth Fowkes Tobin (Aldershot: Ashgate, 2009), 91–108. Hannah Woolley, however, makes a very early reference to the practice of cutting out prints in England 1674. See *A Supplement to the Queen-like Closet* (London, 1674), 70.

71 Pullins, 'The State of the Fashion Plate, circa 1727', 140.

72 The intricate knife work of *Découpure* and dressed prints is also evident in cut paper work, which was popular in England in the eighteenth century. See Madeleine Pelling, 'Crafting Friendship: Mary Delany's Album and Queen Charlotte's Pocketbook', *Journal18* (2018), http://www.journal18.org/2909.

73 An unadorned version of this print can be found in the collections of the British Museum. See 1917,1208.3774.

74 MFA: 44.1221; MoL: 2002.139/356; VAM: 1197-1875. See also Morgan Library: PML 15534-36. LACMA also contains pairs of dressed prints from Holland, which depict a merchant couple and a fashionable couple. Again, it is the communicative properties of dress which are valued in these images. See M.85.124.1a-b and M.85.124.2a-b. Religious subjects were also popular amongst the earlier dressed prints. See Karr Schmidt, *Altered and Adorned*, 67.

75 Another possible example is Winterthur: 1969.0901 A. See also VAM: E.3750-1923. The latter is a print with surface embellishment, rather than cut and recessed fabrics. It is inherently difficult to date many of these images, as earlier prints were often embellished decades later. A print dated to 1790, and in a private collection, has both been dressed with fabrics and decorated with straw work. This gap is partially filled by the continuing popularity of cut paper work, although this technique generally engaged with plain paper rather than printed images. The presence of aniline dyes reveals that an album of prints dating to 1690–1710s in the Victoria and Albert Museum was actually dressed in the nineteenth century. See VAM: E.826-1900–845-1900.

76 Anna Magdelena Braun's *trachtenbuch* is accompanied by four further albums containing her needlework and other crafts. See Germanishes Nationalmuseum: T8182,1–4.

77 For more on German costume books, see Ulinka Rublack and Maria Hayward, eds., *The First Book of Fashion: The Books of Clothes of Matthäus and Veit Konrad Schwarz of Augsburg* (London: Bloomsbury, 2015).

78 See, for example, Germanishes Nationalmuseum: T8182,1, 4.

79 An unembellished version of this print can be found at NLW: 9911461302419.

80 The paper backing on the frame is made from newspaper dating to 1820, implying that the dressing and framing of the print were contemporary to the production of the print itself.

81 Chloe Wigston Smith, 'The Empire of Home: Global Domestic Objects and The Female American (1767)', *Journal for Eighteenth-Century Studies* 40, no. 1 (2017): 67–87, 75.

82 The contemporary framing of the Queen Caroline print implies that display was its intended purpose.

83 For more on pocket books, see Chapter 2.

84 Kent Archives: U951/F24/1-69.

85 A watercolour portrait of the young Fanny Austen Knight, painted by her aunt Cassandra Austen, depicts her painting with watercolours. This portrait is in a private collection.

86 Ramsay MacMullen, *Sisters of the Brush: Their Family, Art, Lives & Letters 1797–1833* (New Haven: Past Times Press, 1997); William Lamson Warren, 'Mary Way's Dressed Miniatures', *The Magazine Antiques* (October 1992): 540–49.

87 George Smart offers a British equivalent. Smart was a tailor who utilized his knowledge of clothing to transform his offcuts into portraits. See Jonathan Christie, *George Smart, The Tailor of Frant: Artist in Cloth & Velvet Figures* (London: Unicorn Press, 2016); Elliot, *Cut and Paste: 400 Years Collage*, 63.

88 Freya Gowerley, 'Collage before Modernism', in *Cut and Paste: 400 Years of Collage*, ed. Peter Elliot (Edinburgh: National Galleries Scotland, 2019): 25–34. On tinsel prints, see Catherine Hindson, 'Grangerising Theatre's Histories: Spectatorship, the Theatrical Tinsel Picture and the Grangerised Book', *Nineteenth Century Theatre and Film* 42, no. 2 (2015): 195–210; Elliot, *Cut and Paste: 400 Years Collage*, 64–65. The three-dimensional dioramas constructed on fashion plates from the 1870s onwards have received no scholarly attention to date. For dioramas on other types of print, see Ibid., 22, 77.

89 WYAS: WYW1352/1/1/4/23. This comment may also relate to Winn's skill as a musician. Winn's harpsicord is still in the possession of the National Trust. See NT: NT 959742.

90 WYAS, WYW1352/3/4/6/1. My thanks to Kerry Bristol for bringing the reference to the tambour frame to my attention.

91 WYAS: WYW1352/1/1/4/15.

92 For example, the character of Emma Mourtray in Elizabeth Hervey's novel *The Mourtray Family* 'had learned to detest all needlework of the notable kind'. See Elizabeth Hervey, *The Mourtray Family*, 2 vols. (London: Faulder, 1800), I, 74. See also the 'Miss Notables' in Frances Burney, *The Witlings*, in *The Witlings and the Woman-Hater*, ed. Peter Sabor and Geoffrey Sill (Peterborough: Broadview, 2002), 48. This text is discussed in Serena Dyer, 'Stitching and Shopping: The Material Literacy of the Consumer', in *Material Literacy in Eighteenth-Century Britain*, ed. Serena Dyer and Chloe Wigston Smith (London: Bloomsbury, 2020), 99–116.

93 See NT: NT 3059746. The Nostell copy is a 1734 edition in French and English, and was probably part of the Nostell library before Sabine Winn's arrival. Intriguingly, it has clearly been used as a pedagogical tool for language learning, as evidenced in the crudely hand-written inscription on the endsheet. My thanks to Edward Potten for bringing this to my attention.

94 Philip A. Wadsworth, 'The Art of Allegory in La Fontaine's Fables', *The French Review* 45, no. 6 (1972): 1125–35.

95 See NT: NT 355692 and NT 38381. Uppark also contains a set of armchairs, dating to the 1750s, upholstered with tapestry depictions of the fables. NT: NT 137632.1-8. Petworth also holds a similar set. NT: NT 485400.1-7

96 Only two other prints from the *Suite de Larmessin* are in the collections of the National Trust. The British Museum contains three. The prints filtered into English homes on ceramics. Meissen used a number of the images on bourdaloue, snuff boxes and teapots, materializing the fables' moral tales. For examples, see the collection of the Holburne Museum, Bath. I am grateful for Patricia Ferguson for bringing these to my attention. A Meissen snuff box depicting '*Contes et Bouvelles*' from *Suite de Larmessin* was sold at Bonhams on 8 October 2014. A stylised version of '*Les Oyes de Frere Philippe*' was even used on Chinese-made export porcelain, produced for the Western market. An example of this is held in a private collection. The image has been simplified and is presented in black and white, with colour added only to the faces.

97 Only a selection of the fables were illustrated in the eighteenth century. The prints were engraved by Nicholas Larmessin (1684–1755), alongside Pierre-Alexandre Aveline (1702–1760), Pierre Filloeul (1696–1754), (Louis Legrand (1723–1808), Dominique Sornique (1708–1756) and Nicolas-Henri Tardieu (1674–1749) were made after paintings by Jean-Baptiste Pater (1695–1736), François Boucher (1703–1770), Sébastien Leclerc (1763–1714), Nicholas Vleughels (1668–1737), Claude Lorrain (1600–1682), Pierre Subleyras (1699–1749) and Pierre Le Mesle (1713–unknown). See also Katharine Baetjer, *French Paintings in The Metropolitan Museum of Art from the Early Eighteenth Century through the Revolution* (London: Yale University Press, 2019), 97–103.

98 This inscription translates as 'Mr Rowland Winn gave me the picture Sabine Winn née d'Herwart'. That Sabine Winn used her married name, and that Rowland is still '*Monsieur*' as opposed to 'Sir Rowland', implies that the inscription was written prior to the 4th baronet's death, and after the couple's marriage.

99 The dressed prints were last on display in 2008 in the 'museum room'.

100 WYAS: WYW1352/1/4/52/171, March 1763. Translated from the French: '*Je ne pui dormir, ni manger, qui étaient les seuls plaisirs comme tu sais qu'on puisse goûter à Badsworth.*'

101 WYAS: WYW1352/1/1/7/19, 12 January 1763.

102 See *Public Advertiser*, 10 August 1758 and 11 December 1760. '*Magnifique estampes*' translates as 'magnificent prints'.

103 On proxy shopping, see Miles Lambert, '"Sent from Town": Commissioning Clothing in Britain During the Long Eighteenth Century', *Costume* 43, no. 1 (2009): 66–84. On the Winns' shopping, see Bristol, 'Between the Exotic and the Everyday'.

104 The the embodiment of emotions in textiles and handiwork, see Alice Dolan and Sally Holloway, 'Emotional Textiles: An Introduction', *Textile: The Journal of Cloth and Culture* 14, no. 2 (2016): 152–59; Johanna Ilmakunnas, 'Embroidering Women and Turning Men: Handiwork, Gender, and Emotions in Sweden and Finland, c. 1720–1820', *Scandinavian Journal of History* 41, no. 3 (2016): 306–31.

105 In *Le Cuvier* (Figure 1.4) the man's apron is made of leather, again demonstrating knowledge of appropriate fabrics.

106 The same textile appears in Figures 4.1, 4.12 and 4.22.

107 For more on elite aprons, see Elizabeth Spencer, '"None but Abigails Appeared in White Aprons": The Apron as an Elite Garment in Eighteenth-Century England', *Textile History* 49, no. 2 (2018): 164–90.

108 Following her self-imposed seclusion at Nostell following the birth of her children, Winn relied on proxy shopping. As well as entrusting Rowland with commissions on his trips away, Winn also wrote directly to retailers. For a detailed analysis of Winn's consumption, see Bristol, 'Between the Exotic and the Everyday'.

109 The most extensive correspondence is with Ann Charlton, a London milliner based on Holles Street. WYAS: WYW1352/3/4/6/8. The printed calicoes were sent from Thomas Yeamans, a local haberdasher from Wakefield. See WYW1352/3/4/6/9.

110 WYAS: WYW1352/3/4/6/8, 30 May 1783, 20 August 1783.

111 WYAS: WYW1352/3/4/6/8, 22 May 1783.

112 Karr Schmidt, *Altered and Adorned*, 67.

113 On quilts, see Sue Prichard, ed., *Quilts, 1700–2010: Hidden Histories, Untold Stories* (London: Victoria and Albert Museum, 2010); Janet Floyd, 'Back into Memory Land? Quilts and the Problem of History', *Women's Studies* 37, no. 1 (2007): 38–56; Mara Witzling, 'Quilt Language: Towards a Poetics of Quilting', *Women's History Review* 18, no. 4 (2009): 619–37.

114 Ellen Weeton, *Miss Weeton's Journal of a Governess, 1807–1825*, ed. Edward Hall (Oxford: Oxford University Press, 1939), II, 325.

115 For a nineteenth-century equivalent, see Elaine Hedges, 'The Nineteenth-Century Diarist and Her Quilts', *Feminist Studies* 8, no. 2 (1982): 293–99; Laura Horton, *Mary Black's Family Quilts: Memory and Meaning in Everyday Life* (Columbia: University of South Carolina Press, 2005).

116 For work on reuse in the eighteenth century, see Ariane Fennetaux, Amélie Junqua, and Sophie Vasset, *The Afterlife of Used Things: Recycling in the Long Eighteenth Century*, ed. Ariane Fennetaux, Amélie Junqua, and Sophie Vasset (London: Routledge, 2014).

117 See Carolyn Dowdell, 'The Multiple Lives of Clothes: Alteration and Reuse of Women's Eighteenth-Century Apparel in England', PhD Thesis, Queens University, 2015.

118 Igor Kopytoff, 'The Cultural Biography of Things: Commoditization as Process', in *The Social Life of Things: Commodities in Cultural Perspective*, ed. Arjun Appadurai (Cambridge: Cambridge University Press, 1986), 64–92. On it-narratives and object-centred stories in literature, see Julie Park, *The Self and It: Novel Objects in Eighteenth-Century England* (Stanford: Stanford University Press, 2010).

119 The original painting is also discussed in Michel Delon, *The Libertine: The Art of Love in Eighteenth-Century France* (New York: Abbeville Press, 2013), 158.

120 See Figures 4.1, 4.10, 4.11, 4.12, 4.16, 4.17, 4.18 and 4.20.

121 WYAS: WYW1352/3/3/1/5/3/43. For analysis of this commission, see Lindsay Boynton and Nicholas Goodison, 'Thomas Chippendale at Nostell Priory', *Furniture History* 4 (1968): 10–61.

122 The inscriptions read 'blue dressing room'. The room was known by this name in the later eighteenth century. See WYAS: WYW1352/3/3/1/5/3/43. By 1806 it was the 'blue sitting room'. See the 1806 inventory of Nostell, WYAS: WYW1352/3/4/1/30. When the 7th baronet inherited in 1818, the paper was painted over in blue, and the room known simply as the 'blue room'. See WYAS: WYW1352/3/3/1/5/6/2.

123 A fruitful route for further enquiry can be found in Winn's making of medicines. See Winn's custom-made apothecary cabinet from Chippendale and her collection of medicinal recipes. For the cabinet, see NT: NT 960400. For the recipes, see, for example, WYAS: WYW1352/1/4/30/2, WYW1352/1/4/30/5, WYW1352/1/4/30/6 and WYW1352/1/4/30/7.

124 This attribution stems from a note (now lost) which was found by a National Trust guide, cited in Maurice Brockwell, *Catalogue of the Pictures and other Works of Art in the Collection of Lord St. Oswald at Nostell Priory* (London: Constable, 1915), 335. Suzannah Henshaw was undoubtedly a skilled maker. Dorothy Richardson

admired an 'exceedingly beautiful' carpet in the drawing room at Nostell in 1761 which had been Henshaw's handiwork. See JRL: MS1122 f.11. Richardson also described the dolls' house on her visit.

125 In the 1840s the Winn daughters invited friends to play with the doll house, according to the National Trust's curatorial notes. There is also clear material evidence of nineteenth-century additions. Specifically, a Berlin work rug and a replaced doll head. For more on dolls' houses, see Halina Pasierbska, *Dolls' Houses* (London: Victoria and Albert Museum, 2014). Elements described by Richardson in 1761, such as the dining room, have now vanished. JRL: MS1122 f.16.

126 It is possible that this was a cooperative project with Winn's daughter, Esther. Mother and daughter certainly engaged in watercolours together, as evidenced by a series of mother–daughter pairs of paintings, each depicting the same scene. These are now held in a private collection. Evidence of Esther's making can also be found in stencils and paints which belonged to her as a child. See WYAS: WYW1352/3/4/8/1. Esther's own daughter, Lousia Winn, painted watercolours of birds collaged with feathers. See WYAS: WYW1352/1/1/13/9.

127 JRL: MS1122 f.11.

128 See LWL: 773.08.00.04. My thanks to Elisabeth Gernerd for her help with this identification.

129 See LWL: 776.04.01.02.

130 This room has previously been misidentified as the 'japan'd' drawing room described by Richardson in 1761. 'Japanning' was often used to describe this decoupage technique in England, but there are a number of discrepancies and this may be a red herring. The Richardson description also mentions a landscape over the fireplace, which is absent from this room, as well as a marble fireplace. It is far more likely that Richardson was describing what is now known as the 'red velvet dressing room', which is decorated with imitation coromandel paper, which also has the appearance of japanning, and contains a fireplace of black Kilkenny marble with a landscape hung above. Richardson describes only six rooms, whereas today the dolls' house has eight, implying that in 1761 some of the rooms may have been unfinished or empty. See JRL: MS1122 f.16.

131 There are twelve surviving examples of these print rooms in Britain and Ireland: Rokeby Park, Castletown, The Vyne, Stratfield Saye, Uppark, Petworth, Woodhall Park, Heveningham Hall, Blickling Hall, Queen Charlotte's Cottage, Calke Abbey and Ston Easton Park. See Chloe Archer, 'Festoons of Flowers ... for Fitting Up Print Rooms', *Apollo* 130 (1989), 386–91.

132 Decoupage, much like quillwork, was a popular way to decorate tea cadies, sewing boxes and other trinkets in the eighteenth century. See, for example, VAM: W.83&A-1919. For more on decoupage on objects and furniture, see Daniëlle O. Kisluk-Grosheide, '"Cutting up Berchems, Watteaus, and Audrans": A Lacca Povera Secretary at The Metropolitan Museum of Art', *Metropolitan Museum Journal* 31 (1996): 81–97.

133 Jane West, *A Tale of the Times* (London, 1803), 224.

134 *Ladies Amusement: Or, The Whole Art of Japanning Made Easy* (London, 1760), 5. Other editions were published in 1758 and 1762. Hannah Robertson also included instructions for japanning. See *The Young Ladies School of Arts* (Edinburgh, 1766), 175.

135 Joseph Antoine Crozat and Pierre Mariette, *Recueil d'estampes d'après Les plus Beaux Tableaux et d'après Les plus Beaux Desseins Qui Sont En France Dans Le Cabinet Du Roi, Dans Celui de Monseigneur Le Duc d'Orleans, & Dans d'autres Cabinets* (Paris, 1763). For the Nostell copy, see NT: NT 3077679. Sadly, there are no missing or cut out prints.

136 Boynton and Goodison, 'Thomas Chippendale at Nostell Priory', 28. For these items, see NT: NT 959750–959752 and 959758.

Chapter 5

1 John Harold Plumb, 'The New World of Children in Eighteenth Century England', in *The Birth of a Consumer Society: The Commercialization of Eighteenth-Century England*, ed. Neil McKendrick, John Brewer, and John Harold Plumb (Bloomington: Indiana University Press, 1982), 286–315.

2 On the fashion doll, see Max von Boehn, *Dolls*, ed. Josephine Nicoll (New York: Dover, 1972), 134–53; Neil McKendrick, 'The Commercialization of Fashion', in *The Birth of a Consumer Society: The Commercialization of Eighteenth-Century England*, ed. Neil McKendrick, John Brewer, and John Harold Plumb (Bloomington: Indiana University Press, 1982), 34–99; Juliette Peers, *The Fashion Doll: From Bébé Jumeau to Barbie* (Oxford: Berg, 2004); Cecilie Stöger Nachman, 'The Queen of Denmark: An English Fashion Doll and Its Connection to the Nordic Countryes', in *Fashionable Encounters: Perspectives and Trends in Textile and Dress in the Early Modern Nordic World*, ed. Tove Engelhardt Mathiassen et al. (Oxford: Oxbow, 2014), 133–40.

3 See, in particular, McKendrick, 'The Commercialization of Fashion'; Plumb, 'The New World of Children in Eighteenth Century England'.

4 For more on the use of dolls as tools for the development of material literacy, see Serena Dyer, 'Stitching and Shopping: The Material Literacy of the Consumer', in *Material Literacy in Eighteenth-Century Britain: A Nationa of Makers*, ed. Serena Dyer and Chloe Wigston Smith (London: Bloomsbury, 2020), 99–116.

5 The Victoria and Albert Museum registry document for the donation records that the museum was offered over fifty dolls, made by Powell as well as her decedents. Not all of the dolls were accepted by the museum, so it is impossible to known whether further dolls by Powell have since been lost. See VAM: MA/1/P1874.

6 Edgar Powell, *The Pedigree of the Powell Family* (London, 1891).

7 Powell's dolls have been briefly discussed in Valerie Cumming, *Understanding Fashion History* (London: Batsford, 2004), 51; Ariane Fennetaux, 'Transitional Pandoras: Dolls in the Longf Eighteenth Century', in *Childhood by Design: Toys and the Material Culture of Childhood, 1700–Present*, ed. Megan Brandow-Faller (London: Bloomsbury, 2018), 47–66, 53.

8 NA: PROB 11/882/126.

9 NA: Register of Clandestine Marriages and Baptisms in the Fleet Prison, 27 August 1737. On Fleet weddings, see Jacob F. Field, 'Clandestine Weddings at the Fleet Prison, c. 1710–1750: Who Married There?', *Continuity and Change* 32, no. 3 (2017): 349–77. For Clark's will, see NA: PROB 11/875/456.

10 *Public Ledger*, 17 August 1761, 2. 'Italian merchant' in this case refers to his occupation and not his nationality.

11 Cited in John Clark's will. See NA: PROB 11/875/456. In 1760 £5,000 was the approximate equivalent of £500,000 in 2017 in terms of purchasing power. Powell's 3 percent annuity would be worth the equivalent of £15,000 per year. Conversion calculated using the National Archives' currency converter, Conversion calculated using the National Archives' currency converter, http://www.nationalarchives.gov.uk/currency-converter.

12 Powell, *The Pedigree of the Powell Family*, 21.

13 This portrait is in a private collection. It is also described in Powell, *The Pedigree of the Powell Family*, 21.

14 An engraving taken from his portrait can be found at the NPG. See NPG: D40456. The original is in the collection of St Luke's Hospital, of which both he and his father were treasurer.

15 *The Times*, 21 May 1832.

16 For more on Whitefriars glass, see Judy Rudoe, *Whitefriars Glass: The Art of James Powell & Sons* (Ilminster: Richard Dennis, 1996).

17 Powell, *The Pedigree of the Powell Family*, 21. See also William Henry Ireland, *England's Topographer: Or A New and Complete History of the County of Kent* (London, 1830), IV, 397.

18 NA: PROB 11/1508/215. This is the equivalent of over £4,000,000 in 2017. Conversion calculated using the National Archives' currency converter, Conversion calculated using the National Archives' currency converter, http://www.nationalarchives.gov.uk/currency-converter.

19 The family bible is in a private collection. It is transcribed in Powell, *The Pedigree of the Powell Family*, 76.

20 This sketch is now in a private collection. It was reproduced in Richard Morris, *The Powells in Essex and Their London Ancestors* (Loughton: Loughton and District Historical Society, 2002), 8. Matching sketches of her husband David and son James are also in a private collection.

21 VAM: W.183:0–11-1919. The dolls are currently split between the textiles and fashion collection and the Museum of Childhood at the Victoria and Albert Museum.

22 VAM: W.183-1919.

23 Paniers were the hooped constructions, usually made from cane, which held out the wide skirts which were fashionable in the mid-eighteenth century.

24 These labels were present when the dolls came into the museum's collection. Many of the earlier dolls also acquired secondary labels in the nineteenth century. On this example, '1754' has been written a second time in a different hand and at a later date.

25 For more on children's clothing and leading strings, see Clare Rose, *Children's Clothes Since 1750* (London: Batsford, 1989), 19.

26 See VAM: W.183:1-1919, W.183:2-1919 and W.183:3-1919.

27 See, for instance, VAM: W.42:6-1922 and MISC.271-1981; MET: 53.179.12a, b; CW: 1958-241; 1971-1739, A-E.

28 Fennetaux, 'Transitional Pandoras', 61.

29 For more on childhood and identity in the eighteenth century, see Anja Müller, 'Fashioning Age and Identity: Childhood and the Stages of Life in Eighteenth-Century English Periodicals', in *Fashioning Childhood in the Eighteenth Century*, ed. Anja Müller (London: Ashgate, 2006).

30 See VAM: W.183:4-1919, W.183:5-1919 and W.183:6-1919.

31 The dolls are all too fragile to be undressed fully. It is therefore unclear whether any of the dolls wear stays.

32 See Chapters 2 and 3 for further discussion of the pocket book.

33 This anecdote is referenced in Fennetaux, 'Transitional Pandoras', 62.

34 Mary Wollstonecraft was especially influential in popularizing the idea that needlework was a frivolous and self-indulgent activity for young women. See *A Vindication of the Rights of Woman*, ed. Janet Todd (Oxford: Oxford University Press, 1999), 192, 275. See also *The New Doll* (London: Ackermann, 1820): 2–3.

35 VAM: W.183:6-1919. Sadly, she is now in fragile and poor condition.

36 VAM: W.183:7-1919.

37 See VAM: MA/1/P1874.

38 Marcia Pointon, '"Surrounded with Brilliants": Miniature Portraits in Eighteenth-Century England', *The Art Bulletin* 83, no. 1 (2001): 48–71. See also Hanneke. Grootenboer, *Treasuring the Gaze: Intimate Vision in Late Eighteenth-Century Eye Miniatures* (Chicago: University of Chicago Press, 2013).

39 Pointon, '"Surrounded with Brilliants"', 64.

40 Susan Stewart, *On Longing: Narratives of the Miniature, the Gigantic, the Souvenir, the Collection* (London: Duke University Press, 1993), 62.

41 This echos the temporal role of the fashion plate. See Timothy Campbell, *Historical Style: Fashion and the New Mode of History, 1740–1830* (Philadelphia: University of Pennsylvania Press, 2016).

42 Sherry Turkle, ed., *Evocative Objects: Things We Think With* (London: MIT Press, 2011), 5; see also Marius Kwint, Christopher Breward, and Jeremy Aynsley, eds., *Material Memories* (Oxford: Berg, 1999); Stephanie Downes, Sally Holloway, and Sarah Randles, 'A Feeling for Things, Past and Present', in *Feeling Things: Objects and Emotions through History*, ed. Stephanie Downes, Sally Holloway, and Sarah Randles (Oxford: Oxford University Press, 2018), 16.

43 YCA: Munby Papers, 54.22 a-m.

44 Amanda Vickery, *Behind Closed Doors: At Home in Georgian England* (London: Yale University Press, 2009), 83–105.

45 The wig is separate from the doll, and it is possible that it is made from Powell's own hair.

46 Another doll in the V&A also wears a miniature quilted petticoat. See VAM: T.137-1929.

47 For Powell's doll, see VAM: W.183:8-1919. For the Brunswick in Johnson's album, see VAM: T.219-1973, 16.

48 For a description of Princess Augusta's outfit which inspired this fashion, see *The London Magazine* (1764), 51.

49 Fennetaux, 'Transitional Pandoras', 54–58. See also Dyer, 'Stitching and Shopping'.

50 VAM: W183:9-1919.

51 This style is generally referred to by dress historians as '*en fourreau*', but this was not a contemporary term used to describe this style.

52 Quoted in Alice Morse Earle, *Costume of Colonial Times* (New York, Charles Scribner, 1894), 152. A similar garment is described thirty years later in *The Lady's Monthly Museum* (London, 1820), 251.

53 I have been unable to trace an extant example of this style of gown.

54 VAM: W.183:10-1919.

55 For more on imagined communities, life-writing and collaborative practices, see Cynthia Anne Huff, ed., *Women's Life Writing and Imagined Communities* (London: Routledge, 2005).

56 The first of the dolls created by Powell's decedents dates to 1814. Many of the later dolls were probably the work of Agnes Powell (1820–1902), Powell's granddaughter by her son David. Agnes married her cousin Nathanael Powell (1813–1906), Powell's grandson by her son James. Harry Powell, who donated the dolls to the Victoria and Albert Museum in 1919, was the couple's son. The note on the 1842 doll explicitly states that Mrs Nathanial Powell was its maker. VAM: 183:15-1919.

57 VAM: MA/1/P1874.

58 Fennetaux, 'Transitional Pandoras', 61.

59 Ibid., 53.

60 Elizabeth Kowaleski-Wallace, *Consuming Subjects: Women, Shopping, and Business in the Eighteenth Century* (New York: Columbia University Press, 1997), 154. See also Miriam Forman-Brunell, *Made to Play House: Dolls and the Commercialization of American Girlhood, 1830–1930* (London: Yale University Press, 1993). William Hogarth's *A Children's Tea Party*, painted in 1730, depicts a doll at a tea table. See National Museum Wales: NGW184284.

61 Wollstonecraft, *A Vindication of the Rights of Woman*, 109.

62 Julie Park, *The Self and It: Novel Objects in Eighteenth-Century England* (Stanford: Stanford University Press, 2010), 81.

63 Fennetaux comments on this correlation between print and doll in 'Transitional Pandoras', 53.

64 Vivienne Richmond, 'Stitching the Self: Eliza Kenniff's Drawers and the Materialization of Identity in Late-19th-Century London', in *Women and Things, 1750–1950: Gendered Material Strategies*, ed. Maureen Daly Goggin and Beth Fowkes Tobin (Aldershot: Ashgate, 2009), 43–54.

65 See, for example, VAM: T.123-1958.

66 See MoL: A21412 and A21160. These dolls garments are discussed in Dyer, 'Stitching and Shopping'.

67 *World and Fashionable Advertiser*, 21 November 1787.

68 Jean-Jacques Rousseau, *Emile, or On Education* (New York: Dover, 2013), 396.

69 Gloucestershire Archives: D2455/F3/7/1/6/5.

70 Ellen Weeton, *Miss Weeton's Journal of a Governess, 1807–1825*, ed. Edward Hall (Oxford: Oxford University Press, 1939), II, 325.

71 Northamptonshire Archives: B(HH)/148.

72 See in particular the doll dressed in a red, striped sack-back gown. NT: 959710.

73 Dorothy Kilner, *The Doll's Spelling Book: Intended as an Assistant to Their Mammas in the Difficult Undertaking of Teaching Dolls to Read* (London: J. Marshall, 1802), v–vi.

74 For further discussion, see Andrew O'Malley, *The Making of the Modern Child: Children's Literature and Childhood in the Late Eighteenth Century* (Abingdon: Routledge, 2011), 114.

75 Kilner, *The Doll's Spelling Book*, 39–40.

76 These were made to accompany Ellenor Fenn, *The Art of Teaching in Sport* (London: John Marshall, 1785).

77 For a surviving example, see VAM: MISC.98-1965.

78 These items are very similar to Jane Johnson's pedagogical cards from the 1730s. LLIU: LMC 1649.

79 For more on the commercialization of childhood, see Plumb, 'The New World of Children in Eighteenth Century England'; Forman-Brunell, *Made to Play House*.

80 McKendrick, 'The Commercialization of Fashion', 43–46.

81 Park, *The Self and It*, 106.

82 For small dolls which are identified as fashion dolls, see MFA: 43.1772a-b; Fashion Museum, Bath: BATMC 93.436, A & B.

83 Only one identified full-sized fashion doll from the eighteenth century survives. It is now in a private collection in Paris, but an image has been reproduced in Jane Munro, *Silent Partners: Artist and Mannequin from Function to Fetish* (London: Yale University Press, 2014), 38.

84 *Oracle and Daily Advertiser*, January 1799; *Morning Post*, February 1800.

85 O'Malley, *The Making of the Modern Child*, 107. For a discussion of these items, see chapter two. LLIU: LMC 1649.

86 *The History of Little Fanny* (London: S & J Fuller, 1810), 2. Hereafter, parenthetical page numbers follow in the text.

87 Patricia Crain, *Reading Children: Literacy, Property, and the Dilemmas of Childhood in Nineteenth-Century America* (Philadelphia: University of Pennsylvania Press, 2016), 92.

88 For example, *The History and Adventures of Little Henry* (London: S & J Fuller, 1810); *Ellen, the Naughty Girl Remembered* (London: S & J Fuller, 1811); *Frank Feignwell's Attempts to Amuse his Friends* (London: S & J Fuller, 1811); *Cinderella* (London: S & J Fuller, 1814).

89 Patricia Crown, 'The Child in the Visual Culture of Consumption 1790–1830', in *Fashioning Childhood in the Eighteenth Century*, ed. Anja Müller (Aldershot: Ashgate, 2006), 63–80.

90 Little biographical information is known about the sisters, but they can be found living together in Shirley Common, Southampton in 1845. See *The London Gazette* (London, 1845), 436. For the manuscript of the book, see VAM: T.360:1 to 3-1998. For the accompanying dolls, see VAM: T.361:1 to 20-1998.

91 VAM: T.360:3-1998.

92 On earlier paper dolls, see Chloe Wigston Smith, *Women, Work and Clothes in the Eighteenth-Century Novel* (Cambridge: Cambridge University Press, 2013), 62–65.

93 McKendrick, 'The Commercialization of Fashion', 45.

94 This doll is held in a private collection.

95 This doll is held in a private collection.

96 Hastings Museum and Art Gallery: HASMG:950.38.12.

97 For further homemade paper dolls, see VAM: MISC.8-1967.

98 See HRP: 1995.123/1-10. A second, remarkably similar set of dolls is in the Victoria and Albert Museum. See VAM: E.1178–1183-1974.

99 One of the dolls in particular resembles the ensemble worn by Queen Charlotte in her 1789 portrait by Sir Thomas Lawrence. For the portrait, see National Gallery, London: NG4257. For the doll, see HRP: 1995.123/5b.

100 Freya Gowerly, 'The Sister Arts: Textile Crafts between Paint, Print and Practice', *Journal for Eighteenth Century Studies* 43, no. 2 (2020): 139–59.

101 BOD: MS. Don. c. 195, ff. 86–89.

102 Peers, *The Fashion Doll*, 3.

Chapter 6

1 VAM: T.219-1973, f. 1; BOD: MS. Don. c. 195, ff. 86–89.

2 Dror Wahrman, *The Making of the Modern Self: Identity and Culture in Eighteenth-Century England* (London: Yale University Press, 2004).

3 Ibid., 289.

4 Felicity Nussbaum, 'Toward Conceptualsing Diary', in *Studies in Autobiography*, ed. James Olney (Oxford: Oxford University Press, 1988), 128–40, 129.

5 Sally Holloway, *The Game of Love in Georgian England: Courtship, Emotions, and Material Culture* (Oxford: Oxford University Press, 2019), 69–70.

6 NA: ZB0702/02; HRP: 1995.123/1-10.

7 WYAS: WYW1352/1/1/13/9.

8 Gerald Egan, *Fashioning Authorship in the Long Eighteenth Century: Stylish Books of Poetic Genius* (London: Palgrave, 2016); Laura Engel, *Fashioning Celebrity: Eighteenth-Century British Actresses and Strategies for Image Making* (Columbus: Ohio State University Press, 2016).

9 James Chandler, *England in 1819: The Politics of Literary Culture and the Case of Romantic Historicism* (Chicago: University of Chicago Press, 1998), 5.

10 Timothy Campbell, *Historical Style: Fashion and the New Mode of History, 1740–1830* (Philadelphia: University of Pennsylvania Press, 2016), 16.

11 Hilary Davidson, *Dress in the Age of Jane Austen: Regency Fashion* (London: Yale University Press, 2019), 51.

12 Suzanne Karr Schmidt, *Altered and Adorned: Using Renaissance Prints in Daily Life* (Chicago: Art Institute of Chicago, 2011).

13 Kate Smith, *Material Goods, Moving Hands: Perceiving Production in England, 1700–1830* (Manchester: Manchester University Press, 2014).

14 Abbé d'Ancourt, *The Lady's Preceptor. Or, a Letter to a Young Lady of Distinction upon Politeness* (London: J. Watts, 1743), 59.

15 George Berkeley, *A Miscellany, Containing Several Tracts on Various Subjects* (Dublin, 1752), 39.

16 Ariane Fennetaux, Amélie Junqua, and Sophie Vasset, eds., *The Afterlife of Used Things: Recycling in the Long Eighteenth Century* (London: Routledge, 2014).

17 Ann Bermingham, *Learning to Draw: Studies in the Cultural History of a Polite and Useful Art* (London: Yale University Press, 2000), 138–39.

18 Amanda Vickery's work on the genteel women of Yorkshire and Lancashire offers the preeminent example of this archival reanimation of women's voices. See *The Gentleman's Daughter* (London: Yale University Press, 1998). More recently, Hallie Rubenhold's book on the victims of Jack the Ripper, and the response it received in the press, demonstrates that this work remains vital. See *The Five: The Untold Lives of the Women Killed by Jack the Ripper* (London: Random House, 2019).

19 See, for example, John Styles' work on the foundling tokens in *The Dress of the People: Everyday Fashion in Eighteenth-Century England* (London: Yale University Press, 2007), 115–19; *Threads of Feeling: The London Foundling Hospital's Textile Tokens, 1740–1770* (London: Foundling Museum, 2010). On the material culture of the enslaved, see Patricia Samford, 'The Archaeology of African-American Slavery and Material Culture', *The William and Mary Quarterly* 53, no. 1 (1996): 87–114; Martha B. Katz-Hyman and Kym S. Rice, *World of a Slave: Encyclopedia of the Material Life of Slaves in the United States* (Santa Barbara: Greenwood, 2011); Robert S. DuPlessis, *The Material Atlantic: Clothing, Commerce, and Colonization in the Atlantic World, 1650–1800* (Cambridge: Cambridge University Press, 2016). See also Robbie Richardson, *The Savage and Modern Self: North American Indians in Eighteenth-Century British Literature and Culture* (Toronto: University of Toronto Press, 2018).

20 For the preeminent study of subversive needlework, see Rozsika Parker, *The Subversive Stitch: Embroidery and the Making of the Feminine* (London: I B Tauris, 2010).

21 VAM: T.6-1956. For discussion of this object, see Maureen Daly Goggin, 'Stitching a Life in "Pen of Steele and Silken Ink": Elizabeth Parker's circa 1830 Sampler', in *Women and the Material Culture of Needlework and Textiles, 1750–1950*, ed. Maureen Daly Goggin and Beth Fowkes Tobin (Aldershot: Ashgate, 2009), 31–50; Nigel Llewellyn, 'Elizabeth Parker's "Sampler": Memory, Suicide and the Presence of the Artist', in *Material Memories*, ed. Marius Kwint, Christopher Breward and Jeremy Aynsley (Oxford : Berg, 1999), 59–68.

22 The sampler measures 85.8 cm by 74.4 cm.

23 Goggin, 'Stitching a Life', 31, 40.

24 For an example of a love token, see National Museum of Australia: 2008.0039.0169.

25 Huntington Library: MAA MO 295.

26 Styles, *Threads of Feeling*, 17.

27 On death and material culture, see Margaret Gibson, *Objects of the Dead: Mourning and Memory in Everyday Life* (Carlton: Melbourne University Press, 2008); Maureen Daly Goggin and Beth Fowkes Tobin, *Women and the Material Culture of Death* (Aldershot: Ashgate, 2009).

Bibliography

Published primary sources

Cinderella. London: S & J Fuller, 1814.
Ellen, the Naughty Girl Remembered. London: S & J Fuller, 1811.
Frank Feignwell's Attempts to Amuse His Friends. London: S & J Fuller, 1811.
Harris's Original British Ladies Complete Pocket Memorandum Book. London: J. W. Pasham, 1782.
Ladies Amusement: Or, The Whole Art of Japanning Made Easy. London, 1760.
The History and Adventures of Little Henry. London: S & J Fuller, 1810.
The History of Little Fanny. London: S & J Fuller, 1810.
The Important Pocket Book. London: John Newbery, 1765.
The Ladies Compleat Pocket Book. London: John Newbery, 1753.
The New Doll. London: Ackermann, 1826.
The Repository of Arts, Literature, Commerce, Manufactures, Fashions, and Politics. London, 1809–1829.
Abbé d'Ancourt, *The Lady's Preceptor. Or, a Letter to a Young Lady of Distinction upon Politeness*. London: J. Watts, 1743.
Aikin, Lucy. 'On Miss Linwood's Admirable Pictures in Needle-work'. *Monthly Magazine*, March 1798.
Bennis, Elizabeth. *The Journal of Elizabeth Bennis, 1749–1779*, ed. Rosemary Raughter. Dublin: Columba Press, 2007.
Beresford, James. *The Miseries of Human Life*. London: William Miller, 1806.
Berkeley, George. *A Miscellany, Containing Several Tracts on Various Subjects*. Dublin, 1752.
Brookshaw, George. *A New Treatise on Flower Painting, or, Every Lady Her Own Drawing Master*. London: Longman, 1816.
Burney, Frances. *Diary and Letters of Madame D'Arblay*, ed. Charlotte Barret. London, 1842.
Burney, Frances. *The Witlings*, in *The Witlings and the Woman-Hater*, edited by Peter Sabor and Geoffrey Sill. Peterborough: Broadview, 2002.
Campbell, Richard. *London Tradesman*. London: T. Gardener, 1747.
Cappe, Catherine. *Memoirs of the Late Mrs Catherine Cappe*. London, 1823.
Charnock, John. *Biographia Navalis: Or, Impartial Memoirs of the Lives and Characters of Officers of the Navy of Great Britain*. London: R. Faulder, 1797.
Crozat, Joseph Antoice and Pierre Mariette. *Recueil d'estampes d'après Les plus Beaux Tableaux et d'après Les plus Beaux Desseins Qui Sont En France Dans Le Cabinet Du Roi, Dans Celui de Monseigneur Le Duc d'Orleans, & Dans d'autres Cabinets*. Paris, 1763.
Edgeworth, Maria and Richard Lovell Edgeworth. *Practical Education*. London, 1798.
Fénelon, François and George Hickes. *Instructions for the Education of a Daughter Done into English, and Revised by Dr George Hickes*. London: James Reid, 1713.
Fenn, Ellenor. *The Art of Teaching in Sport*. London: John Marshall, 1785.

Hervey, Elizabeth. *The Mourtray Family*. London: Faulder, 1800.
Hort, Josiah. *Sixteen Sermons by Josiah, Lord Bishop of Kilmore and Ardagh*. Dublin: George Grierson, 1738.
Hutton, Catherine. *Reminiscences of a Gentlewoman of the Last Century*, ed. C. H. Beale. Birmingham: Cornish Brothers, 1891.
Ireland, William Henry. *England's Topographer: Or A New and Complete History of the County of Kent*. London, 1830.
Kilner, Dorothy. *The Doll's Spelling Book: Intended as an Assistant to Their Mammas in the Difficult Undertaking of Teaching Dolls to Read*. London: J. Marshall, 1802.
Locke, John. *The Works of John Locke*, vol. 8. London: Rivington, 1824.
Robertson, Hannah. *The Young Ladies School of Arts*. Edinburgh, 1766.
Rousseau, Jean-Jacques. *Emile, or On Education*. 1763; New York: Dover, 2013.
Stuart, Louisa. *Gleanings from an Old Portfolio, 1785–1799*. Edited by Godfrey Clark. Edinburgh: D. Douglas, 1895.
Swan, Abraham. *The British Architect*. London, 1750.
Walker, Adam. *A Complete System of Family Book-Keeping*. London: T. Kinnersly, 1758.
Weeton, Ellen. *Miss Weeton's Journal of a Governess, 1807–1825*, edited by Edward Hall. Oxford: Oxford University Press, 1939.
West, Jane. *A Tale of the Times*. London, 1803.
Wodhull, Michael. *Poems*. London: W. Bower and J. Nichols, 1772.
Wollstonecraft, Mary. *A Vindication of the Rights of Woman*, edited by Janet Todd. Oxford: Oxford University Press, 1999.

Secondary sources

Adburgham, Alison. *Women in Print: Writing Women and Women's Magazines from the Restoration to the Accession of Victoria*. London: Allen and Unwin, 1972.
Anderson, Misty G. *Imagining Methodism in Eighteenth-Century Britain: Enthusiasm, Belief, and the Borders of the Self*. Baltimore: Johns Hopkins University Press, 2012.
Archer, Chloe. 'Festoons of Flowers . . . for Fitting Up Print Rooms', *Apollo* 130 (1989), 386–91.
Arianne Baggerman. 'The Moral of the Story: Children's Reading and the Catechism of Nature around 1800'. In *Making Knowledge in Early Modern Europe: Practices, Objects, and Texts, 1400–1800*, edited by Pamela H. Smith and Benjamin Schmidt, 143–63. London: University of Chicago Press, 2007.
Arizpe, Evelyn, Morag Styles, and Shirley Brice Heath. *Reading Lessons from the Eighteenth Century: Mothers, Children and Texts*. Lichfield: Pied Piper Publishing, 2006.
Backscheider, Paula R. *Eighteenth-Century Women Poets and Their Poetry: Inventing Agency, Inventing Genre*. Baltimore: Johns Hopkins University Press, 2005.
Baetjer, Katharine. *French Paintings in The Metropolitan Museum of Art from the Early Eighteenth Century through the Revolution*. London: Yale University Press, 2019.
Barreto, Cristina and Martin Lancaster. *Napoleon and the Empire of Fashion: 1795–1815*. Milan: Skira, 2010.
Batchelor, Jennie. 'Fashion and Frugality: Eighteenth-Century Pocket Books for Women'. *Studies in Eighteenth Century Culture* 32 (2003): 1–18.
Batchelor, Jennie. *Dress Distress and Desire: Clothing and the Female Body in Eighteenth-Century Literature*. London: Palgrave Macmillan, 2005.
Batchelor, Jennie. *Women's Work: Labour, Gender and Authorship, 1750–1830*. Manchester: Manchester University Press, 2010.
Batchelor, Jennie and Manushag N. Powell, eds. *Women's Periodicals and Print Culture in Britain, 1690–1820s: The Long Eighteenth Century*. Edinburgh: Edinburgh University Press, 2018.

Beaudry, Mary Carolyn. *Findings: The Material Culture of Needlework and Sewing*. London: Yale University Press, 2006.

Beetham, Margaret. *A Magazine of Her Own?: Domesticity and Desire in the Women's Magazine, 1800–1914*. Abingdon: Routledge, 1996.

Bendoni, Wendy. *Social Media for Fashion Marketing: Storytelling in a Digital World*. London: Bloomsbury, 2017.

Bennett, Judith M. and Amy M. Froide, eds. *Singlewomen in the European Past, 1250–1800*. Philadelphia: University of Pennsylvania Press, 1999.

Berg, Maxine. *The Age of Manufactures, 1700–1870*. London: Routledge, 1985.

Bermingham, Ann. *Learning to Draw: Studies in the Cultural History of a Polite and Useful Art*. London: Yale University Press, 2000.

Berry, Helen. 'Polite Consumption: Shopping in Eighteenth-Century England.' *Transactions of the Royal Historical Society* 6, no. 12 (2002): 375–94.

Black, Jeremy. *The British Abroad: The Grand Tour in the Eighteenth Century*. London: Sutton, 1997.

Blackman, Cally. 'Walking Amazons: The Development of the Riding Habit in England during the Eighteenth Century'. *Costume* 35, no. 1 (2001): 47–58.

Borzello, Frances. *Seeing Ourselves: Women's Self-Portraits*. London: Thames and Hudson, 1998.

Bowden, Will. *Industrial Society in England Towards the End of the Eighteenth Century*. London: Frank Cass, 1965.

Boynton, Lindsay and Nicholas Goodison. 'Thomas Chippendale at Nostell Priory', *Furniture History* 4 (1968): 10–61.

Brewer, John and Roy Porter, eds. *Consumption and the World of Goods*. London: Routledge, 1993.

Bristol, Kerry. 'A Tale of Two Sales: Sir Rowland Winn and No. 11 St James's Square, London, 1766–1787'. *History of Retailing and Consumption* 2, no. 1 (2016): 9–24.

Bristol, Kerry. 'Between the Exotic and the Everyday: Sabine Winn at Home 1765–1798'. In *A Taste for Luxury in Early Modern Europe Display, Acquisition and Boundaries*, edited by Johanna Ilmakunnas and Jon Stobart, 161–78. London: Bloomsbury, 2017.

Brockwell, Maurice. *Catalogue of the Pictures and other Works of Art in the Collection of Lord St. Oswald at Nostell Priory*. London: Constable, 1915.

Burman, Barbara, and Ariane Fennetaux. *The Pocket: A Hidden History of Women's Lives, 1660–1900*. London: Yale University Press, 2019.

Byrne, Paula. *The Real Jane Austen: A Life in Small Things*. London: Harper Press, 2013.

Calahan, April. *Fashion Plates: 150 Years of Style*, edited by Karen Trivette Cannell. London: Yale University Press, 2015.

Callan, Hilary and Shirley Ardene. *The Incorporated Wife*. London: Croom Helm, 1984.

Campbell, Timothy. *Historical Style: Fashion and the New Mode of History, 1740–1830*. Philadelphia: University of Pennsylvania Press, 2016.

Chandler, James. *England in 1819: The Politics of Literary Culture and the Case of Romantic Historicism*. Chicago: University of Chicago Press, 1998.

Chrisman-Campbell, Kimberly. *Fashion Victims: Dress at the Court of Louis XVI and Marie-Antoinette*. London: Yale University Press, 2015.

Christie, Jonathan. *George Smart, The Tailor of Frant: Artist in Cloth & Velvet Figures*. London: Unicorn Press, 2016.

Clayton, Tim. *The English Print, 1688–1802*. London: Yale University Press, 1997.

Colley, Linda. *Britons: Forging the Nation, 1707–1837*. London: Yale University Press, 1992.

Connor, Rebecca Elisabeth. *Women, Accounting and Narrative: Keeping Books in Eighteenth-Century England*. London: Routledge, 2004.

Cook, Daniel and Amy Culley, eds. *Women's Life Writing, 1700–1850*. London: Palgrave, 2012.

Coutu, Joan Michèle. *Then and Now: Collecting and Classicism in Eighteenth-Century England*. London: McGill-Queen's University Press, 2015.

Crain, Patricia. *Reading Children: Literacy, Property, and the Dilemmas of Childhood in Nineteenth-Century America*. Philadelphia: University of Pennsylvania Press, 2016.

Crown, Patricia. 'The Child in the Visual Culture of Consumption 1790–1830'. In *Fashioning Childhood in the Eighteenth Century*, edited by Anja Müller, 63–80. Aldershot: Ashgate, 2006.

Culley, Amy. *British Women's Life Writing, 1760–1840: Friendship, Community, and Collaboration*. London: Palgrave, 2014.

Cumming, Valerie. *Understanding Fashion History*. London: Batsford, 2004.

Dannehl, Karin. 'Object Biographies: From Production to Consumption'. In *History and Material Culture*, edited by Karen Harvey, 123–38. Abingdon: Routledge, 2009.

Davidson, Hilary. *Dress in the Age of Jane Austen: Regency Fashion*. London: Yale University Press, 2019.

Day, Carolyn. *Consumptive Chic: A History of Beauty, Fashion, and Disease*. London: Bloomsbury, 2017.

Day, Julie. *Elite Women's Household Management: Yorkshire, 1680–1810*, PhD Thesis, University of Leeds, 2007.

de Vries, Jan. *The Industrious Revolution: Consumer Behaviour and the Household Economy, 1650–Present*. Cambridge: Cambridge University Press, 2008.

Deetz, James. *In Small Things Forgotten: The Archaeology of Early American Life*. New York: Anchor Books, 1977.

Delon, Michel. *The Libertine: The Art of Love in Eighteenth-Century France*. New York: Abbeville Press, 2013.

Desnoyers, Rosika. *Pictorial Embroidery in England: A Critical History of Needlepainting and Berlin Work*. London: Bloomsbury, 2019.

Dolan, Alice. 'An Adorned Print: Print Culture, Female Leisure and the Dissemination of Fashion in France and England, around 1660–1779'. *V&A Online Journal* 3 (2011), http://www.vam.ac.uk/content/journals/research-journal/issue-03/an-adorned-print-print-culture,-female-leisure-and-the-dissemination-of-fashion-in-france-and-england,-c.-1660-1779/.

Dolan, Alice. 'Touching Linen: Textiles, Emotion and Bodily Intimacy in England C. 1708–1818'. *Cultural and Social History* 16, no. 2 (2019): 145–64.

Dolan, Alice and Sally Holloway. 'Emotional Textiles: An Introduction'. *Textile: The Journal of Cloth and Culture* 14, no. 2 (2016): 152–59.

Dowdell, Carolyn. 'The Multiple Lives of Clothes: Alteration and Reuse of Women's Eighteenth-Century Apparel in England'. PhD Thesis, Queens University, 2015.

Downes, Stephanie, Sally Holloway, and Sarah Randles. 'A Feeling for Things, Past and Present'. In *Feeling Things: Objects and Emotions through History*, edited by Stephanie Downes, Sally Holloway, and Sarah Randles, 8–23. Oxford: Oxford University Press, 2018.

Downes, Stephanie, Sally Holloway, and Sarah Randles eds. *Feeling Things: Objects and Emotions through History*. Oxford: Oxford University Press, 2018.

DuPlessis, Robert S. *The Material Atlantic: Clothing, Commerce, and Colonization in the Atlantic World, 1650–1800*. Cambridge: Cambridge University Press, 2016.

Dyer, Serena. 'Fashioning Consumers: Ackermann's *Repository of Arts* and the Cultivation of the Female Consumer'. In *Women's Periodicals and Print Culture in Britain, 1690–1820s*, edited by Jennie Batchelor and Manushag N Powell, 474–87. Edinburgh: Edinburgh University Press, 2018.

Dyer, Serena. 'Stitching and Shopping: The Material Literacy of the Consumer'. In *Material Literacy in Eighteenth-Century Britain: A Nation of Makers*, edited by Serena Dyer and Chloe Wigston Smith, 99–116. London: Bloomsbury, 2020.

Dyer, Serena and Chloe Wigston Smith, eds. *Material Literacy in Eighteenth-Century Britain: A Nation of Makers*. London: Bloomsbury, 2020.

Earle, Alice Morse. *Costume of Colonial Times*. New York, Charles Scribner, 1894.

Egan, Gerald. *Fashioning Authorship in the Long Eighteenth Century: Stylish Books of Poetic Genius*. London: Palgrave, 2016.

Elliot, Patrick, ed. *Cut and Paste: 400 Years of Collage*. Edinburgh: National Galleries Scotland, 2019.

Engel, Laura. *Fashioning Celebrity: Eighteenth-Century British Actresses and Strategies for Image Making*. Columbus: Ohio State University Press, 2016.

Fennetaux, Ariane. 'Female Crafts: Women and Bricolage in Late Georgian Britain, 1750–1820'. In *Women & Things, 1750–1950: Gendered Material Strategies*, edited by Maureen Daly Goggin and Beth Fowkes Tobin, 91–108. Aldershot: Ashgate, 2009.

Fennetaux, Ariane. 'Transitional Pandoras: Dolls in the Long Eighteenth Century'. In *Childhood by Design: Toys and the Material Culture of Childhood, 1700–Present*, edited by Megan Brandow-Faller, 47–66. London: Bloomsbury, 2018.

Fennetaux, Ariane, Amélie Junqua, and Sophie Vasset, eds. *The Afterlife of Used Things: Recycling in the Long Eighteenth Century*. London: Routledge, 2015.

Festa, Lynn. 'Person, Animal, Thing: The 1796 Dog Tax and the Right to Superfluous Things'. *Eighteenth-Century Life* 33 (2009): 1–44.

Field, Jacob F. 'Clandestine Weddings at the Fleet Prison, c. 1710–1750: Who Married There?'. *Continuity and Change* 32, no. 3 (2017): 349–77.

Fine, Ben and Ellen Leopold. 'Consumerism and the Industrial Revolution'. *Social History* 15, no. 2 (1990): 151–79.

Finn, Margot. 'Working-Class Women and the Contest for Consumer Control in Victorian County Courts'. *Past & Present*, no. 161 (1998): 116–54.

Finn, Margot. 'Men's Things: Masculine Possession in the Consumer Revolution'. *Social History* 25, no. 2 (2000): 133–55.

Finn, Margot. *The Character of Credit: Personal Debt in English Culture, 1740–1914*. Cambridge: Cambridge University Press, 2003.

Finn, Margot C. and Kate Smith, eds. *The East India Company at Home, 1757–1857*. London: UCL Press, 2018.

Flood, Catherine and Sarah Grant, *Style and Satire: Fashion in Print, 1777–1927*. London: Victoria and Albert Museum, 2014.

Floyd, Janet. 'Back into Memory Land? Quilts and the Problem of History'. *Women's Studies* 37, no. 1 (2007): 38–56.

Ford, John. *Ackermann, 1783–1983*, London: Ackermann, 1983.

Forman-Brunell, Miriam. *Made to Play House: Dolls and the Commercialization of American Girlhood, 1830–1930*. London: Yale University Press, 1993.

Froide, Amy M. *Never Married: Singlewomen in Early Modern England*. Oxford: Oxford University Press, 2005.

Froide, Amy M. *Silent Partners: Women as Public Investors during Britain's Financial Revolution, 1690–1750*. Oxford: Oxford University Press, 2017.

Fuentes, Marisa J. *Dispossessed Lives: Enslaved Women, Violence, and the Archive*. Philadelphia: University of Pennsylvania Press, 2016.

Fuhring, Peter, Louis Marchesano, Rémi Mathis, and Vanessa Selbach, eds. *A Kingdom of Images: French Prints in the Age of Louis XIV, 1660–1715*. Los Angeles: Getty Publications, 2015.

Garvey, Ellen Gruber. *Writing with Scissors: American Scrapbooks from the Civil War to the Harlem Renaissance*. Oxford: Oxford University Press, 2012.

Gernerd, Elisabeth. 'Têtes to Tails: Eighteenth-Century Underwear and Accessories in Britain and Colonial America'. PhD Thesis, University of Edinburgh, 2015.

Gibson, Margaret. *Objects of the Dead: Mourning and Memory in Everyday Life*. Carlton: Melbourne University Press, 2008.

Ginsburg, Madeleine. 'Barbara Johnson and Fashion'. In *Barbara Johnson's Album of Fashions and Fabrics*, edited by Natalie Rothstein, 18–28. London: Thames and Hudson, 1987.

Goggin, Maureen Daly. 'Stitching a Life in "Pen of Steele and Silken Ink": Elizabeth Parker's circa 1830 Sampler'. In *Women and the Material Culture of Needlework and Textiles, 1750–1950*, edited by Maureen Daly Goggin and Beth Fowkes Tobin, 31–50. Aldershot: Ashgate, 2009.

Goggin, Maureen Daly and Beth Fowkes Tobin, eds. *Women and the Material Culture of Needlework and Textiles, 1750–1950*. Aldershot: Ashgate, 2009.

Goggin, Maureen Daly and Beth Fowkes Tobin, eds. *Material Women, 1750–1950: Consuming Desires and Collecting Practices*. Aldershot: Ashgate, 2009.

Goggin, Maureen Daly and Beth Fowkes Tobin, eds. *Women and Things, 1750–1950*. Aldershot: Ashgate, 2009.

Goggin, Maureen Daly and Beth Fowkes Tobin, eds. *Women and the Material Culture of Death*. Aldershot: Ashgate, 2010.

Gowerly, Freya. 'Collage before Modernism', in *Cut and Paste: 400 Years of Collage*, ed. Peter Elliot, 25–34. Edinburgh: National Galleries Scotland, 2019.

Gowerly, Freya. 'The Sister Arts: Textile Crafts between Paint, Print and Practice'. *Journal for Eighteenth Century Studies* 43, no. 2 (2020): 139–59.

Green, David R. and Alastair Owens. 'Gentlewomanly Capitalism? Spinsters, Widows, and Wealth Holding in England and Wales, c. 1800–1860'. *The Economic History Review* 56, no. 3 (2003): 510–36.

Greig, Hannah. 'Dressing for Court: Sartorial Politics and Fashion News in the Age of Mary Delany'. In *Mrs Delany and Her Circle*, edited by Mark Laird and Alicia Weisberg-Roberts, 80–93. London: Yale University Press, 2009.

Greig, Hannah. *The Beau Monde: Fashionable Society in Georgian London*. Oxford: Oxford University Press, 2013.

Greig, Hannah, Jane Hamlett, and Leonie Hannan, eds. *Gender and Material Culture in Britain since 1600*. London: Palgrave, 2016.

Grootenboer, Hanneke. *Treasuring the Gaze: Intimate Vision in Late Eighteenth-Century Eye Miniatures*. Chicago: University of Chicago Press, 2013.

Guest, Harriet. *Small Change: Women, Learning, Patriotism, 1750–1810*. Chicago: University of Chicago Press, 2000.

Hannan, Leonie and Sarah Longair, eds. *History Through Material Culture*. Manchester: Manchester University Press, 2017.

Hannan, Leonie et al. '"A View from Old Age": Women's Lives as Narrated through Objects'. *Life Writing* 16, no. 1 (2019): 51–67.

Harris, Eileen. *The Genius of Robert Adam: His Interiors*. London: Yale University Press, 2001.

Harrison, Colin. *John Malchair of Oxford: Artist and Musician*. Oxford: Ashmolean Museum, 1998.

Harvey, Karen ed. *History and Material Culture*. London: Routledge, 2009.

Harvey, Karen. *The Little Republic: Masculinity and Domestic Authority in Eighteenth-Century Britain*. Oxford: Oxford University Press, 2012.

Harvey, Karen. 'Craftsmen in Common: Objects, Skills and Masculinity in the Eighteenth and Nineteenth Centuries'. In *Gender and Material Culture in Britain since 1600*, edited by Hannah Greig, Jane Hamlett, and Leonie Hannan, 68–89. London: Palgrave, 2016.

Haywood, Ian. '"A Metropolis in Flames and a Nation in Ruins": The Gordon Riots as Sublime Spectacle'. In *The Gordon Riots: Politics, Culture and Insurrection in Late Eighteenth-Century Britain*, edited by Ian Haywood and John Seed, 117–43. Cambridge: Cambridge University Press, 2012.

Hedges, Elaine. 'The Nineteenth-Century Diarist and Her Quilts'. *Feminist Studies* 8, no. 2 (1982): 293–99.

Hills, Richard. *Papermaking in Britain, 1488–1988*. London: Athlone, 1988.

Hindson, Catherine. 'Grangerising Theatre's Histories: Spectatorship, the Theatrical Tinsel Picture and the Grangerised Book'. *Nineteenth Century Theatre and Film* 42, no. 2 (2015): 195–210.

Holland, Vyvyan. *Hand Coloured Fashion Plates, 1770–1899*. London: Batsford, 1988.

Hollander, Anne. *Seeing Through Clothes*. Los Angeles: University of California Press, 1993.

Holloway, Sally. *The Game of Love in Georgian England: Courtship, Emotions, and Material Culture*. Oxford: Oxford University Press, 2019.

Horton, Laura. *Mary Black's Family Quilts: Memory and Meaning in Everyday Life*. Columbia: University of South Carolina Press, 2005.

Huff, Cynthia Anne ed. *Women's Life Writing and Imagined Communities*. London: Routledge, 2005.

Hussey, David and Margaret Ponsonby. *The Single Homemaker and Material Culture in the Long Eighteenth Century*. London and New York: Routledge, 2016.

Ilmakunnas, Johanna. 'Embroidering Women and Turning Men: Handiwork, Gender, and Emotions in Sweden and Finland, c. 1720–1820'. *Scandinavian Journal of History* 41, no. 3 (2016): 306–31.

Jajdelska, Elspeth. *Speech, Print and Decorum in Britain, 1600–1750: Studies in Social Rank and Communication*. Abingdon: Routledge, 2016.

Johnston, Lucy. 'Clothing in Context: Nineteenth-Century Dress and Textiles in the Thomas Hardy Archive', *Costume* 52, no. 2 (2018): 261–84.

Katz-Hyman, Martha B. and Kym S. Rice. *World of a Slave: Encyclopedia of the Material Life of Slaves in the United States*. Santa Barbara: Greenwood, 2011.

Kisluk-Grosheide, Daniëlle O. '"Cutting up Berchems, Watteaus, and Audrans": A Lacca Povera Secretary at The Metropolitan Museum of Art'. *Metropolitan Museum Journal* 31 (1996): 81–97.

Klekar, C. ed. *The Culture of the Gift in Eighteenth-Century England*. London: Palgrave Macmillan, 2009.

Kopytoff, Igor. 'The Cultural Biography of Things: Commoditization as Process'. In *The Social Life of Things: Commodities in Cultural Perspective*, edited by Arjun Appadurai, 64–92. Cambridge: Cambridge University Press, 1986.

Kowaleski-Wallace, Elizabeth. *Consuming Subjects: Women, Shopping, and Business in the Eighteenth Century*. New York: Columbia University Press, 1997.

Kwint, Marius, Christopher Breward, and Jeremy Aynsley, eds. *Material Memories*. Oxford: Berg, 1999.

Laing, Alastair. 'Sir Rowland and Lady Winn: A Conversation Piece in the Library at Nostell Priory'. *Apollo* 152, no. 458 (2000): 14–18.

Lambert, Miles. '"Sent from Town": Commissioning Clothing in Britain During the Long Eighteenth Century'. *Costume* 43, no. 1 (2009): 66–84.

Landes, David S. *The Unbound Prometheus: Technological Change and Industrial Development in Western Europe from 1750 to the Present*. Cambridge: Cambridge University Press, 1969.

Leis, Arlene. 'Displaying Art and Fashion: Ladies' Pocket-Book Imagery in the Paper Collections of Sarah Sophia Banks'. *Journal of Art History* 82, no. 3 (2013): 252–71.

Lejeune, Philippe. *Le Pacte Autobiographique*. Paris: Seuil, 1975.

Lemire, Beverly. *Fashion's Favourite: The Cotton Trade and the Consumer in Britain, 1660–1800*. Oxford: Oxford University Press, 1991.

Lemire, Beverly ed. *The Force of Fashion in Politics and Society*. Farnham: Ashgate, 2010.

Levy, Alison ed. *Widowhood and Visual Culture in Early Modern Europe*. London: Routledge, 2003.

Llewellyn, Nigel. 'Elizabeth Parker's "Sampler": Memory, Suicide and the Presence of the Artist'. In *Material Memories*, edited by Marius Kwint, Christopher Breward and Jeremy Aynsley, 59–68. Oxford: Berg, 1999.

Lloyd, Stephen and Kim Sloan. *The Intimate Portrait: Drawings, Miniatures and Pastels from Ramsay to Lawrence*. Edinburgh: National Galleries Scotland, 2008.

Loske, Alexandra. *Colour: A Visual History*. London: Tate Publishing, 2019.

MacGregor, Arthur. *Curiosity and Enlightenment: Collectors and Collections from the Sixteenth to the Nineteenth Century*. London: Yale University Press, 2007.

MacGregor, Neil. *A History of the World in 100 Objects*. London: Allen Lane, 2010.

MacMullen, Ramsay. *Sisters of the Brush: Their Family, Art, Lives & Letters 1797–1833*. New Haven: Past Times Press, 1997.

Major, Emma. *Madam Britannia: Women, Church, and Nation, 1712–1812*. Oxford: Oxford University Press, 2011.

Mascuch, Michael. *The Origins of the Individualist Self: Autobiography and Self-Identity in England, 1591–1791*. Cambridge: Polity Press, 1997.

Mauss, Marcel. *The Gift: The Form and Reason for Exchange in Archaic Societies*. Abingdon: Routledge, 2002.

McCormack, Matthew. *Embodying the Militia in Georgian England*. Oxford: Oxford University Press, 2015.

McCormack, Matthew. 'Boots, Material Culture and Georgian Masculinities'. *Social History* 42, no. 4 (2017): 307–1022.

McCreery, Cindy. *The Satirical Gaze: Prints of Women in Late Eighteenth-Century England*. Oxford: Oxford University Press, 2004.

McKendrick, Neil. 'The Commercialization of Fashion'. In *The Birth of a Consumer Society: The Commercialization of Eighteenth-Century England*, edited by Neil McKendrick, John Brewer, and John Harold Plumb, 34–99. Bloomington: Indiana University Press, 1982.

McKendrick, Neil, John Brewer, and John Harold Plumb. *The Birth of a Consumer Society: The Commercialization of Eighteenth-Century England*. Bloomington: Indiana University Press, 1982.

McNeil, Peter. *Pretty Gentlemen: Macaroni Men and the Eighteenth-Century Fashion World*. London: Yale University Press, 2018.

McNeil, Peter and Patrik Steorn. 'The Medium of Print and the Rise of Fashion in the West'. *Journal of Art History* 82, no. 3 (2013): 135–56.

Metken, Sigrid. *Geschnittenes Papier: Eine Geschichte Des Ausschneidens in Europa von 1500 Bis Heute*. Munich: Callwey, 1978.

Mingay, G. E. *Parliamentary Enclosure in England: An Introduction to Its Causes, Incidence, and Impact, 1750–1850*. Abingdon: Routledge, 2014.

Moore, Doris Langley. *Fashion through Fashion Plates, 1771–1970*. London: Ward Lock, 1971.

Morris, Richard. *The Powells in Essex and Their London Ancestors*. Loughton: Loughton and District Historical Society, 2002.

Müller, Anja. 'Fashioning Age and Identity: Childhood and the Stages of Life in Eighteenth-Century English Periodicals'. In *Fashioning Childhood in the Eighteenth Century*, edited by Anja Müller, 91–100. London: Ashgate, 2006.

Munro, Jane. *Silent Partners: Artist and Mannequin from Function to Fetish*. London: Yale University Press, 2014.

Murphy, Anne L. *The Origins of English Financial Markets: Investment and Speculation before the South Sea Bubble*. Cambridge: Cambridge University Press, 2009.

Nachman, Cecilie Stöger. 'The Queen of Denmark: An English Fashion Doll and Its Connection to the Nordic Countryes'. In *Fashionable Encounters: Perspectives and Trends in Textile and Dress in the Early Modern Nordic World*, edited by Tove Engelhardt Mathiassen et al., 133–40. Oxford: Oxbow, 2014.

Nussbaum, Felicity. 'Toward Conceptualising Diary'. In *Studies in Autobiography*, edited by James Olney, 128–40. Oxford: Oxford University Press, 1988.

Nussbaum, Felicity. *The Autobiographical Subject: Gender and Ideology in Eighteenth-Century England*. London: Johns Hopkins University Press, 1989.

O'Malley, Andrew. *The Making of the Modern Child: Children's Literature and Childhood in the Late Eighteenth Century*. Abingdon: Routledge, 2011.

Park, Julie. *The Self and It: Novel Objects in Eighteenth-Century England*. Stanford: Stanford University Press, 2010.

Parker, Rozsika. *The Subversive Stitch: Embroidery and the Making of the Feminine*. London: I B Tauris, 2010.

Pasierbska, Halina. *Dolls' Houses*. London: Victoria and Albert Museum, 2014.

Peers, Juliette. *The Fashion Doll: From Bébé Jumeau to Barbie*. Oxford: Berg, 2004.

Pelling, Madeleine. 'Crafting Friendship: Mary Delany's Album and Queen Charlotte's Pocketbook'. *Journal18* (2018), http://www.journal18.org/2909.

Plumb, John Harold. 'The New World of Children in Eighteenth Century England'. In *The Birth of a Consumer Society: The Commercialization of Eighteenth-Century England*, edited by Neil McKendrick, John Brewer, and John Harold Plumb, 286–315. Bloomington: Indiana University Press, 1982.

Pointon, Marcia. *Strategies for Showing: Women, Possession, and Representation in English Visual Culture 1665–1800*. Oxford: Oxford University Press, 1997.

Pointon, Marcia. 'Materializing Mourning: Hair, Jewellery, and the Body'. In *Material Memories*, edited by Marius Kwint, Jeremy Aynsley, and Christopher Breward, 39–71. London: Bloomsbury, 1999.

Pointon, Marcia. '"Surrounded with Brilliants": Miniature Portraits in Eighteenth-Century England'. *The Art Bulletin* 83, no. 1 (2001): 48–71.

Powell, Edgar. *The Pedigree of the Powell Family*. London, 1891.

Prichard, Sue ed. *Quilts, 1700–2010: Hidden Histories, Untold Stories*. London: Victoria and Albert Museum, 2010.

Prown, Jules David. 'Mind in Matter: An Introduction to Material Culture Theory and Method'. *Winterthur Portfolio* 17, no. 1 (1982): 1–19.

Prown, Jules David. 'The Truth of Material Culture', in *American Artifacts: Essays in Material Culture*, edited by Jules David Prown, Kenneth Haltman, 1–19. East Lansing: Michigan State University Press, 2000.

Pullins, David. 'The State of the Fashion Plate, circa 1727: Historicizing Fashion between 'Dressed Prints and Dezallier's Recueils'. In *Prints in Translation, 1450–1750: Image, Materiality, Space*, edited by Suzanne Karr Schmidt and Ed Wouk, 136–57. London: Routledge, 2017.

Rabow-Edling, Susanna. *Married to the Empire: Three Governors' Wives in Russian America 1829–1864*. Fairbanks: University of Alaska Press, 2015.

Rendell, Jane. *The Pursuit of Pleasure: Gender, Space & Architecture in Regency London*. London: Athlone, 2002.

Richardson, Robbie. *The Savage and Modern Self: North American Indians in Eighteenth-Century British Literature and Culture*. Toronto: University of Toronto Press, 2018.

Richmond, Vivienne. 'Stitching the Self: Eliza Kenniff's Drawers and the Materialization of Identity in Late-19th-Century London'. In *Women and Things, 1750–1950: Gendered Material Strategies*, edited by Maureen Daly Goggin and Beth Fowkes Tobin, 43–54. Aldershot: Ashgate, 2009.

Riello, Giorgio. *Cotton: The Fabric That Made the Modern World*. Cambridge: Cambridge University Press, 2013.

Riello, Giorgio and Tirthankar Roy, eds. *How India Clothes the World: The World of South Asian Textiles, 1500–1850*. Leiden: BRILL, 2009.

Riley, Noel. *The Accomplished Lady: A History of Genteel Pursuits, c. 1660–1860*. Huddersfield: Oblong, 2017.

Rose, Clare. *Children's Clothes Since 1750*. London: Batsford, 1989.

Rothstein, Natalie ed. *Barbara Johnson's Album of Fashions and Fabrics*. London: Thames & Hudson, 1987.

Rubenhold, Hallie. *Lady Worsley's Whim: An Eighteenth-Century Tale of Sex, Scandal and Divorce*. London: Random House, 2011.

Rubenhold, Hallie. *The Five: The Untold Lives of the Women Killed by Jack the Ripper*. London: Random House, 2019.

Rublack, Ulinka and Maria Hayward, eds. *The First Book of Fashion: The Books of Clothes of Matthäus and Veit Konrad Schwarz of Augsburg*. London: Bloomsbury, 2015.

Rudoe, Judy. *Whitefriars Glass: The Art of James Powell & Sons*. Ilminster: Richard Dennis, 1996.

Samford, Patricia. 'The Archaeology of African-American Slavery and Material Culture'. *The William and Mary Quarterly* 53, no. 1 (1996): 87–114.

Sands, Frances. 'Nostell Priory: History of a House, 1730–85'. PhD, University of York, 2012.

Savile, Gertrude. *Secret Comment: The Diaries of Gertrude Savile, 1721–1757*, edited by Alan Saville. Kingsbridge: Kingsbridge History Society, 1997.

Schmid, Susanne. 'Mary Berry's "Fashionable Friends" (1801) on Stage'. *The Wordsworth Circle* 43 (2012): 172–77.

Schmidt, Suzanne Karr. *Altered and Adorned: Using Renaissance Prints in Daily Life*. Chicago: Art Institute of Chicago, 2011.

Schrift, Alan. *The Logic of the Gift: Toward an Ethic of Generosity*. London: Routledge, 1997.

Secord, James A. 'Scrapbook Science: Composite Caricatures in Late Georgian England'. In *Figuring It Out: Science, Gender, and Visual Culture*, edited by Ann B. Shtier and Bernard V. Lightman, 164–91. Hanover: Dartmouth College Press, 2006.

Shepard, Alexandra. *Accounting for Oneself: Worth, Status, and the Social Order in Early Modern England*. Oxford: Oxford University Press, 2015.

Shevelow, Katherine. *Women and Print Culture: The Construction of Femininity in the Early Periodical*. Abingdon: Routledge, 1989.

Sloan, Kim. *'A Noble Art': Amateur Artists and Drawing Masters, c. 1600–1800*. London: British Museum, 2000.

Sloan, Kim and Andrew M. Burnett. *Enlightenment: Discovering the World in the Eighteenth Century*. London: British Museum Press, 2003.

Smith, Chloe Wigston. *Women, Work and Clothes in the Eighteenth-Century Novel*. Cambridge: Cambridge University Press, 2013.

Smith, Chloe Wigston. 'The Empire of Home: Global Domestic Objects and The Female American (1767)'. *Journal for Eighteenth-Century Studies* 40, no. 1 (2017): 67–87.

Smith, Chloe Wigston. 'Fast Fashion: Style, Text, and Image in Late Eighteenth-Century Women's Periodicals'. In *Women's Periodicals and Print Culture in Britain, 1690–1820s*, edited by Jennie Batchelor and Manushag N. Powell, 440–57. Edinburgh: Edinburgh University Press, 2018.

Smith, Kate. 'Sensing Design and Workmanship: The Haptic Skills of Shoppers in Eighteenth-Century London'. *Journal of Design History* 25 (2012): 1–10.

Smith, Kate. *Material Goods, Moving Hands: Perceiving Production in England, 1700–1830.* Manchester: Manchester University Press, 2014.

Smith, Kate and Leonie Hannan. 'Return and Repetition: Methods for Material Culture Studies'. *The Journal of Interdisciplinary History* 48, no. 1 (2017): 1–17.

Smith, Simon. *Slavery, Family, and Gentry Capitalism in the British Atlantic: The World of the Lascelles, 1648–1834.* Cambridge: Cambridge University Press, 2006.

Spacks, Patricia Ann Mayer. *Imagining a Self: Autobiography and Novel in Eighteenth-Century England.* Cambridge, MA: Harvard University Press, 1976.

Spencer, Elizabeth. '"None but Abigails Appeared in White Aprons": The Apron as an Elite Garment in Eighteenth-Century England'. *Textile History* 49, no. 2 (2018): 164–90.

Stabile, Susan. *Memory's Daughters: The Material Culture of Remembrance in Eighteenth-Century America.* London: Cornell University Press, 2018.

Stewart, Susan. *On Longing: Narratives of the Miniature, the Gigantic, the Souvenir, the Collection.* London: Duke University Press, 1993.

Stobart, Jon and Mark Rothery. *Consumption and the Country House.* Oxford: Oxford University Press, 2016.

Strasdin, Kate. *Inside the Royal Wardrobe: A Dress History of Queen Alexandra.* London: Bloomsbury, 2017.

Strobel, Heidi A. 'Mary Linwood, Thomas Gainsborough, and the Art of Installation Embroidery'. In *Materializing Gender in Eighteenth-Century Europe*, edited by Jennifer G. Germann and Heidi A. Strobel, 173–91. London: Routledge, 2016.

Styles, John. *The Dress of the People: Everyday Fashion in Eighteenth-Century England.* London: Yale University Press, 2007.

Styles, John. *Threads of Feeling: The London Foundling Hospital's Textile Tokens, 1740–1770.* London: Foundling Museum, 2010.

Tague, Ingrid H. *Animal Companions: Pets and Social Change in Eighteenth-Century Britain.* Pennsylvania: Pennsylvania State University Press, 2015.

Taylor, Lou. *Mourning Dress: A Costume and Social History.* London: George Allen and Unwin, 1983.

Tobin, Beth Fowkes and Maureen Daly Goggin. 'Introduction: Materializing Women'. In *Women & Things, 1750–1950: Gendered Material Strategies*, edited by Maureen Daly Goggin and Beth Fowkes Tobin, 1–14. Aldershot: Ashgate, 2009.

Todd, Christopher. 'A Swiss Milady in Yorkshire: Sabine Winn of Nostell Priory'. *Yorkshire Archaeological Journal* 77 (2005): 205–24.

Todd, Christopher and Sophie Raikes. 'Love, Rebellion and Redemption: Three Generations of Women at Nostell Priory'. In *Maids and Mistresses: Celebrating 300 Years of Woman and the Yorkshire Country House*, edited by Ruth M. Larson, 77–88. York: Yorkshire Country House Partnership, 2004.

Trentmann, Frank. 'Beyond Consumerism: New Historical Perspectives on Consumption'. *Journal of Contemporary History* 39 (2004): 373–401.

Trentmann, Frank. *The Making of the Consumer: Knowledge, Power and Identity in the Modern World.* London: Berg, 2006.

Trentmann, Frank. 'Materiality in the Future of History: Things, Practices, and Politics'. *Journal of British Studies* 48, no. 2 (2009): 283–307.

Trentmann, Frank. *Empire of Things: How We Became a World of Consumers, from the Fifteenth Century to the Twenty-First.* London: Allen Lane, 2016.

Troughton, Jane Elizabeth. 'The Role of Music in the Yorkshire Country House, 1770–1850'. PhD Thesis, University of York, 2014.

Turkle, Sherry ed., *Evocative Objects: Things We Think With* (London: MIT Press, 2011).
Ulrich, Laurel Thatcher. *The Age of Homespun: Objects and Stories in the Creation of an American Myth*. London: Vintage Books, 2002.
Van Horn, Jennifer. *The Power of Objects in Eighteenth-Century British America*. Chapel Hill, NC: University of North Carolina Press, 2017.
Veblen, Thorstein. *Theory of the Leisure Class*. London: George Allen and Unwin, 1925.
Vickery, Amanda. *The Gentleman's Daughter*. London: Yale University Press, 1998.
Vickery, Amanda. 'His and Hers: Gender, Consumption and Household Accounting in Eighteenth-Century England'. *Past & Present* 1 (2006): 12–38.
Vickery, Amanda. 'The Theory and Practice of Female Accomplishment'. In *Mrs Delany and Her Circle*, ed. Mark Laird and Alicia Weisberg-Roberts, 94–109. London: Yale University Press, 2009.
Vickery, Amanda. *Behind Closed Doors: At Home in Georgian England*. London: Yale University Press, 2009.
Vickery, Amanda. 'Mutton Dressed as Lamb? Fashioning Age in Georgian England'. *Journal of British Studies* 52 (2013): 858–86.
von Boehn, Max. *Dolls*, edited by Josephine Nicoll. New York: Dover, 1972.
Wadsworth, Philip A. 'The Art of Allegory in La Fontaine's Fables'. *The French Review* 45, no. 6 (1972): 1125–35.
Wahrman, Dror. *The Making of the Modern Self: Identity and Culture in Eighteenth-Century England*. London: Yale University Press, 2004.
Warren, William Lamson. 'Mary Way's Dressed Miniatures'. *The Magazine Antiques* (October 1992): 540–49.
Watson, Victor. 'Jane Johnson: A Very Pretty Story to Tell Children'. In *Opening the Nursery Door: Reading, Writing, and Childhood, 1600–1900*, edited by Mary Hilton, Morag Styles, and Victor Watson, 31–46. London: Routledge, 1997.
Weatherill, Lorna. 'Consumer Behaviour, Textiles and Dress in the Late Seventeenth and Early Eighteenth Centuries'. *Textile History* 22, no. 2 (1991): 297–310.
Weatherill, Lorna. *Consumer Behaviour and Material Culture in Britain, 1660–1760*, 2nd ed. London: Routledge, 1996.
Wennerlind, Carl. *Casualties of Credit: The English Financial Revolution, 1620–1720*. Cambridge, MA: Harvard University Press, 2011.
Whyman, Susan. *Pen and the People: English Letter Writers, 1660–1800*. Oxford: Oxford University Press, 2011.
Williams, Louise. '"To Amuse for an Hour"? Materiality, Femininity and Performance in the Scrapbook of Lady Maxwell'. *Scottish Archives* 19 (2013): 106–18.
Wirz, Charles ed. *Annales de La Société Jean-Jacques Rousseau*. Geneva: Librairie Jullien, 1992.
Witzling, Mara. 'Quilt Language: Towards a Poetics of Quilting'. *Women's History Review* 18, no. 4 (2009): 619–37.
Zionkowski, Linda. *Women and Gift Exchange in Eighteenth-Century Fiction: Richardson, Burney, Austen*. London: Routledge, 2016.

Index

Page numbers for illustrations are in *italics*. Page numbers in the format 209 n.50 indicate a note, and in the format 195g indicate a glossary entry.

accessories
    fans, *117*
    fichus, *169*, 171, 175, *175*, 195g
    girdles, *97*, 99
    jewellery, *115*
    sashes, *101*, 173, *174*
    shawls, *169*, 171, 175, *175*
    shoes, *92*, *105*, *108*, 172
    veils, *101*, 186–7
    See also hats; muffs
accomplishments, 78–89
    See also art; embroidery; needlework; watercolours
account books, 36
accounting
    family, 37
    financial, 21, 32, 34–5, 57
    material, 2, 16–17, 21–2
Ackermann, Rudolph, 82
    The New Doll, or Grandmama's Gift, 183
    Repository of Arts, 41–3, 74
        fabric swatches, *42*, 208 n.36
        mourning dress, 106
        Promenade Dress plate, 74, *76*, *77*, 209 n.50
        shop and school, 82
Adam, Robert, 128, *129*
adorned prints. *See* dressed prints
agency, 3
    of consumers, 39
    creative, 154, 191
    and dolls, 177
    of things, 153
    of women, 18, 177, 191
Aikin, Lucy, 114

albums, 38, 45–6, 74
    See also Johnson, Barbara: Album
allegory, 88–9
alphabet cards, 30–2
apparel. *See* clothing
appearance, legibility of, 36, 181–3
aprons, *73*, 85, 99, *100*, 136
Armagnac, Mademoiselle d' (Charlotte of Lorraine), *134*, 135
art
    amateur versus professional, 82
    collage, 140
    commercialization of, 82
    decoupage, 157, 220 n.130, 220 n.132
    découpure, 135 (*See also* dressed prints)
    education in, 78, 82
    miniatures, 140, 170
    painting, 80–2, 114
    supplies, 82
    See also watercolours
Augusta of Brunswick-Wolfenbüttel, 171
authenticity, 63, 65, 171
autobiography. *See* life writing

Badsworth (Yorkshire), 127, 142
Banks, Sarah Sophia, 38, 45, *46*
Barnard, Lady Anne, 93
Bath, 26, 28, 201 n.29
Beach, Thomas, *The Honourable Mrs Craven*, *27*
beading, *116*
Belle Assemblée, La (periodical), 74, *79*, 82–5, 106
Benham Park (Berkshire), 26
Beresford, James, *Miseries of Human Life*, 14

Bermingham, Ann, 80
Berry, Agnes, 74
Berry, Helen, 10
Berry, Mary, 74
biography. *See* life writing
Blickling Hall (Norfolk), 141
bodices, 173, 175, *175*, 184, *185*
Boitard, Louis Peter, 47
book-keeping. *See* accounting
books
    account, 36
    albums, 38, 45–6, 74
    for children, 180
    commonplace, 37
    scrapbooks, 38
    See also pocket books
Borzello, Frances, 99
Boucher, François, *Le Fleuve Scamandre*, 146
Bowles, William, 54
Braun, Anna Magdalena, *Trachtenbuch*, 136, *137*, 216 n.76
Bristol, Kerry, 128
brocade, 40, *52*, *145*, *149*, 152, 154
Brookshaw, George, 78
Brown, Capability, 26
browsing, 10–11
brunswicks, 46, 171–2, 195g
Brunswick-Wolfenbüttel, Augusta of, 171
Burman, Barbara, 3
Burney, Frances, 95
Burton sisters, 184
Byrne, Paula, 7

Campbell, Timothy, 63
capes, *90*, *119*
Cappe, Catherine, 127–8, 130
caps, *169*, 171, 184, *185*
Caroline of Brunswick (Queen of England), 136, *138*
Cavendish, Georgiana (Duchess of Devonshire), 94
Cavendish, Margaret (Duchess of Portland), 193
charity, 30
Charlotte Augusta (Princess of Wales), 106
Charlotte of Mecklenburg-Strelitz (Queen of Great Britain), 37–8, 184, *185*
Charlton, Ann, 152
Cheltenham, 57–8
childhood, 161, 166, 180
children, *110*, 161
    accounting by, 32
    books for, 180
    clothes for, 33, 165, 177–9
    in fashion plates, 177–9
    girls, 179–80
    as makers, 21–2, 165–6, 174
    material life writing of, 130
Chippendale, Thomas, 128, *129*
Clark, John, 162
Clark, Laetitia (born Kipling), 162
Clark, Laetitia (later Powell). *See* Powell, Laetitia
class
    aspirations, 93
    clothes, legible through, 181–3
    education in, 31–2
    elite, 93, 128
        in dressed prints, 135, 136
        fashions of, 26, 28, 184, 186–7
        social life, 54–6
    and interior design, 128
    merchant, 162–3
    and textile choice, 151, 154
clothing
    amounts purchased, 33, 44, 170
    biographical function of, 7
    capes, *90*, *119*
    children's, 33, 165, 177–9
    cuffs, 169, *169*, 171, 184, *185*
    for dolls, 165, 168–9, 171–2, 175, *175*
    engageantes, 169, *169*, 171, 184, *185*, 195g
    fastenings, 33, 168–9
    for older age, 44
    recycling, 153
    sleeves, 171, 173, *174*, 175, *175*
    and social difference, 181–3
    stomachers, 49, *134*, 135, 165
    trousseaux, 170
    undergarments, 165–6, 168–9, 171, 203 n.59, 222 n.31
    See also aprons; bodices; coats; dresses; hats; mourning dress; petticoats; robes
coats, 33, 195g
    pelisses, 44, 102–6, *113*, *118*, 195g
    See also jackets
Colby, Mary, 56
collaboration, 153–4, 174–5, 176, 190
collage, 140
collections, 38
    albums, 38, 45–6, 74
    fashion plates, 45–6

See also Johnson, Barbara: Album; Powell, Laetitia: dolls
Collett, John, *An officer in the light infantry*, 96
colonialism, 53–4
colours
    black, *86*, 102, *103*, *105*, 106
    blue, 98–9, *100*, *101*, *112*, 153
    brown, *120*
    choices of, 44
    coral, *120*
    dark, 44
    gold, 98–9, *115*
    patriotic, 98–9
    pink, *86*, *108*
    red, 93–5, 98–9, 156
    teal, *105*, *108*
    white, 98–9, *104*, *108*, *115*
    yellow, 153–4, 157
commonplace books, 37
compere front, 49, *51*, 172, 195g
consumption
    and agency, 39
    and making, 3, 9–14, 114, 159, 161, 191–2
    material literacy of, 9–10
    patriotic, 40–1, 43
    rational, 10–11
    and self-regulation, 35–6
    and taste, 128
    and women, 3, 8, 10–11, *12*, 26
    See also shopping
copying, 74, *76*, 78
Cornewell, Harriet (later Lewis), 57
cottons, 40–1, *71*, *104*, *108*
    printed, 173, *174*
Coxheath, 94–5, *96*
Craven, Anna Rebecca (later Johnson), 26, 186
Craven, Mary, 27
Craven, Sir William, 26
credit, 35–7
crêpe, 98
Cruikshank, Isaac, *Miseries of Human Life*, 11, *12*
cuffs, 169, *169*, 171, 184, *185*
Culley, Amy, 8

Dalrymple, John Hamilton, 186
Darly, Matthew and Mary, 82
death, 102, 130–1
debt, 35–7, 130

decoupage, 157, 220 n.130, 220 n.132
découpure, 135
    See also dressed prints
Deetz, James, 3, 18
Delany, Mary, 93
Devonshire, Duchess of (Georgiana Cavendish), 94
d'Hervart (Herwart), Jacques Philippe, 125, 126
d'Hervart (Herwart), Jeanne Esther (born Dunz), 125
d'Hervart (Herwart), Marianne-Ursule, 125
d'Hervart (Herwart), Philibert, 125
d'Hervart (Herwart), Sabine. *See* Winn, Sabine
diaries, 37
disease/illness, 130–1
dishabille, 65, *67*, 85, 195g
display, 93
dogs, 74, *75*, 88, *101*, *108*
Dolan, Alice, 133
dolls, 2, 17–18, 161–2, *178*
    and agency, 177
    as chronicles of fashion, 173, 187
    clothes for, 165, *169*, 171, 172
    dressing of, 165, 179–80
    fashion, 181, 224 n.83
    fashion plates, relation to, 167–8, 176, 177–9
    hats for, 175, *175*
    life writing through, 164–5, 170, 176–7
    and material literacy, 180
    paper, 181–7
    as pedagogical tools, 172–3, 179–80, 181–3
    petticoats for, 165, 168–9, 171–2, 175, *175*
    shoes for, 172
    stomachers for, 165
    as time capsules, 170, 181, 187
    for women, 180–1
    women as, 177
    See also Powell, Laetitia: dolls
dolls' houses, 156–9, 176, 180, 220 n.125, 220 n.130
dressed prints, 131–54
    history of, 131–40
    and original compositions, 153–4
    Trouvain, Antoine, *Mademoiselle d'Armagnac en Robe de Chambre*, *134*
    See also Winn, Sabine: dressed prints
dresses, 33, *52*, 154
    closed-front, *134*, 135
    compere front, 49, *51*, 172, 195g
    court, *72*, *79*, 167, *167*, 184, *185*

dishabille, 65, *67*, 85, 195g
evening, *83*, 116
half-dresses, *73*
levites, 173, *174*, 195g
mantuas, *91*, 167, *167*
masculine, *71*, 93–9
negligées, 33, 49, 168–9, 171, 195g
nightgowns, 33, *97*, 98–9, 195g
promenade, 74, *76*, *77*
redingotes, *87*
restoration, *98*
riding habits, 43–4, *69*, 93–5
round-gowns, 44, 195g
undress, 167–8, 173, *174*
visiting, 175–6
walking, *79*
wedding, 169–71
'Windsor Uniform', 95, *97*
See also morning dresses; mourning dress; petticoats; robes
dressmaking, 11, *13*
costs of, 43–4
knowledge of, 168–9, 173, 179
See also needlework
Duff, Mary Caroline, 186
Dunz, Jeanne Esther (later d'Hervart), 125

Edgeworth, Richard and Maria, 78–80
education, 30–3, 176
in art, 78, 82
in fashion, 31–2, 33, 172–3
of girls, 179–80
materials of, 30–2
moral, 181–2
by mothers, 30–2, 172–5
sartorial, 179–81
social, 31–2, 177, 180
Egremont, 2nd Earl of (Charles Wyndham), 36
embellishments, *91*, 98–9, *112*, *120*
beading, *116*
feathers, *66*, *91*, 93
flounces, 49, *118*, *119*, *169*, 171, 173
fly-fringes, *169*, 171, 195g
fur, *90*, 184, *185*
lace, *118*, *119*, *169*, 171, 184, *185*
ribbons, *71*, *86*
robings (robins), 49, *169*, 171, 195g
tassels, *97*, 98–9, *134*, 135

embroidery, *116*, 141
on dressed prints, 151–2
samplers, 114, 192–3
on satin prints/medallions, 89
whitework, *104*, 175
emotion, 34, 99, 102, 192–3
performed through creative practice, 106, 114
engageantes, 169, *169*, 171, 184, *185*, 195g
Engelbrecht, Martin, *Une Vendeuse des Images*, 131, *132*
English Ladies Pocket Companion, 45
eroticism, 142, 153–4

Falmouth, Lady, 156
fans, *117*
fashion, 17–18, 44–7
among elite classes, 26, 28, 184, 186–7
chronicles of, 45–7, 173, 187
criticism of, 44–5
dolls, 181
education in, 31–2, 33, 179–81
in interior design, 128
knowledge of, 46, 65
military style, 94–9
and places of entertainment, 54–6
terminology of, 46
fashion periodicals, 49, 58–63
See also Ackermann, Rudolph; *Belle Assemblée, La*; *Gallerie des Modes*; *Gallery of Fashion*; *Lady's Magazine*; *Lady's Monthly Museum*; pocket books
fashion plates, 45–7, 58–63, 65, 82–5, 206 n.1
in Barbara Johnson's Album, 22–3, 32, 34, 45–7, *168*
children in, 177–9
colouring of, 78
composition of, 65
copying of, 74, *76*, 78
dolls, relation to, 167–8, 176, 177–9
Dress of the Year 1766, *62*
as historiography, 63
and making, 74, 78
and material literacy, 59
memorialization through, 59, 63
temporality of, 191
watercolours of, 74, *76*
fastenings, 33, 168–9
feathers, *66*, *91*, 93
femininity, 80, 88–9
Fénelon, François, 30

Fenn, Ellenor (Mrs Teachwell), 180
Fennetaux, Ariane, 3, 165
fichus, *169*, 171, 175, *175*, 195g
Filloeul, Pierre
    Le Coccu Battu et Content, 147
    Le Glouton, 146
    La Matrone d'Ephes, 145
Finn, Margot, 36
Fleming, Seymour (Lady Worsley), 54, 93–4, *95*
flounces, 49, *118*, *119*, *169*, 171, 173
fly-fringes, *169*, 171, 195g
Foundling Hospital tokens, 38–9
France
    culture, 142, 152
    language, 126–7
Frankland, Amelia, 80, *81*, 102
Frankland, Ann. *See* Lewis, Ann Frankland
Frankland, Charlotte, 54, 102
Frankland, Dinah, 54
Frankland, Dorothy (born Smelt), 99
Frankland, Grace, 54
Frankland, Harriet, 56
Frankland, Henry, 53–4
Frankland, Katherine, 54, 102
Frankland, Marianne, 80, *81*
Frankland, Mary (Lady Roche), 54, 57
Frankland, Sarah Rhett, 54, *55*
Frankland, Admiral Sir Thomas (5th Baronet, 53–4, 57, 102
Frankland, Sir Thomas (6th Baronet), 54, 80
Frankland-Russell, Robert, 80
French culture, 142, 152
French language, 126–7
fringes, *97*, *169*, 171
Fuller, Samuel and Joseph, *The History of Little Fanny*, 82, 182–3, 184
fur, *90*, 93, *118*, 184, *185*

Gallerie des Modes (periodical), 65, *71*, 74, *90*, 106, 177–9
Gallery of Fashion (periodical), 65, *68*, 74, 106, *107*
garments. *See* clothing
gender, 14
    disruption of, 94–5, *96*
    femininity, 80, 88–9
    masculinity, *71*, 93–9
George III (King of England), 95, 98
Germany, 136
Gillray, James, 80

girdles, *97*, 99
girls, 179–80
Goggin, Maureen Daly, 192–3
Gordon Riots, 56
Gosset, Matthew (Viscount of Jersey), 54
gowns. *See* dresses
Great House (Olney), 23, *24*
Grey, Thomas de (2nd Baron Walsingham), 36
grief, 34, 102, 106
    See also mourning
Guise, John, 125

hair
    as relic, 130
    styles, 44, 49, *66*, *109*, *111*
    unpowdered, *109*
Hamilton, Hugh Douglas, *Sir Rowland Winn and his wife Sabine Winn*, 128, *129*
Hannan, Leonie, 7
Hardy, Katharine, 37, 38
Hardy, Mary, 37, 38
Hare, Ann. *See* Lewis, Ann Frankland
Hare, Robert, 57–8
Harpton Court (Radnor), 56, 57
Hartshorne, Catherine Milburgha, 38
hats, *87*, 89, 93, *94*, *169*, 171
    caps, *169*, 171, 184, *185*
    for dolls, 175, *175*
    and mourning, *86*, 102
    turbans, *105*, 186–7
Hayslip, Annie, 37, 38
Heinel, Anne Frédérique, 156
Henshaw, Katherine, 156
Henshaw, Suzannah (later Winn), 156
Herstmonceux (Sussex), 58
Herwart (d'Hervart), Jacques Philippe, 125, 126
Herwart (d'Hervart), Jeanne Esther (born Dunz), 125
Herwart (d'Hervart), Marianne-Ursule, 125
Herwart (d'Hervart), Philibert, 125
Herwart (d'Hervart), Sabine. *See* Winn, Sabine
Hicks, Anne, 179
historiography, 182–3
    of fashion, 45–7, 173, 187
    through dolls, 173, 187
    through fashion plates, 63
Holland, Henry, 26
Hollander, Anne, 63
Hope (figure), 88

Hoppner, John, *The Frankland Sisters*, 80–2
Hort, Josiah, *Of Righteousness in Paying Debts*, 36–7
Huguenots, 125
Hutton, Catherine, 46

Ilive, Elizabeth, 36
imagination, 165, 167
indexes, material, 38
Inglis, Sir Hugh, 41
Ingram, Catherine (later Wodhull), 26, 28, *29*, 43
Ingram, Mary, 28
inheritance, 25, 28, 57–8, 125
    of clothing, 34
interior design, 128, 157–9
    in dolls' houses, 156
Irby, Augusta (Lady Walsingham), 36

jackets, 153–4, 175, *175*, 184
    brunswicks, 46, 171–2, 195g
jewellery, *115*
Johnson, Anna Rebecca (born Craven), 26, 186
Johnson, Barbara, 2–3, 16–17, 21–47, 186, 189, 201 n.29
    Album, *2*, 8–9, *22*, *168*, 203 n.59, 206 n.126
        beginnings of, 21–2
        fashion plates in, 22–3, 32, 34, 45–7, *168*
        financial accounting in, 32
        gaps in, 34
        gifts and purchases, *43*
        A Lady in the Dress of the Year 1758, 168
        organization of, 33–4, *35*
        silk and cotton in, *40*
    amounts of clothing purchased, 44
    archive, 16
    biography, 23–8
    Catherine Wodhull, friendship with, 26, 28
    colour choices of, 44
    education, 30–3
    family tree, *24*
    and fashion, 44–7
    gifts to, 43–4
    as maker, 39
    material literacy of, 39–45
    poems, 26
    political views of, 41
    self-regulation, financial, 32–3
    wealth, 26, 28
Johnson, George, 28, 37
Johnson, George Wolsey, 38

Johnson, Harriet, 184–7
Johnson, Jane, 23–5, 30–1, 37–8
    Jane Johnson's Nursery Library, 30–2
    A Very Pretty Story to Tell Children, 30, 32
Johnson, Maria, *185*, 186
Johnson, Robert, 26, 37
Johnson, Robert Augustus, 186
Johnson, Thomas, 36
Johnson, Woolsey, 23, 36, 201 n.11
journals. *See* diaries; fashion periodicals

Kauffmann, Angelica, 106
Kilner, Dorothy, *The Doll's Spelling Book*, 180
Kipling, Laetitia (later Clark), 162
Knight, Fanny Austen, 136, 140, 217 n.85
knitting, 85, *87*
knowledge
    of dressmaking, 168–9, 173, 179
    of fashion, 46, 65
    haptic, 10–11
    material, 10–11
    sartorial, 133–5, 136, 151, 165, 168–9, 176
    of terminology, 39
    of textiles, 151

la Fontaine, Jean de, *Fables*, 141, 142, 150
lace, *118*, *119*, *169*, 171, 184, *185*
lacing, 33
Ladies Complete Pocket Book, 45, *139*
Ladies Museum or Complete Pocket Memorandum Book, 45
Lady's Magazine, 59
    Fashionable Dresses in the Rooms at Weymouth, 49, *50*, 56
    The Ladies in the newest Dress, 60
Lady's Monthly Museum (periodical), 74, *75*, 106, 114
Lancret, Nicolas
    Le Cuvier, 5
    Les Deux Amis, *148*, 151
    La Faucon, 145
    Le Gascon Puni, 142, *147*
    Nicaise, *150*, 151
    Les Oyes de Frere Philippe, 144
    Les Rémois, 142, *143*
    La Servante Justifiee, *149*, 153–4, *155*
    Les Troqueurs, *124*
Lane's Pocket Book, 45
Larmessin, Nicolas, IV

Suite de Larmessin, 141–50, 218 n.96
    Les Aveux Indiscrets, 149
    Le Coccu Battu et Content, 151
    Le Cuvier, 5
    Les Deux Amis, 148, 151
    La Faucon, 145
    Le Fleuve Scamandre, 142, 146
    Frere Luce, 144
    Le Gascon Puni, 142, 147
    La Jument de Compere Pierre, 142, 148
    Nicaise, 150, 151
    Les Oyes de Frere Philippe, 144
    Les Rémois, 142, 143
    La Servante Justifiee, 149, 153–4
    Les Troqueurs, 124
leading strings, 165
leisure, 10, 50, 168
Lejeune, Philippe, 7–8
Lemire, Beverly, 38
levites, 173, *174*, 195g
Lewis, Ann (1779-93), 56, 57, 102
Lewis, Ann Frankland, 2–3, 17, 49–120, 189
    biography, 50–8
    family tree, *53*
    family wealth, 53–4
    social life, 89–94, 211 n.102, 211 n.103
    watercolours, 49–50, 206 n.5, 208 n.32, 208 n.43
        The Dress of the Year 1774, 49, *51*
        The Dress of Year 1775, *4*
        The dress of year 1776, *61*
        The dress of year 1777, *66*
        The dishabille of year 1778, 65, *67*, 85
        1779, *69*, 93–4, 211 n.95
        1780, *70*
        The dress of year 1781, *72*
        The dress of year 1782, *73*
        The dress of year 1784, *86*, 102
        Morning dress of the year 1785, 85, *87*, 89
        Morning dress January 1786, *90*
        The Court dress of the year 1787, *91*
        Morning dress 1788, *92*
        The Windsor Uniform 1789, *97*
        The Half dress of the year 1790, 65, *100*
        Morning dress 1791, 65, *100*
        untitled (1792), 102, *103*
        1793, *104*
        May 1794, 102, *105*
        Morning dress 1795, *108*
        1796, *109*
        1797, 102, *110*
        1798, 102, *111*
        1799, *112*
        Morning dress December 1800, 102, *113*
        1801, *115*
        1802, *116*
        1803, *117*
        Morning dress 1804, 102, *118*
        March 1806, 102, *119*
        Morning dress January 1807, *120*
        fashion plates, relation to, 65, *103*, 114, *117*
        titles, 65
Lewis, Elizabeth, 56
Lewis, Harriet (born Cornewell), 57
Lewis, Harriet Cornewell, 57
Lewis, John, 56, 57, 102
Lewis, Louisa, 57, 106, *111*, *120*
Lewis, Marianne, 56
Lewis, Sarah, 56
Lewis, Sir Thomas Frankland, 56, 57, 106
life writing
    clothing as signifier in, 99
    material, 1–2, 7–9, 189–91
        audiences for, 190
        of children, 130
        by men, 8
        privacy of, 152–3, 190
        through dolls, 164–5, 170, 176–7
    portraits as, 63, 65, 99
    sartorial, 161–2
    through things, 7–9, 153
linen, 151, 152
Linwood, Mary, 114
literacy, economic, 21
literacy, material, 6–7, 9–10, 39–45, 59, 88
    development of, 17–18, 161, 172–3, 180
    and dressed prints, 140, 151
Locke, John, 32
London, 56, 89–93, 127, 162–3, 164
lustring (lutestring), 31, 34, 39, 40, 195g
luxury, 10, 74, 82

MacGregor, Neil, 7
making
    by children, 21–2, 165–6
    of clothes, 11, *13*
    and consumption, 3, 9–14, 114, 159, 161, 191–2

experiments in, 140
and fashion plates, 74, 78
knitting, 85, *87*
and material life writing, 123
skill in, 11, 141, 150–1, 156–7
by women, 9, 78–89
See also dressmaking; embroidery
Malchair, John, 80
Manners, Laura, 186
Mansfield, 2nd Earl of (David Murray), 41
mantuas, *91*, 167, *167*
Marie Antoinette (Queen of France), 38
Mariette, Pierre, *Recueil d'Estampes*, 157
marriage, 169–71
Marshall, John, 180
Mascuch, Michael, 8
masculinity, in women's dress, *71*, 93–9
material accounting, 2, 16–17, 21–2
material culture, 3–5
material indexes, 38
material knowledge, 10–11
material life writing, 1–2, 7–9, 189–91
audiences for, 190
of children, 130
by men, 8
privacy of, 152–3, 190
through dolls, 164–5, 170, 176–7
material literacy, 6–7, 9–10, 39–45, 59, 88
development of, 17–18, 161, 172–3, 180
and dressed prints, 140, 151
May, Gabriel, 125–6
medallions, silk, 85–9, 210 n.77
memorialization, 106, 170, 176, 190, 193
of sartorial moments, 173
of self, 38–9
through dressed prints, 152–3
through fashion plates, 59, 63
memory quilts, 38
men
as consumers, 14
material life writing practices, 8
military style, 94–9
Miller, Lady Anna, 26
miniatures, 140, 170
Molyneux, Maria, Countess of Sefton, 186
money
accounting, 21, 32, 34–5, 57
debt, 35–7, 130

inheritance, 25, 28, 57–8, 125
of women, 25–6, 28
See also wealth
Montague, Elizabeth, 193
morality
and debt, 36–7
education in, 181–2
morning dresses, *68*, *75*, *84*
in Ann Frankland Lewis's watercolours
Morning dress of the year 1785, 85, *87*, 89
Morning dress January 1786, *90*
Morning dress 1788, *92*
Morning dress 1791, 65, *100*
Morning dress 1795, *108*
Morning dress December 1800, 102, *113*
Morning dress 1804, 102, *118*
Morning dress January 1807, *120*
mothers, as educators, 30–2, 172–5
Mountjoy, Lord (Herbert Windsor), 31, *31*
mourning, *86*, 102–14
national, 106
mourning dress, 102–14
in Ann Frankland Lewis's watercolours, *66*, *86*, *103*, *107*, *113*
in Barbara Johnson's Album, 33, 34
hats, *86*, 102
partial, *86*, 106, *111*
muffs, *68*, *72*, *75*, *76*, *77*, 88
fur, *90*, *118*
with silk medallions, 85–9
Murray, David (2nd Earl of Mansfield), 41
muslins, 44, *83*, 85, 173, *175*, *175*, 184

needlework, 14, *15*, *67*, *83*, 85
mourning, 106, 114
painting, 114
quilting, 171
skills in, 88, 165–6, 171, 172, 175–6, 179–80
work baskets, 85, *87*, 89
See also embroidery
negligées, 33, 49, 168–9, 171, 195g
Newbery, John, 32, 203 n.59
Nicholas, Robert, 54
nightgowns, 33, *97*, 98–9, 195g
Nostell (Yorkshire), 127, 128, *129*, 130, 156, 157–9
dolls' house, 156–9, 180, 220 n.125, 220 n.130

Nuremburg (Germany), 136
Nussbaum, Felicity, 8
Nutt, Betsy, 180

objects, 3–5
    agency of, 153
    language of, 6–7
    and life writing, 7–9, 153
    material culture, 3–5
    memorializing function of, 193
    personal meaning of, 190
Olney (Buckinghamshire), 23, *24*

Page, R., *Caroline, Queen of England*, 136, *138*
Paine, James, 128
painting, 80–2, 114
    See also portraits; watercolours
paper
    cutting, 157
    dolls, 181–7
    dolls' clothes, 165
    and textiles, 131–3, 140
    See also dressed prints; prints
Park, Julie, 181
Parker, Elizabeth, 192–3
Parker, Rozsika, 9, 80
patchwork quilts, 38, 152–3
Pater, Jean-Baptist
    Les Aveux Indiscrets, 149
    Le Glouton, 146
    La Matrone d'Ephes, 145
patriotism, 88, 94–9
    through consumption, 40–1, 43
Paulin, Henry, 43–4
pelisses, 44, 102–6, *113*, *118*, 195g
periodicals, 49, 58–63
    See also Ackermann, Rudolph; *Gallerie des Modes*; *Gallery of Fashion*; *Lady's Magazine*; *Lady's Monthly Museum*; pocket books
petticoats, 33, 49, *52*, *101*, *134*, 135, 153–4
    brunswicks, 46, 171–2, 195g
    for dolls, 165, 168–9, 171–2, 175, *175*
play, 176, 177, 180, 183
pleats, 171, 173, *174*
Plumb, John Harold, 161
pocket books, 32, 45–7, 59, 63, 140
    English Ladies Pocket Companion, 45
    Ladies Complete Pocket Book, 45, 140

    Ladies Museum or Complete Pocket Memorandum Book, 45
    Lane's Pocket Book, 45
    Polite and Fashionable Ladies Companion, 45
    Wayland's Annual Present or Pocket Book, 45
Pointon, Marcia, 99–102
Polite and Fashionable Ladies Companion, 45
Portland, Duchess of (Margaret Cavendish), 193
portraits, 99
    dressed, 140
    Hamilton, Hugh Douglas, *Sir Rowland Winn and his wife Sabine Winn*, 128, *129*
    Hoppner, John, *The Frankland Sisters*, 80–2
    as life writing, 63, 65, 99
    miniatures, 140, 170
    Reynolds, Joshua, *Seymour, Lady Worsley*, 94–5
    self-portraits, 169–71, 176
    Zoffany, Johan, *Mrs Wodhull*, 28, *29*
Powell, Baden, 163–4
Powell, David (1725-1810), 162–3, *164*
Powell, David (1764-1832), 163
Powell, Edward, 163
Powell, Harry, 176
Powell, James, 163–4
Powell, John Clark, 163
Powell, Laetitia, 2–3, 9, 17–18, 161–87, 189
    biography, 162–4
    dolls, 6, 161–2, 164–76, 222 n.31
        1785, 173–5
        Doll dressed in a brunswick, 171–2
        Fashionable Full Dress for Spring 1759, 165–6, *167*
        Fashionable Full Dress for Young Lady, 1754, 164–5
        Fashionable Undress for Spring 1759, 167–8
        Fashionable visiting dress, 175–6
        Mrs Powell's Wedding Suit, 169–71
        Undress called a Levite, 173, *174*
    family tree, *163*
    as maker, 164–77
    wealth, 162–3
prices, 22, 32, 34, 40
print culture, 45–7, 65
    as creative influence, 191–2
    engagement with, 133
print rooms, 157, 220 n.131
prints, 80
    colouring of, 78, 153

compositional style of, 136
decoupage, 157
découpure, 135
in dolls' houses, 156–7
Engelbrecht, Martin, *Une Vendeuse des Images*, 131, 132
sale of, 150
See also dressed prints; Larmessin, Nicolas, IV; medallions, silk; Winn, Sabine: dressed prints
production. *See* making
Prown, Jules David, 7, 102
Pullins, David, 135
Pyne, William Henry, *Miseries of Human Life*, 14, 15

quilting/quilts, 38, 152–3, 171

reading
    for children, 180
    by women, 25
    See also fashion periodicals; pocket books
redingotes, 87
replication, 177–9
Reynolds, Joshua, 102
    Seymour, Lady Worsley, 94–5
Rhett, Sarah (later Frankland), 54, 55
ribbons, 71, 86
riding habits, 43–4, 69, 93–5
Riello, Giorgio, 3
Robertson, Hannah, 85
robes, 105
    à la française, 195g
    à la Polonaise, 70, 71
    à l'anglaise, 195g
    See also dresses
robings (robins), 49, 169, 171, 195g
Roche, Lady (Mary Frankland), 54, 57
Roche, Sir Boyle, 54
round-gowns, 44, 195g
Rousseau, Jean-Jacques, 179
Russell, Jane. *See* Johnson, Jane

sack-back gowns. *See* negligées
samplers, 114, 192–3
sarsanet, 43, 44, 195g
sashes, 101, 173, 174
satin, 40, 195g
    prints/medallions, 85–9, 210 n.77

satire, 80
Say, Lady (Elizabeth Twistelton), 44–5
Schwarz, Matthäus, 8
scrapbooks, 38
Scudéry, Madeleine de, 168
selfhood, 189–90
    constructed through creative practice, 80, 85, 150–1, 176–7
    constructed through portraiture, 99–102
    and life transitions, 170
    mirroring, 177–9, 180
    and time, 190–1
self-memorialization, 38–9
self-portraits, 169–71, 176
self-regulation, 30, 32, 35–6, 190
self-representation, 17, 169–70
    miniature, 177–9, 187
selvedges, 169, *169*, 171, 195g
sewing. *See* dressmaking; embroidery; needlework
sex, 142, 153–4
shawls, *169*, 171, 175, *175*
shoes, *92*, *105*, *108*
    for dolls, 172
shopping, 3, 9–10, *12*
    browsing, 10–11
    correspondence, 14
    proxy, 150, 218 n.108
silk, 34, 40, *40*, *73*, *86*, 100
    brocade, 40, *52*, *145*, *149*, 152, 154
    for dolls' clothes, *169*, 171, 172
    in dressed prints, 151, 152
    lustring (lutestring), 31, 34, 39, 40, 195g
    medallions, 85–9
    popularity of, 43
    sarsanet, 43, 44, 195g
    from Spitalfields weavers, 41–3
    taffety, 34, 195g
    See also satin
skills
    development of, 167–8, 176
    lack of, 136, 140, 174
    in making, 11, 141, 150–1, 156–7
    needlework, 167–8, 171, 172, 175–6, 179–80
slave trade, 54
sleeves, 171, 173, *174*, 175, *175*
Smelt, Dorothy (later Frankland), 99
Smith, Kate, 7
social class. *See* class

social life, 54–6, 89–94
spickelbilder, 133
Stahl, Johann Ludwig, *La Poupée anglaise, a diverse modes*, 183
Stock, Mary, 179–80
stomachers, 49, *134*, 135
    for dolls, 165
Strasdin, Kate, 7
Stuart, Lady Louisa, 98–9
stuff, 195g
    See also textiles
Suite de Larmessin. See Larmessin, Nicolas, IV
Swan, Abraham, 28
Switzerland, 125–6
Sykes, Anne, 37, 38

tabby (textile), 40
taffety, 34, 195g
tassels, *97*, 98–9, *134*, 135
taste, 128, 153
temporality, 170, 181, 187, 190–1
terminology, 39, 41–3, 46
textile industry, 40–1
textile swatches, 32, 37–9, *42*, 152, 208 n.36
    See also Johnson, Barbara: Album
textiles
    choice of, 175
    crêpe, 98
    imported, 40, 43
    knowledge of, 151
    linen, 151, 152
    muslins, 44, *83*, 85, 173, *175*, *175*, 184
    and paper, 131–3, 140
    plush, 41
    prices, 22, 32, 34, 40
    selvedges, 169, *169*, 171, 195g
    tabby, 40
    vocabulary of, 39, 41–3
    wool, 135
    See also cottons; satin; silk
Thenford (Northamptonshire), 26, 28
things, 3–5
    agency of, 153
    language of, 6–7
    and life writing, 7–9, 153
    material culture, 3–5
    memorializing function of, 193
    personal meaning of, 190

Thirkelby Hall (Yorkshire), 53–4
time, 170, 181, 187, 190–1
Todd, Christopher, 126
touch, 10–11, 14, 183
Town and Country Magazine, 156
toys, 180
    See also dolls
Trimmer, Sarah, 180
trimmings. See embellishments
trousseaux, 170
Trouvain, Antoine, *Mademoiselle d'Armagnac en Robe de Chambre*, *134*
turbans, *105*, 186–7
Twistleton, Elizabeth (Lady Say), 44–5

undergarments, 165–6, 168–9, 171, 203 n.59, 222 n.31
undress, 167–8, 173, *174*
Uppark (Sussex), 141

Veblen, Thorstein, 10
veils, *101*, 186–7
Vevey (Switzerland), 125–6
Vickery, Amanda, 35–6, 44, 170
virtue, 88–9
Vleugels, Nicolas
    Frere Luce, 144
    La Jument de Compere Pierre, 148

Wahrman, Dror, 189
Walker, Adam, 37
Walker, George, *Industrious Jenny*, 11, *13*
Walker, Jane, 11, *13*
Wallis, John, 184
Walsingham, 2nd Baron (Thomas de Grey), 36
Walsingham, Lady (Augusta Irby), 36
Walton, Henry, 99
watercolours, 2, 37
    of fashion plates, 74, *76*
    materials of, 82
    prints, colouring of, 78, 153
    Pyne, William Henry, *Miseries of Human Life*, 14, *15*
    by women, 80, *83*
    See also Lewis, Ann Frankland
Way, Mary, 140
Wayland's Annual Present or Pocket Book, 45
wealth
    of Ann Frankland Lewis, 53–4
    of Barbara Johnson, 26, 28

inherited, 25, 28, 57–8, 125
    of Laetitia Powell, 162–3
    of Sabine Winn, 125
Weeton, Ellen, 152–3
West, Jane, 157
Whinyates, Thomas, 54
White, Mary, 45–6
widows/widowhood, 57, 106, 130
Wilson, Anne Sanders, *The History of Miss Wildfire*, 183
Windsor, Herbert (Lord Mountjoy), 31, *31*
Winn, Esther, 128, 130, 220 n.125
Winn, George Allanson, 141
Winn, Sabine, 2–3, 17, 123–59, 189, 218 n.108
    biography, 125–31, 213 n.8
    clothes of, 152
    dressed prints, 140–54
        Les Aveux Indiscrets, 149
        Le Coccu Battu et Content, *147*, 151
        Le Cuvier, 5
        Les Deux Amis, *148*, 151
        La Faucon, 145
        Le Fleuve Scamandre, 146
        Frere Luce, 144
        Le Gascon Puni, 147
        Le Glouton, 146
        La Jument de Compere Pierre, 148
        La Matrone d'Ephes, 145
        Nicaise, *150*, 151
        Les Oyes de Frere Philippe, 144
        Les Rémois, 143
        La Servante Justifiee, *149*, 153–4
        Les Troqueurs, 124
    English language, lack of, 126–7, 142
    family tree, *127*
    as maker, 123, 141, 150–2, 153–4, 156–7
    Swissness of, 125, 127, 141, 142
    wealth, 125
Winn, Sir Rowland (4th Baronet), 126, 128
Winn, Sir Rowland (5th Baronet), 14, 17, 54–6, 123, *129*, 214 n.31, 215 n.49
    gifts to Sabine, 142, 150
Winn, Sir Rowland (6th Baronet), 130, *131*

Winn, Suzannah (born Henshaw), 156
wives, 141, 159, 170, 201 n.15
Woburn Abbey (Bedfordshire), 141
Wodhull, Catherine (born Ingram), 26, 28, *29*, 43
Wodhull, Michael, 26, 28, 43
Wollstonecraft, Mary, 177, 222 n.34
women
    accomplishments of, 78–89
    agency of, 18, 177, 191
    communities among, 8–9
    as consumers, 3, 8, 10–11, *12*, 26
    creative practice of, 78–89, 93
    as dolls, 177
    dolls for, 180–1
    education of, 179–80
    girls, 179–80
    making by, 9, 78–89
    and money, 25–6, 28
    mothers, 30–2, 172–5
    never-married, 25–6
    watercolours by, 80, *83*
    widows/widowhood, 57, 106, 130
    wives, 141, 159, 170, 201 n.15
    writing by, 25
    See also femininity
Woodhouse, Elizabeth, 11, 170
Woodward, George Moutard, *Fashions of the Day*, 63, *64*
wool, 135
work baskets, 85, *87*, 89
Worsley, Lady (Seymour Fleming), 54, 93–4, *95*
Worsley, Sir Richard, 93
Wyndam, Charles (2nd Earl of Egremont), 36
Wyndham, Lady Ann, 186

York, 54–6, 93
Yorkshire, 53–4, 127–8, 142
    See also Nostell

Zoffany, Johan, *Mrs Wodhull*, 28, *29*
Zucchi, Antonio, 128, *129*